THE GREAT SOCIETY

THE MACMILLAN COMPANY
NEW YORK · BOSTON · CHICAGO
DALLAS · ATLANTA · SAN FRANCISCO

MACMILLAN & CO., LIMITED
LONDON · BOMBAY · CALCUTTA
MELBOURNE

THE MACMILLAN CO. OF CANADA, LTD.
TORONTO

THE
GREAT SOCIETY

A Psychological Analysis

BY

GRAHAM WALLAS

AUTHOR OF "HUMAN NATURE IN POLITICS," ETC.

New York
THE MACMILLAN COMPANY
1923

PREFACE

DEAR WALTER LIPPMANN,

This book develops the material of that discussion-course ("Government 31") which you joined during my stay at Harvard in the spring of 1910.

Now that the book is finished, I can see, more clearly than I could while I was writing it, what it is about; and in particular what its relation is to my *Human Nature in Politics* (1908). I may, therefore, say briefly that the earlier book was an analysis of representative government, which turned into an argument against nineteenth-century intellectualism; and that this book is an analysis of the general social organisation of a large modern state, which has turned, at times, into an argument against certain forms of twentieth-century anti-intellectualism.

I send it to you in the hope that it may be of some help when you write that sequel to your *Preface tc Politics* for which all your friends are looking.— Sincerely yours,

GRAHAM WALLAS.

THE LONDON SCHOOL OF ECONOMICS
AND POLITICAL SCIENCE,
CLARE MARKET, LONDON, W.C.

v

CONTENTS

PART I

CHAPTER I

CHAPTER II

CHAPTER III

CHAPTER IV

CHAPTER V

CHAPTER VI

CHAPTER VII

CHAPTER VIII

CHAPTER IX

CHAPTER X

PART II

CHAPTER XI

CHAPTER XII

CHAPTER XIII

SYNOPSIS

PART I

CHAPTER I. (*The Great Society*).—The extension of social scale which created the Great Society was mainly due to certain mechanical inventions. Those who first developed these inventions expected that their results would be entirely good. But we now feel some misgiving when we compare the states of consciousness typical of the Great Society with those typical of more primitive social organisations; or when we estimate the forces making for its coherence or dissolution. This misgiving leads to an effort to understand the problems of the Great Society as a whole, which runs counter to the intellectual specialisation of the nineteenth century. To that effort the study of psychology has as yet made little effective contribution.

CHAPTER II. (*Social Psychology*), page 20.—Social Psychology deals with those more conscious facts of the human type which are relevant to the behaviour of mankind in society. It is convenient to call such inherited type-facts "dispositions," and to leave to philosophy their relation to the general problem of free-will and determinism. The type-facts dealt with by Social Psychology may be divided either into elementary or into complex dispositions. The complex dispositions are generally the more important in social analysis; though they are not easily examined by those laboratory methods which have been so successful in other branches of the science.

CHAPTER III. (*Instinct and Intelligence*), page 32.—The complex human dispositions may be divided into the Instincts, and Intelligence. All Instincts are to some extent adaptable, and their action may in the higher animals be accompanied by consciousness, and, as life goes on, memory and imagination. Intelligence is not a subordinate "apparatus" set in action by Instinct; and the tendency so to treat it constitutes a real social danger. Curiosity, Trial and Error, Thought, and Language are intelligent dispositions acting as "naturally" as any of the Instincts. The whole body of complex dispositions (instinctive and intelligent) forms a series of increasing consciousness and decreasing fixity. Social Psychology is not a safe guide for social action unless it is combined with personal experience, and the study of history, eugenics and other human sciences.

them, and to substitute a more complex conception of the stimulation (conscious and unconscious) of all our dispositions by our social environment.

CHAPTER IX. (*Love and Hatred*), page 139.—Is love of our fellows natural to us? Mother-Love is certainly natural; and so are the weaker forms of Love arising from Fatherhood, Sex, and Fellow-membership of the human species. Philanthropy, however, in order to become the Public Spirit required in the Great Society, must be strengthened by Imagination, Knowledge, Habit, the æsthetic emotion, and other dispositions. Hatred is as natural as Love, and had its own "survival-value" in the course of evolution. But the biological and psychological arguments advanced against the possibility of organised peace among the Great Powers seem insufficient.

CHAPTER X. (*Thought*), page 176.—Is there an art of Thought? Modern Psychology, with its insistence upon the essential identity and subconscious action of Memory, Imagination, and Reasoning, might seem to answer, No. But though we cannot control the moment of Thought, we can control (a) the material circumstances necessary for Thought; (b) the mental attitudes which are favourable or unfavourable to Thought; (c) our relation to the subject-matter of Thought. This last consists of (1) Memory and Record (each of which has its own advantages and dangers); (2) the alterations which we may deliberately produce in our environment, in order more effectively to think about it; and (3) the Logical rules and terms by which we may direct Attention. Modern improvements in Logic are mainly mathematical, and that fact has helped in the reaction towards Intuition (Instinctive Inference) in the moral sciences. But the most effective relation between Thought and Intuition in the work of organising the Great Society will give the pre-eminence to Thought with its appropriate passion.

PART II

CHAPTER XI. (*The Organisation of Thought*), page 235.—The analysis of the forms of Organisation in the Great Society may be conveniently based, not upon our structural dispositions, but upon the three forms of consciousness (Cognition, Conation, and Feeling) one of which may be dominant in any Organisation. The simplest form of Thought-Organisation is oral group-dialectic, which is now unduly neglected in favour of the impersonal organisation of Thought made possible by the printing press. But the English use the oral discussions of Committees, Councils, and Parliament for most of their political work, though with a certain loss of efficiency due to a neglect of the necessary psychological conditions. The Cabinet corresponds more closely to the psychological conditions of effective discussion, but may be transformed in the future by the increasing pressure of its work. The present organisation of the Civil Service has psychological advantages and disadvantages of its own. The Thought-Organisation of business is often inefficient; and the Organisation, personal or impersonal, of the Thought of the ordinary working citizen is limited by many incidents of modern industrial life, and is only now beginning to be seriously studied.

PART I

PART I

CHAPTER I

THE GREAT SOCIETY

"Yesterday, and ever since history began, men were related to one another as individuals. . . . To-day the every-day relationships of men are largely with great impersonal concerns, with organisations, not with other individual men.

"Now this is nothing short of a new social age, a new era of human relationships, a new stage-setting for the drama of life."—President WOODROW WILSON, *The New Freedom*, 1913, pp. 6 and 7.

DURING the last hundred years the external conditions of civilised life have been transformed by a series of inventions which have abolished the old limits to the creation of mechanical force, the carriage of men and goods, and communication by written and spoken words. One effect of this transformation is a general change of social scale. Men find themselves working and thinking and feeling in relation to an environment, which, both in its world-wide extension and its intimate connection with all sides of human existence, is without precedent in the history of the world.

Economists have invented the term The Great Industry for the special aspect of this change which is dealt with by their science, and sociologists may conveniently call the whole result The Great Society. In those countries where the transformation first began a majority of the inhabitants already live either in huge commercial cities, or in closely populated industrial

3

districts threaded by systems of mechanical traction and covering hundreds of square miles. Cities and districts are only parts of highly organised national states, each with fifty or a hundred million inhabitants; and these states are themselves every year drawn more effectively into a general system of international relationships.

Every member of the Great Society, whether he be stupid or clever, whether he have the wide curiosity of the born politician and trader, or the concentration on what he can see and touch of the born craftsman, is affected by this ever-extending and ever-tightening nexus. A sudden decision by some financier whose name he has never heard may, at any moment, close the office or mine or factory in which he is employed, and he may either be left without a livelihood or be forced to move with his family to a new centre. He and his fellows can only maintain their standard wage or any measure of permanency in their employment if the majority of them judge rightly on difficult questions put to them by national political parties and national or international Trade Unions. Even in those English villages into which the Great Industry may seem to have scarcely penetrated the change of scale is already felt. The widow who takes in washing fails or succeeds according to her skill in choosing starch or soda or a wringing-machine under the influence of half-a-dozen competing world-schemes of advertisement. The boys playing football on the village green think of themselves as possible members of a champion English team. The spectacled young schoolmaster who looks on is brooding, with all his future happiness consciously at stake, on his chances of advancement in the Transvaal or West Australia, or on the relation between his own religious opinions and an analysis of Hebrew eschatology by a German professor.

The English factory girl who is urged to join her Union, the tired old Scotch gatekeeper with a few pounds to invest, the Galician peasant when the emigration agent calls, the artisan in a French provincial town whose industry is threatened by a new invention, all know that unless they find their way successfully among world-wide facts which reach them only through misleading words they will be crushed. They may desire to live the old life among familiar sights and sounds and the friends whom they know and trust, but they dare not try to do so. To their children, brought up in the outskirts of Chicago or the mean streets of Tottenham or Middlesbrough, the old life will have ceased to exist, even as an object of desire.

Fifty years ago the practical men who were bringing the Great Society into existence thought, when they had time to think at all, that they were thereby offering an enormously better existence to the whole human race. Men were rational beings, and, having obtained limitless power over nature, would certainly use it for their own good. In 1867, for instance, Bernard Cracroft described the intense optimism of the typical English manufacturer of his time:

The mercantile feeling and fever, the ardent faith in progress, the belief . . . in a mercantile millennium, to be obtained partly by the boundless development of human energy striving like fire ever upwards, partly by unforeseen but probable discoveries, which at any moment may throw additional millions into the lap of human comfort, and so

raise humanity another stage above the gulf of wretched-
ness and want.[1]

The Great Society, even if it should deprive men of
some of the romance and intimacy of life, must, they
thought, at least give them such an increase of security
as would be far more than an equal return. Famine
would be impossible when any labourer could buy
flour and bacon from the world-market in his village
shop. Wars would be few and short if they meant disaster to an international system of credit.

Now, however, that the change has come, hardly
any one thinks of it with the old undoubting enthusiasm. Actual famine has, it is true, disappeared from
the Great Society, but there remains the constant possibility of general and uncontrollable depressions of
trade. The intervals between great wars are apparently becoming longer, but never has the expenditure
on armaments been so great or the fear of war so constant.

Wars, however, and commercial crises may be
thought of as merely accidental interruptions to a
social development which steadily advances in spite
of them. The deeper anxiety of our time arises from
a doubt, more or less clearly realised, whether that
development is itself proceeding on right lines.

We come back perhaps to London or Leeds after a
visit to a place where a simpler form of life is still in
some degree possible. We may have been watching
a group of Cornish fishermen, who have forgotten the
fish-steamer and the London market, and are mend-
ing their nets while the children play by the boats; or

---

[1] *Essays on Reform* (1867), p. 169.

we have been talking day by day with a Yorkshire sheep-farmer whose father and grandfather held the same land as himself. On the morning after our return, we notice from a fresh point of view the men and women who hurry with us out of the trains, or bend over ledgers in banks and offices, or stand tired and vacant outside factories in the dinner hour. Here and there we see an eager dark-haired boy, who seems to have found the environment that fits him best. He has perhaps been taken on as an assistant porter at King's Cross, and is irradiated, not only with confidence in his own future, but with a glorious sense of identity between himself and the Great Northern Railway. Such faces are, however, rare exceptions. Of the rest, not many perhaps are consciously unhappy, but there are strangely few signs of that harmony of the whole being which constitutes happiness.

In the presence of mere stupid social inequality we feel comparatively hopeful. We can contrive schemes for dealing with the row of broken men waiting for the casual ward to open, or the dull fat women who pass in their uselessly efficient motor cars. But all our schemes involve an increase in the number of clerks and mechanics and teachers with no essential change in their way of life. Even the parks and picture galleries and libraries and the other mitigations of the new environment, for which during the rest of the year we are working and voting, seem to us, for the moment, to be tragically inadequate.

Those who have watched the more rapid change from the old to the new in the East describe themselves as having the same feeling in a sharper form. A Hindoo peasant, who exchanges the penury and uncertainty of village agriculture for the steadier work and better pay of a Bombay cotton factory, never looks, they say, as if he had thereby attained greater satisfaction for the inner needs of his nature. Lafcadio Hearn wrote in 1894, when the resolute determination of the Japanese to enter the Great Society was already beginning to take effect, "The new Japan will be richer and stronger and in many things wiser, but it will neither be so happy nor so kindly as the old." [1]

Our fathers, under the influence of Herbert Spencer and the popular science of 1850, could trust that, even if the members of a single generation should find it difficult to adapt their nervous structure to the new conditions, yet that adaptation when once it had been achieved by habit would be handed on to succeeding generations by biological inheritance. The biologists of our time have forced us to realise that such "acquired characteristics" are not inherited. Each generation, except in so far as we create by selective breeding a somewhat better, or by the sterility of the finer individuals a somewhat worse, human type, will start, we are told, in essentials, not where their fathers left off, but where their fathers began.

And we find ourselves sometimes doubting, not only as to the future happiness of individuals in the Great Society, but as to the permanence of the Great Society itself. Why should we expect a social organisation to endure, which has been formed in a moment of time by human beings, whose bodies and minds are the result of age-long selection under far different conditions?

Social organisation on a large scale is not a wholly

[1] Quoted in *Collier's Weekly*, March 7, 1910.

new thing. For certain restricted purposes—chiefly the levying of taxes and the gathering of armies—the empires of Assyria, Persia, and Rome organised men on a scale not less than that of a modern state. Any one of those empires, at the moment of its greatest efficiency, must have seemed to the statesmen who were directing it from the centre to fulfil all the conditions of permanency. Each of them possessed not only irresistible military power, but a monopoly of all means of rapid communication, and the control of the only important body of accumulated wealth in the world which they knew. Yet the systems which created these powerful cohesive forces created at the same time disruptive forces which proved even more powerful. As the ancient empires became larger they became too distant and too unreal to stimulate the affection or pride of their subjects. The methods of their agents became more mechanical and inhuman, and the passions which grouped themselves round smaller units, local or racial or religious, produced an ever-increasing inner strain. In Hosea, or Daniel, or Revelations, or almost any of the scriptures of that tiny East-Mediterranean people who were incorporated into all the ancient empires in succession, we can feel the tension which ultimately broke up the systems of Nineveh and Rome. And in the colder analysis of Thucydides' Corcyrean chapters we can estimate the passions of class and city which prevented the formation, even for a single generation, of a purely Hellenic national state.

Are there any signs of such an inner strain resulting from the size and impersonal power of the Great Society? Has the invention of representative government, as its advocates used to argue, prevented the forces of class or race or religion or self from ever again thrusting against the larger cohesion of the State? No one who tries to interpret the obscure feelings of half-articulate men and women will say so. France is a representative republic, and that republic is supported by a stronger feeling of political solidarity than is to be found in any other European nation. But who can be sure that the forces represented by the "sabotage" of the French railway servants or the turbulence of the vine-growers are declining? In America the racial and class feeling of the new immigrants shows itself unexpectedly resistant to the dissolving force of national consciousness. In England the "particularism" of trades and professions and the racial feeling of Wales or Ulster, of Scotland or Catholic Ireland, seem to be growing stronger and not weaker.

More threatening still to the cohesion of the Great Society are the motives openly avowed by some of the American and European masters of concentrated capital, the men who direct enormous social power without attempting to form a social purpose, who smash working-class Unions with no idea of any system which may take their place, who boast that their trade is their politics, and corrupt whole parties merely to increase the personal wealth which they will waste in making or buying things that they hardly desire. The "cash nexus" has no more than the "voting nexus" secured that common membership of the Great Society shall mean a common interest in its solidarity. Even the Churches which claim to be Catholic, and whose formulas imply that it is their first duty to see ecumenical society as a whole, too often seem to put up their political and social influence to be sold to the highest bidder, and swing from side to side in the ship of state like a loose gun. And everywhere the preachers of Syndicalism and "direct action," the editors of clerical-ist newspapers, the owners of "predatory wealth," claim to represent the real and growing social forces as against the phrase-makers, the undenominationalists, the bloodless traitors to class or church, who stand for the community as a whole.

If one looks from the forces acting within the sepa-rate states to the forces which bear upon that relation between states without which world-industry and world-commerce cannot exist, one sees there too that the "Realpolitiker," the men who claim to voice in England or in Germany the living human passions, stand not for European unity but for European dis-ruption.

When, indeed, one gets behind the mechanical ar-rangements of railways and telegraphs, or of laws and treaties and elections, what are the real forces on which our hopes of national or international solidarity de-pend? One remembers afternoons spent in canvassing along the average streets of a modern city, and the words and looks which showed how weak are the feel-ings which attach the citizen to a society whose power he dimly recognises, but which he often seems to think of merely with distrust and dislike.

And if, once more, we turn away from Europe and the United States to the beginnings of the Great So-ciety in South America or China, the question whether the new system is creating sufficient cohesive force to ensure its own permanence becomes even more difficult to answer with confident hope.

But, owing to the very complexity of the relations which bind us to the Great Society, we stand to lose much more by any failure in its cohesion than did the subjects of the ancient empires. Up till our own time the vast majority of the inhabitants of the world lived in little, almost self-supporting, villages. If an empire broke up, some of these villages might be wasted by war, but the rest, like the cells of a divided rotifer, grouped themselves easily enough as part of a new body. If, at the capital of the empire, a population had been brought together which depended on a more intricate form of social organisation, that population was destroyed or scattered. Some day the Assyriologists will reconstruct for us the industrial and financial system, which enabled the inhabitants of Nineveh or Babylon to be fed and employed, and we shall then be able to imagine the sufferings which left those cities mere piles of ruins surrounded by a few peasants' huts. When the corn-ships of Egypt and the tribute-money of Gaul and Spain ceased to come to Rome, the population of the city sank from about a million to perhaps a third of that number. But now, thirty-five out of the forty-five million inhabitants of the United Kingdom depend for their food upon a system of world-relations far more complex than that which was built up by Assyria or Rome for the supply of their capitals. Let a European war break out—the war, perhaps, between the Triple Alliance and the Triple Entente, which so many journalists and politicians in England and Germany contemplate with criminal levity. If the combatants prove to be equally balanced, it may, after the first battles, smoulder on for thirty years. What will be the population of London, or Manchester, or Chemnitz, or Bremen, or Milan, at the end of it? Or what would be the condition of New York if a social war in Nevada between Trade Unionists and mine-owners should slowly spread over the Union and should last for a generation of recurrent fighting? The writers who are most fond of calling attention to the possibility of England becoming a thinly populated agricultural country like Denmark, or of New York being ruined by social unrest, generally do so in order to support some proposal for increased national armaments or for increased internal coercive authority in the hands of an undemocratic executive. England, for instance, is to enact compulsory service, build an ever vaster fleet, and challenge Germany by a more vigorous foreign and imperial policy. But if the problem is that of increasing the cohesive forces in the vaguely defined economic and political organisation of which both Germany and ourselves are part, we shall not solve it either by piling up armaments or by strengthening our police. Worldwide coercion, like Archimedes' lever, requires a fulcrum, and the believers in "strong government" never tell us where that fulcrum is to be found.

It is by imagining the effect of an actual dissolution of the Great Society that we can make most clear to ourselves the nature of our fears for its future. But even if the forces of cohesion and dissolution remain as evenly balanced as they are now, our prospects are dark enough. The human material of our social machinery will continue to disintegrate just at the points where strength is most urgently required. Men whom we are compelled to trust will continue to prefer the smaller to the larger good. The director will sacrifice the interest of his shareholders to his own or that of his family, the statesman will sacrifice his country to his party or his constituency or his Church, the Concert of Europe will remain helpless because each of its constituent nations refuses to work for the good of the whole. And the results of a system which we are not strong enough either to remodel or to control will continue to be seen in the slum and the sweating shop, the barracks and the base-hospital.

Throughout the politics and literature of the twentieth century one traces this fear, conscious or half-conscious, lest the civilisation which we have adopted so rapidly and with so little forethought may prove unable to secure either a harmonious life for its members or even its own stability. The old delight in the "manifest finger of destiny" and "the tide of progress," even the newer belief in the effortless "evolution" of social institutions are gone. We are afraid of the blind forces to which we used so willingly to surrender ourselves. We feel that we must reconsider the basis of our organised life because, without reconsideration, we have no chance of controlling it. And so behind the momentary ingenuities and party phrases of our statesmen we can detect the straining effort to comprehend while there is yet time. Our philosophers are toiling to refashion for the purposes of social life the systems which used so confidently to offer guidance for individual conduct. Our poets and playwrights and novelists are revolutionising their art in the attempt to bring the essential facts of the Great Society within its range.

All these efforts run counter to the intellectual habits in which our generation was brought up. On its intellectual side the Great Society was the work of specialists. During its formation we and our fathers learnt to admire, without a trace of that scorn which Jesus ben Sirach caught from his Greek masters, the leaders of specialised science—the chemists who are "wakeful to make clean the furnace," and the biologists "whose discourse is of the stock of bulls." Each of them became "wise in his own work." "Without them," we said, "shall not a city be inhabited, and we shall not sojourn nor walk up and down therein. . . . They will maintain the fabric of the world; and in the handy-work of their craft is their prayer." If we added: "They shall not be sought for in the council of the people, and in the assembly they shall not mount on high," [1] our scorn was meant, not for them, but for the politician and the generaliser.

We are forced, however, now to recognise that a society whose intellectual direction consists only of unrelated specialisms must drift, and that we dare not drift any longer. We stand, as the Greek thinkers stood, in a new world. And because that world is new, we feel that neither the sectional observations of the special student, nor the ever-accumulating records of the past, nor the narrow experience of the practical man can suffice us. We must let our minds play freely over all the conditions of life till we can either justify our civilisation or change it.

The Greek thinkers, with all their magnificent courage and comprehensiveness, failed in the end either to understand or to guide the actual social forces of their time. Our own brains are less acute, our memories less retentive than those of the Greeks, while the body of relevant fact which we must survey has been increased ten-thousand-fold. How are we to have any

[1] Ecclesiasticus, chap. xxxviii. (R.V.).

chance of success? I shall discuss in a later chapter the detailed expedients by which the peculiar knowledge of each among an organised body of men can be used to control their common action.[1] But the efficiency of such expedients is limited. In laboratories and universities and Government offices we can test hypotheses and compare results by means of the subdivided labour of hundreds of observers to whom each other's knowledge is unknown. But the formation of the original hypothesis, the inventive moment on which successful action depends, must take place in an individual brain. If we wish to estimate the real possibility of using the ever-growing mass of recorded fact for the guidance of organised social action, we must think, not of the long rows of tables and microscopes in a scientific laboratory, nor of the numbered stacks of books and maps in the British Museum or the Library of Congress, but of a minister or responsible official when he has put back his books on their shelves, has said good-bye to his last expert adviser, and sits with shut eyes at his desk, hoping that if he can maintain long enough the effort of straining expectancy some new idea will come into his mind. Can the conclusions of the specialist then reach him? In the case of the natural sciences we can see that they do, and we can watch the process by which this has been made possible. Between the original specialist and the man who applies his results to the organised conduct of life there exists a whole hierarchy of intellectual workers, turning out a series of text-books and Encyclopædia articles, each covering a wider field with less intensive treatment and fitting together isolated fragments of

[1] See Chapter XI.

knowledge into subordinate groups, as children do when they arrange the pieces of a picture puzzle. Their work is put out of date by every advance in the knowledge gained by original research, but while it lasts it makes that knowledge part of the effective intellectual machinery of each generation. A statesman, however little of a scientific specialist he may be, is not now likely to spend time or energy in speculation about engines driven by perpetual motion, or armies paid with gold produced by the formulas of the alchemists. Nor will he, like Pericles, plan a system of national defence which involves the bringing, year by year, of the population of a whole country-side to spend their summers in an undrained and already crowded city.

But in one important field extraordinarily little has been done to make the results of research available for the guidance of social action. During the last twenty years psychology has been applying new and more exact methods to the examination of the human mind. Throughout that time there has also been an immense output of books dealing with the general conditions of social organisation, many of them being based upon the opinions of the writers as to psychological facts. Much of the speaking and writing even of practical politicians has taken the form of psychological generalisations as to "human nature" and the rest. The influence, however, of the professed psychologists upon either the sociological writers or the practical politicians has been curiously small.

Colonel A. C. Yate, M.P., for instance, wrote not long ago, from the Athenæum Club, to the *Times*, to complain that Mr. Carnegie had called War a degrading evil. "Does Mr. Carnegie," he asked, "really understand human nature and the immutable laws which govern and guide it? Is the grand law of the 'selection of the fittest' to give way to the miserable mediocrity of compromise fostered by charity?" [1] Colonel Yate might perhaps find it more difficult than he would expect to put his "immutable laws" into explicit language. But if he did so, I am sure that they would not be found in any treatise by a competent psychologist.

If he, or any other member of the Athenæum, had written to the *Times* to ask whether Mr. Carnegie really understood the immutable laws which govern and guide electric dynamos, either he would have been referring to laws set out in accepted text-books, or, if he claimed to have discovered new laws, he would have set out his claim with a full sense of responsibility and have started an immediate and well-informed discussion. But though the laws which govern human nature are at least as important as those which govern dynamos, no one wrote to the *Times* to ask Colonel Yate what they were, and no other member of the Athenæum Club probably expressed any curiosity about them. Looseness of thought and language on the subject is taken for granted.

This book, therefore, like its predecessor,[2] is written with the practical purpose of bringing the knowledge which has been accumulated by psychologists into touch with the actual problems of present civilised life. My earlier book dealt in the main with the problem of representative government. This will deal with general social organisation, considered with special refer-

---

[1] *Times*, December 27, 1910.
[2] *Human Nature in Politics*, Constable, 1908.

ence to the difficulties created by the formation of what I have called the Great Society. I offer it to my readers in the hope that it may soon be superseded both by the discovery of new psychological facts and by the suggestion of more fertile applications.

CHAPTER II

SOCIAL PSYCHOLOGY

BEFORE indicating the lines on which the science of social psychology may, in my judgment, be made most useful for the organisation of the Great Society, I shall attempt in the two following chapters to give a rough indication of the subject-matter and terminology of the science itself.

The human species, like all other species of living things, consists of individuals no one of whom is exactly like any other, but all of whom conform more or less nearly to a common type. The science of social psychology aims at discovering and arranging the knowledge which will enable us to forecast, and therefore to influence, the conduct of large numbers of human beings organised in societies. It is accordingly concerned mainly with the type, and treats individual variations from it rather as instances of a general tendency to vary than as isolated facts.

Psychology, however, does not deal with all the human type-facts, and the first difficulty, both of general and of social psychology, is to limit in that respect its subject-matter, and to distinguish it from the subject-matter of physiology and anatomy.

There is no human type-fact which may not at some time or other influence the history of societies, from the liability of man to sunburn and frost-bite, or his fitness for animal and vegetable food, to his highest intellectual and emotional faculties. A general science of social anthropology might indeed be undertaken which should survey all the facts of human anatomy, physiology, and psychology as they bear on social organisation. Social psychology is not, however, that science. It deals, within limits which are felt by all psychologists to exist although there is little agreement on their details, only with the higher and more conscious facts of human behaviour.

Social psychology, like all other sciences, attempts to connect the events which it observes with antecedent causes. When these causes are facts of the human type, psychologists now tend to call them by the general term "disposition." When we observe that human beings are normally liable to fall in love, or to feel hunger or curiosity, we say that man has certain "dispositions" which cause these results. It is further convenient to use the term "human nature" as meaning the sum-total of the human "dispositions."

A "disposition" is sometimes obviously connected with a material fact in human anatomy. A visible injury, for instance, to a particular region of the brain is found to impair a particular intellectual faculty or to distort the normal action of some instinct. More often no such material relation can be demonstrated, and therefore most psychologists prefer not to dogmatise as to whether an infinitely strong microscope would reveal a material "cause" of all psychological dispositions, or whether indeed, in the ultimate analysis of the universe, there is such a thing as "matter" at all.[1]

---

[1] Mr. McDougall, in his *Social Psychology* (*e.g.* p. 29), in order to emphasise his refusal to dogmatise on the point whether all psychological dispositions have a material basis, calls them "psychophysical dispositions."

The next difficulty is one of terminology. At any given moment every human being has innumerable psychological tendencies. Some of these are inherited and some are acquired; or, to be more exact, all our inherited tendencies are modified by acquired experience. Shall the terms "disposition" and "nature" include the acquired as well as the inherited elements? I propose to use them so as to exclude the acquired elements. It follows, of course, that at no period of his life does a man's "nature" (as I shall use the term) actually exist. Inherited psychological dispositions reveal themselves, not all at birth, but gradually during life and growth. The man has already been changed by experience before most of his dispositions appear, and after its appearance each disposition is constantly influenced by further experience. A man's nature, that is to say, or any one of his dispositions, is an imaginary point, from which the effects of experience are assumed to start. The man, at any given moment, is the result of the action of his experience on his nature.

This use of words has the advantage of enabling the social psychologist to project, so to speak, all his facts on to one terminological plane. Both the habits of ordinary speech and the traditional presentation of their subject by writers on psychology have made it unnecessarily difficult to combine and compare such facts as that men feel pain, make calculations, and act in obedience to the impulse of anger. Pain is generally examined by close introspective attention to its momentary character, and is therefore generally spoken of as a fact in consciousness. Rational calculation is generally approached by the "logical" method of testing the validity of its various forms. It is therefore spoken of as a process. Anger is one of those instincts which have been "explained" during the last fifty years by reference to the course of human evolution. It is therefore spoken of as a fact in human or animal inherited structure. It is only when we project all three facts on the single plane of structure, and speak of the three *dispositions* to feel pain, to reason, and to become angry that the combination and comparison of such factors in any given social problem become easy.[1]

The statement, however, that psychological events are the result of the relation between our experience and our nature raises the metaphysical and ethical objection that those who make it seem to deny free will and therefore to paralyse human energy. An able and temperate writer, for instance, in the *Manchester Guardian*, when reviewing a treatise on social psychology, urged: "It is apt to take us perilously near to the sort of determinism which sets out an array of independent warring motives, each fighting on its own account, with the ego or self keeping the ring and registering the victory of the stronger."[2]   And a clerical

---

[1] A corresponding difficulty of language caused endless confusion during that "age of faith," between 1820 and 1870, when men really attempted to apply Political Economy to the conduct of social life. Payment for the use of land had been habitually considered from the point of view of the landlord, who reckons his possessions in units of area, and was called "rent." Payment for the use of "capital," of a railway, for instance, had been habitually considered from the point of view of the investor, who reckons his savings in units of value, and was called "interest." It was therefore extraordinarily difficult for the practical man, who "believed in political economy," to treat "rent" and "interest" as comparable things, unless he forced himself to realise that the income derived from ownership of a railway could be calculated as rent per acre of track, and the income from land as interest per hundred pounds invested. Only within the last few years have American reformers, after wandering for a generation between Henry Georgism and Marxism, begun to use phrases like "the physical valuation of railways," which make it possible to project statements about "land" and "capital" on to one plane.

[2] *Manchester Guardian*, Dec. 14, 1908.

speaker in the Cambridge Senate House strongly opposed the establishment of a special examination in Psychology, on the ground that Psychology was "immoral and mischievous, a blinding of man to the responsibility of his actions." [1]

This objection has always been brought against any intrusion of cause and effect into regions hitherto assigned to the free activity of human or superhuman will. Aristophanes attacked Socrates for impiety and materialism in teaching that the clouds were mechanical emanations and not divine persons. Socrates himself, in Plato's *Phædo*, attacks the physiological studies of Anaxagoras on the same ground. He is explaining to his disciples why he refused to take the hint conveyed to him by the Athenian Government that his escape would be connived at. Anaxagoras, he says, would argue

. . . that I am sitting here because my body is composed of bones and muscles, and that the bones are hard and separated by joints, while the muscles can be tightened and loosened. . . . But he would quite forget to mention the real cause, which is that, since the Athenians thought it right to condemn me, *I* have thought it right and just to sit here and to submit to whatever sentence they may think fit to impose. For, by the dog of Egypt, I think that these muscles and bones would long ago have been in Megara or Bœotia, prompted by *their* opinion of what is best, if *I* had not thought it better and more honourable to submit to whatever penalty the State inflicts rather than escape by flight. [2]

The philosophical answer to this objection may be left to the philosophers, with the proviso that they

---

[1] *Westminster Gazette*, Nov. 3, 1910.
[2] *Phædo* (p. 179, Golden Treasury Series).

shall give us a conception of the relation between freedom and determinism which shall apply to the whole living universe, and that they shall not draw an arbitrary line, as some of them seem inclined to do, dividing certain facts of psychology, which are legitimate subjects of scientific enquiry, from others which are not. It may be sufficient here to urge the empirical consideration that, throughout the history of mankind and in every branch of science, those who have really advanced our knowledge of causes and effects have felt their energy, and even their sense of "freedom," to be increased rather than paralysed by what they have learnt.

When these philosophical and terminological difficulties have been overcome or avoided, we are in a position to consider what should be the actual choice and arrangement of human psychological dispositions in that working "projection" (to use again the mapmakers' term) of human nature, which is most convenient for the special applied science of social psychology. The facts when chosen will, of course, include only a very small fraction of our recorded knowledge as to the human type. Not only will a vast number of facts be excluded as more appropriate to the sciences of anatomy and physiology, but a large proportion even of known psychological facts will be left to the general science of psychology. Each social psychologist will, that is to say, place on his working projection only those facts which he believes to be relevant to the social problems of his age, although he will, from time to time, dip, and urge others to dip, into the sea of hitherto irrelevant facts, with the hope of discovering new causal relationships between some of them and the subject-matter of his own work. Speaking generally, he will find that, while certain broad facts of human psychology are relevant to all the applied psychological sciences—pedagogic, or pathological, or social—each of the applied sciences must make its own choice of details.

But as soon as he begins his provisional selection of facts, the social psychologist will meet with a further question of arrangement. Shall he separate his psychological facts as far as possible into their ultimate elements, or gather them into the largest groups which can be shown to have a causal connection with each other? If I let a drop of hot sealing-wax fall on my finger, I feel a momentary sensation of touch followed by a prolonged sensation of pain. I jerk my hand off the table, shake it, and put my finger to my mouth. Then I look round the room, with a vague hope of finding something to cure the pain and prevent bad results. I open perhaps a drawer in which I keep odds and ends. As I do so I remember being told that boracic powder is good for a burn, and that there is some in a room upstairs, to which I accordingly go. Any other normal human being will act more or less in the same way, and the whole process may be conceived of as the result of the nearer environmental fact of the hot sealing-wax, and of the more distant environmental facts stored in my memory, acting on the inherited dispositions which make up my "nature." But it is clear that my "nature" may be divided either into such "elementary" dispositions as those which make me successively feel pain, start, jerk my hand, etc., or into more "complex" dispositions producing connected series of such events. If we confine ourselves, for in-

stance, to the series of events beginning with the drop-
ping of the sealing-wax and ending with the bringing of
the finger to the mouth, they may all be referred to
one complex disposition which inclines me to bring
any part of my body that feels a burning pain to my
mouth.

The same is true of my later action. It may be
treated either as the result of many elementary dispositions to perceive, to remember, to decide, etc.; or as
the one result of a single complex disposition to search,
with the help both of the senses and of the memory, for
means of relieving pain.

The series of events chosen might have been even
more complex than those which normally follow an accidental burn, and the same statement would have
been true. The behaviour of mothers in bringing up
children, or of men in the long process of making fortunes, or of astronomers discovering planets, may be
treated as instances either of innumerable elementary
dispositions, or of the three complex dispositions of
mother-love, acquisitiveness, and curiosity.

In dealing with particular problems the social
psychologist will of course use whichever method is
most convenient for his particular purpose. I shall,
for instance, mainly use the complex analysis in the
first part of this book, and a particular elementary analysis is in the second part. But for that preliminary
view of his subject-matter, which he will carry half-
consciously in his mind and use for his wider specula-
tions, the social psychologist will, I believe, be wise
to explain human conduct rather by the complex dispositions, which are the Greatest Common Measures

of human nature, than by the elementary dispositions, which are its Least Common Measures.

With regard, therefore, to our elementary dispositions I do not propose to do more here than indicate the character of the most important of them. They are described at length in all the text-books of psychology, and include the senses, and such measurable facts as memory and association, habit and fatigue. They may be arranged on several schemes of classification, either, for instance, as physiological facts observed from outside, or (in the scheme which I shall use in the second part of this book) as forms of consciousness, such as cognition, conation (or "Will"), and feeling, observed from within. The social psychologist must know about them, but he will often get his knowledge most conveniently from books written without any special reference to social organisation. For the special needs of his science he will find that the most important point for him to realise about these elementary dispositions is the quantitative limitations of them all, the fact, for instance, that we cannot see or hear or remember much more than was required by our earliest human ancestors, or endure much more exertion than was necessary for them in gathering food.

The complex dispositions with which the social psychologists have mainly to deal may be roughly grouped as Instinct and Intelligence, and one of the reasons why social psychology has had so little influence on social organisation is that it is extremely difficult to apply to the study of Instinct and Intelligence the exact methods of modern natural science. Certain elementary dispositions—the senses, the reflexes, memory, and so on—have been examined during the last thirty years by trained experimentalists, using mechanical apparatus in specially equipped laboratories. These men have been able to arrange innumerable tests under identical conditions, and therefore to compare results with confidence and to compile exact statistical records. Their success has been unmistakable and progressive. They have made scores of well-established discoveries on such points as the limitations and illusions of sight and hearing and touch, or of those newly observed "ampullar" and "vestibular" senses which guide some of our subconscious movements. Elementary mental processes, like association or memory, which we are apt to take for granted, have been also shown to be capable of precise measurements.[1] The experimentalists have been assisted by the immense progress which has recently taken place in the general physiology of the nervous system, and indeed their greatest successes have been made in the frontier region between physiology and psychology. Many of these discoveries are being applied, or soon will be applied, to practical purposes. The schoolmaster is already arranging his lessons with a view to economy of effort, and will soon use immensely more effective means in testing the fitness of each pupil for any particular course.[2] The nerve-doctor no longer gives his advice wholly in the dark. It is becoming possible for the men who have to handle machines or choose and employ others to do so—the aviator, the typewriter, the factory manager—to acquire a working knowledge, not only of wheels and bands and valves,

[1] See, e.g., C. S. Myers, *Text-book of Experimental Psychology*, and E. B. Titchener, *Text-book of Psychology*.
[2] See, e.g., Cyril Burt, "Experimental Tests of General Intelligence," *British Journal of Psychology*, December, 1909.

but also of the nervous systems which are to co-operate with them. The advertisement manager is learning how to secure that his placards shall be both noticed and remembered.[1]

The social psychologist, when he is dealing with those facts in human nature on which the experimentalists have worked, receives invaluable guidance both from their results and from their method and spirit. He can now use words like pain or pleasure or habit in a clearer sense than that given by the loose associations of ordinary speech. Human instincts have been made much more intelligible by recent experimental work on the instinctive behaviour of other animals. Even when he deals with reason he finds that the still more recent experimental enquiries into the forms of consciousness which accompany thought are rich in both positive and negative suggestions.

But the facts of human nature which are of the greatest importance to the social psychologist are just those to which laboratory methods are least applicable. It is almost impossible to arrange a series of identical experiments to illustrate the working of patriotism or ambition or the property instinct or artistic and intellectual creativeness. In such matters the social psychologist must be content with the instances which arise in ordinary life, and must examine them by the older methods of introspection, personal evidence, and analogy. In so doing he knowingly lays himself open to the contempt of the experimentalist. Professor E. B. Titchener of Cornell, for instance, who is one of the

[1] See, e.g., many ingenious suggestions for the practical application of psychology to business in Professor Muensterberg's *American Problems* and *Psychology and Industrial Efficiency*.

most fruitful and devoted of experimental psychologists, says:

For the past two thousand years psychology has been resting upon plausibilities and probabilities. Now that we are beginning to have a psychology of facts, it is both honesty and policy to state where the facts end and speculative construction begins.[1]

Contempt of this kind will do the social psychologist no harm, and may help to guard him against that facility in *ad hoc* psychological generalisation, of which current sociological literature is full. Much indeed that is now written by sociologists on such psychological points as "Imitation," or "Sympathy," or "The Psychology of the Crowd," [2] gives Professor Titchener ample justification for the statement that:

So far is applied psychology from reliance upon the parent discipline, that some of its most widely used and most strongly emphasised ideas contravene established scientific principle.[3]

But the purpose of social psychology is to guide human action; and human action takes place in a world which pays little attention to the exact degrees of our knowledge and our ignorance. It is clear that we do possess the more complex dispositions, and that they do exercise an important influence on our social conduct; and important causes will, in every social problem, remain important, however inadequate our means of examining them may be, while unimportant causes will remain unimportant, however accurately we observe and measure them.

[1] Titchener, *Text-book of Psychology*, p. 457.
[2] See *infra*, Chapter VIII.
[3] Titchener, "The Past Decade in Experimental Psychology," *American Journal of Psychology*, 1910, xxi, pp. 404-421.

CHAPTER III

IN approaching the complex dispositions into which the facts of human nature can be divided for the purposes of social psychology, it is convenient to begin with the Instincts. Every treatise on psychology has its list of human instincts, and every list varies somewhat from the others. Most of them, however, include hunger, parental affection, play, pugnacity, sex, hunting, curiosity, fear, gregariousness, shyness, cleanliness, acquisitiveness, display, and constructiveness. To such a list each applied psychological science will make its own additions. The future science, for instance, of architectural psychology will add the æsthetic sense of symmetry, and the queer little instinct which makes us desire to sleep with our feet towards the light; while the psychology of baby-minding will emphasise the instinct which inclines a baby to put any small newly-observed object into its mouth. Social psychology for its part will add certain instincts which are developed at rather late periods of our growth. Among these, for instance, will be what the Germans call Wanderlust—the desire which comes on the growing boy to leave the family and set up for himself—and the two instincts which Mr. McDougall calls negative and positive "self-feeling," but which I prefer to call the conflicting instincts (both of them being necessary in a gregarious or semi-gregarious society) to "give a lead" to others, and "to take a lead" from others. It will also include a number of extremely intricate facts, which I shall deal with in a later chapter,[1] and which are usually ascribed to instincts of "Imitation" and "Sympathy."

The best definition which I know of the whole class of instincts is that given by Mr. McDougall in his *Social Psychology:*

We may, then, define an instinct as an inherited or innate psycho-physical disposition which determines its possessor to perceive and to pay attention to objects of a certain class, to experience an emotional excitement of a particular quality upon perceiving such an object, and to act in regard to it in a particular manner, or at least to experience an impulse to such action.[2]

As this definition indicates, the normal course by which an instinctive disposition reveals itself is the impact on our nervous system of some appropriate external or internal physical occurrence (called the "stimulus") followed, either simultaneously, or in succession to each other, by conscious feeling and muscular movement. A full psychological terminology ought

[1] *Infra,* Chapter VIII.
[2] W. McDougall, *Social Psychology,* p. 29. There are two dictionary meanings of the words "instinct," "instinctive," "instinctively," etc., in both of which they may be correctly used. The first meaning follows from the definition of innate instinct which I have quoted above. The second meaning is "like an innate instinct" (in respect of prerational impulse, etc.), as in the statement, quoted by Mr. McDougall, that a drunkard fed on fruit "becomes instinctively a teetotaler" (*Social Psychology,* p. 21). The two meanings are, as he points out, often confused; and, therefore, though I think that he is wrong in holding the second to be illegitimate, it is best in psychological writing to confine oneself, as I shall do, strictly to the first.

(as Mr. McDougall also points out) to contain, in the case of each instinct, separate names for the disposition itself and for both the feeling and the action which result from its stimulation. Ordinary language, however, is not so exact. We name the Hunger instinct from the feeling, the Play instinct from the action, and Pugnacity or Acquisitiveness from the disposition itself.

If we look at the phenomena of Instinct throughout the whole animal world, we find that they fall into two main groups: one group being best illustrated by the behaviour of insects and certain other animals which have their hard tissues on the surface of the body, and the other group apparently diverging at the point in evolution represented by the appearance of an internal skeleton, and best illustrated by the behaviour of man and the other higher mammals.[1] A solitary wasp will seize a caterpillar of one particular species, will sting it in a particular way, lay her egg on it, and carry it to her nest to be walled in in a particular manner. She will do this only once, and after her death the wasp hatched from her egg will go through the same ritual. Her action is not "mechanical" in the ordinary sense of the term, because it is characterised by a rapid and successful adaptation to such details as the position of the caterpillar, the obstacles to be surmounted, and the

---

[1] "Zoologists divide the animal kingdom into two great groups, whose lines of descent are distinct as far down as the flat-worms. The one of these leads through the unsegmented and segmented worms to the insects, spiders, and crustaceans; the other leads through various invertebrate forms, largely extinct, to the vertebrates, and so finally to men. Students of animal behaviour also divide the animals into two great groups, those that are markedly plastic in their responses to stimulation, and those that are markedly fixed. The interesting point to us is that these groupings coincide" (Titchener, *Text-book of Psychology*, 1910, p. 457).

character of the soil in which the burrow is formed. We have no evidence as to the conscious feeling which may accompany it. It may be one of conscious adaptation while acting and of delight in success. But it is difficult to believe that the wasp's action, performed as it is once for all by an animal which has never seen it done before, can be accompanied by any conscious elements of memory or association or imaginative forecasting of the result.

Vertebrate animals perform in early youth actions which are analogous to the instinctive performances of the wasp. Chickens, newly hatched from the shell, all peck at seeds in the same way. Children, who have never seen other children crawling, will, at the appropriate age, begin to crawl by making preordained movements of the legs and arms. Later on, a carefully brought-up child, who has perhaps never been really afraid before, or seen anyone really afraid, will in the presence of a runaway horse or of the blood from a wound, perform the purely instinctive acts of running away, screaming, hiding, etc. When such instinctive acts are gone through for the first time by a child (and, if we may argue from analogy, when they are gone through for the first time by any one of the higher vertebrates) the performer is fully aware of what he is doing, and even of his effort to adapt his action to the details of his surroundings, though he has no knowledge of what he will do next.

But in the normal course of vertebrate life the chief instinctive actions are performed, not once for all, as in the case of the wasp, but repeatedly. At each repetition, even in the case of birds and non-human mammals, memory and acquired habit must enter as forces modifying both the action itself and the forms of consciousness which accompany the action. Not long, therefore, after birth, men, and apparently the other higher vertebrates, begin to live in an atmosphere of organised ideas, of memory, that is to say, association and imagination. An Esquimaux or Indian hunter, and, to a less degree, perhaps, an experienced old wolf, follows, it is true, an imperious instinct in seeking game, but he does so with an ever-growing memory of earlier hunts, with an exact conception of what he is going to do next, and with some prevision of the probable result.

In the case of man, this irradiation of instinctive action by intelligence shades into processes in which intelligence acts as an independent directing force. Instead, for instance, of a purely instinctive impulse to hunt being made more effective by intelligence, our decision to hunt may itself be due to a preliminary process of reflection upon our future wants and the possible ways of satisfying them.

This independent action of Intelligence is, I believe, in its simplest forms as "natural" to us, as much due to inherited disposition, as is the working of any one of the usual list of instincts. The traditional terminology, however, of the moral sciences makes it extraordinarily difficult either to recognise this fact or even to state it clearly.

A hundred years ago professors and schoolmasters taught that men were completely "rational," and that the other animals were completely "instinctive." Men, and men alone, were born with the power of learning from experience; and the power of learning from experience was at birth their whole psychological equipment. If different men tended to behave in the same way under the same circumstances, it was not because they were born with the same instincts, but because they had gone through the same experiences, and, through association and inference, had formed the same habits. Animals were as completely instinctive as men were rational. Some theologians and philosophers declared that all animals were unconscious automata. Even those who allowed them a degree of consciousness were apt to state or imply that their conduct under any given circumstances was absolutely fixed by instincts on whose perfection and independence of experience the defenders of Final Causes were never tired of dwelling. A boy who had been brought up among dogs and ferrets, or a girl who had helped to manage her baby brothers and sisters, would never have dared to introduce their knowledge either of animal intelligence or of human instincts into an essay on "Instinct and Reason."

It did not occur, therefore, to any one except the eccentric Lord Monboddo, or Erasmus Darwin, the precursor of evolution, that a student of human psychology could learn anything from the psychology of animals. Jeremy Bentham troubled himself as little about the relation between animal instinct and human intelligence as he did about the relation between eighteenth century institutions and medieval history. The word "instinct" does not occur in the enormous index to his collected works. If, however, one translates Bentham into the terms of modern psychology, one may say that he divided the whole nature of man into two parts: an irresistible instinctive disposition to seek pleasure and avoid pain, and a passionless faculty of ascertaining through reason the means by which that disposition can be satisfied. William Godwin, in a passage in his diary, written possibly after he had been reading Bentham, puts this position quite clearly:

Reason, accurately speaking, has not the smallest degree of power to put any one limb or articulation of our bodies into motion. Its province in a practical view is wholly confined to adjusting the comparison between different objects of desire, and investigating the most successful mode of attaining those objects. It proceeds upon the assumption of their desirableness or the contrary, and neither accelerates nor retards the vehemence of their pursuit, but merely regulates its direction and points the road by which we shall proceed to our goal.[1]

But Bentham and Godwin, while thus apparently disparaging Reason by denying it any power over human conduct, were really exaggerating its functions. If so general a thing as Happiness is taken as the sole end of action, and if Reason alone chooses the means of reaching that end, Reason becomes all-important. The utilitarians are therefore rightly called "intellectualists," and their "intellectualism" was the more misleading because they sometimes argued as if Reason always drew conclusions from its premises with mechanical perfection, and as if those premises as they stood in the mind of any reasoning being were identical with the objective facts in the world outside him.

Since Darwin, however, the study of human nature on lines suggested by comparative psychology has shown that we have many different instincts, and that they dispose us not merely to search through reason for the means of satisfying them, but directly to perform certain appropriate actions. We have learnt that

[1] *Life of Godwin* (C. K. Paul), vol. i, p. 294, under date 1798.

if we see a man run away or burst into tears, we are not bound to infer that he does so because his reason has selected that action for him as the best way of securing pleasure or avoiding pain.

But in criticising the Intellectualism of the Utilitarians, modern social psychologists are apt to fall into a kind of anti-intellectualism which involves a curiously similar fallacy. Mr. McDougall, for instance, in his *Social Psychology*, gives a list of "the principal human instincts." It consists (pp. 45-89) of Flight, Repulsion, Curiosity, Pugnacity, Self-abasement, Self-assertion, the Parental Instinct, Reproduction, the Gregarious Instinct, Acquisitiveness, Constructiveness.

With regard to the whole list he writes, in an eloquent passage:

We may say, then, that, directly or indirectly, the instincts are the prime movers of all human activity; by the conative or impulsive force of some instinct (or of some habit derived from an instinct) every train of thought, however cold and passionless it may seem, is borne along towards its end, and every bodily activity is initiated and sustained. The instinctive impulses determine the end of all activities, and supply the driving power by which all mental activities are sustained; and all the complex intellectual apparatus of the most highly developed mind is but a means towards these ends, is but the instrument by which those impulses seek their satisfactions, while pleasure and pain do but serve to guide them in their choice of the means.

Take away these instinctive dispositions with their powerful impulses, and the organism would become incapable of activity of any kind; it would lie inert and motionless like a wonderful clockwork whose mainspring had been removed, or a steam-engine whose fires had been drawn.[1]

[1] *Social Psychology*, p. 44.

The first defect, as it seems to me, in this statement is that Mr. McDougall does not project his facts as to Reason and Instinct on to one plane. He distinguishes between "instinctive impulses" and "intellectual apparatus." Fear, for instance, he would apparently say, is "impulse," and Thought is "apparatus." But Fear and Thought, if we project our dispositions on to the plane of consciousness, are both impulses; and if we project them on to the plane of structure they are both of them "apparatus." Both, that is to say, to quote again Mr. McDougall's own definition of Instinct, are "psychophysical dispositions, which determine their possessors to . . . pay attention to objects of a certain class . . . and to act in regard to them in a particular manner." [1] Mr. McDougall indeed himself includes Curiosity in his list of Instincts, although he would find it difficult to say that the "particular manner" in which Curiosity inclines us to "act" does not involve "mental activity" and the use of "intellectual apparatus." But behind this (as it seems to me) formal fallacy lies, I believe, a real difference between Mr. McDougall and myself. Mr. McDougall does not hold, as I hold, that we are born with a tendency, under appropriate conditions, to think, which is as original and independent as our tendency, under appropriate conditions, to run away.

The anti-intellectualism of M. Ribot's *Psychology of the Emotions* does not involve the same formal fallacy as that which appears to me to be contained in the passage which I have quoted from Mr. McDougall. He dwells on a true and regrettable fact of human

---

[1] *Ante,* p. 33.

nature, that the physiological and instinctive dispositions have more compelling force than the intelligent dispositions; although he seriously exaggerates its truth. "Who does not know," he says, "that intellectual passions are mere phantoms which a real passion sweeps away like a gust of wind?" [1] And again, "What is fundamental in the character is the instincts, tendencies, impulses, desires, and feelings, all these and nothing else." [2]

But when Mr. Leslie Stephen wrote: "Men are not governed by their abstract principles, but by their passions and emotions," [3] one recognises that his distrust of rationalism again uses the fallacy of the two planes to give itself an apparent logical cogency, as when a farmer's distrust of book-learning makes him say: "Lads get on in the world not by algebra, but by hard work."

[1] *Psychology of the Emotions* (Eng. Trans.), p. 393.
[2] *Ibid.*, p. 390.
[3] *The English Utilitarians*, vol. ii, p. 329. I turned, when writing the passage above, somewhat anxiously to the pages of my *Human Nature in Politics*, in which I myself attacked the intellectualism of Bentham and his followers, to see whether I there fell into the same kind of anti-intellectualism which I here criticise. I find there little or nothing which I should like to withdraw. I should, however, for my present purpose, write with a somewhat different emphasis. And there is one sentence which I should wish to modify, that in which I say: "Impulse, it is now agreed, has an evolutionary history of its own earlier than the history of those intellectual processes by which it is often directed and modified" (p. 25). This distinction between instinctive "impulse" and intellectual "process" seems to me to be open to the same accusation of projection on two planes which I have made above against Mr. McDougall's statement. I should now write it: "Instinctive impulses, it is now agreed, have an evolutionary history of their own earlier than the history of those intellectual impulses by which they are often directed and modified." I am the more inclined to make this correction after reading the headlines of a review of my *Human Nature in Politics* in the *New York City Mail*, where it is described as a "Startling analysis" of "a field of action into which reason seldom enters."

Professor E. Ray Lankester rightly told the Biological Society of Paris, in 1899, that "the mechanisms of intelligence" are "later in the history of the development of the brain" than "the mechanisms of instinct," but I know of no evidence to justify his further statement that the latter "can only develop in proportion as the former become feeble and defective."[1]

All social historians who treat of the nineteenth century are agreed as to the practical evils which resulted from the intellectualist bias of utilitarian politics and economics. The horrors of the early factory system were prolonged by the authoritative doctrine that both parties in any industrial contract might be trusted to secure their own "interest"; while those who "believed in Political Economy" tended to inhibit their own disposition towards pity for the victims of industrial processes, because of a confused theory that disinterested pity either did not exist, or existed without

---

[1] *Nature,* April 26, 1900, pp. 624, 625.—The present position of the controversy as to the relation between Instinct and Reason is admirably illustrated by a symposium held in July, 1910, at a joint meeting of the Aristotelian Society and the British Psychological Association, and reported in the *British Journal of Psychology* for October, 1910. Professor C. S. Myers, who opened the discussion, took, as I read him, essentially the position which I have adopted in this chapter, *i.e.,* that the various types of "instinctive" and "intelligent" behaviour all involve a "conscious awareness of end," and all are plastic under the influence of experience and effort, but that "instincts" are relatively more fixed and less conscious, and the intelligent dispositions relatively more conscious and less fixed. "In what," he says, "is ordinarily called instinctive behaviour, the innate mechanism is relatively fixed and given; in what is ordinarily called intelligent behaviour the mechanism is relatively plastic and acquired" (p. 270). And again: "Thus the psychology and physiology of instinct are inseparable from the psychology and physiology of intelligence. There is not one nervous apparatus for instinct and another for intelligence. We ought to speak, not of instinct and intelligence, but of instinct-intelligence, treating the two as one indivisible mental function, which, in the course of evolution, has approached now nearer to so-called instinct, now nearer to so-called intelligence" (p. 267). He suggests that the word "Instinct" might

any scientific right to do so. Electoral systems both in England and America were during the nineteenth century often constructed on the assumption that any voter would certainly choose, among a long and complicated list of candidates, or in a chaos of overlapping authorities, the representative who would bring about his greatest happiness—and the slums of London and New York are in part the consequence. One of the reasons of the failure of the revolutionary martyrs of 1848, and of two generations of Russian reformers, was that many of them assumed that, as soon as they issued a proclamation, it would be known, understood, and acted upon by every one concerned.

But the loose anti-intellectualism which now threatens to take the place of the old intellectualism may prove to be infinitely more dangerous in the twentieth century. An internecine European war is the one enormous disaster which overhangs our time; and such a war is made more possible whenever thought is represented as the mere servant of the lower passions, and

---

be used, as I use the word "disposition" for the whole Instinct-Intelligence series. "In one book," he says (Kirkpatrick, *Fundamentals of Child Study*), "I find enumerated the instincts of imitation, curiosity, and play; the expressive, æsthetic, moral, and religious instincts; the parental and social instincts; the collecting, constructive, destructive, and fighting instincts. May we not complete the list by adding the instincts of thought, reason, intelligence?" (p. 215).

But he suddenly, and, as it seems to me, quite unnecessarily, falls into what I have called the "two planes fallacy." Having carefully explained that the difference between the instinctive and intelligent dispositions is a quantitative one, *i.e.*, consists in the relative importance of certain factors in each, he goes on to say: "These two terms (Instinct and Intelligence) we must recognise as pure abstractions relating to different aspects of the same mental processes, not to different mental processes" (*ibid.*, p. 268); and (p. 218), "Instinct regarded from within becomes intelligence; intelligence regarded from without becomes instinct."

A difference of aspect is for the purpose of his argument no difference at all.

a cynical struggle for life as the only condition which
answers to the deeper facts of our nature. The French
syndicalist writers, as I shall show in a later chapter,[1]
have constructed a whole philosophy of anarchism on
an anti-intellectualist basis. In England, perhaps the
most obvious effect of the new trend of thought is seen
in current ecclesiastical apologetic. An able reviewer,
for instance, in the *Church Times* of September 9,
1910, writes:

> On the whole, it is true to say that in the great decisions
> of life, when we have to choose between Christianity and
> infidelity; between Anglicanism and Romanism; between
> Conservatism and Socialism—the decision is only made
> superficially on intellectual grounds, *and would be made all
> the same however much weaker the evidence was.* With the
> increase in our knowledge of psychology, which is to be an-
> ticipated in the next few years, this will probably become
> much clearer.[2]

Dr. A. W. Robinson spoke even more clearly to the
Church Congress in 1909:

> The function of the intellect is to find reasons for a
> course of action which, on other than intellectual grounds,
> we are inclined to desire or approve.[3]

One is curiously reminded of certain advice which
that old fox, King Leopold I. of Belgium, gave to his
niece Victoria on her accession to the English throne:

> A rule which you may thus early impress on your mind
> is, that people are far from acting generally according to

[1] Chapter XII.
[2] *Church Times*, September 9, 1910. The italics are my own.
[3] *Ibid.*, October 8, 1909.

the dictation of their interest, but oftener in consequence of their passions.

And

> The Established Church I also recommend strongly. You cannot, without pledging yourself to anything in particular, say too much on the subject.[1]

The philosophy of syndicalism constitutes, I believe, a very real danger to Trade Unionism in France. An anti-intellectualist apologetic may in the end prove to be an equally real danger to the Church in England. Thought may be late in evolution, it may be deplorably weak in driving power, but without its guidance no man or organisation can find a safe path amid the vast impersonal complexities of the universe as we have learnt to see it.

But even if, as I believe, Intelligence is as truly a part of our inherited nature, and as independent a cause of human action as any of the traditional list of instincts, it is not a sufficient analysis of the facts merely to add a single disposition to the rest and call it Intelligence. There are at least two dispositions, Curiosity and "Trial and Error," which sometimes cause action which is rather instinctive than intelligent, and sometimes action which is rather intelligent than instinctive. And there are two other dispositions (which I shall call Thought and Language) whose action is normally, if not invariably, intelligent.

Curiosity may be placed almost exactly on the doubtful line which divides Instinct from Intelligence. In its simplest form this disposition was apparently

---

[1] *Queen Victoria's Letters,* February 3, 1837, and June 23, 1837.

evolved as a means of enabling living beings to avoid
danger, or gain advantage, from objects which were
too unusual to excite, at their first appearance, any
one of the more specific instincts, but which might do
so on nearer inspection. Under its influence a human
being or other higher animal experiences a strong impulse to go cautiously up to the unusual object, and
to examine it by touch, smell, etc., as well as by the
sense (usually sight or hearing) by which it was first
observed. During the approach and examination, the
larger muscles are tightened, so as to be ready for in-
stantaneous reaction when the more specific instinct
(fear, for instance, or hunger, or the hunting instinct)
shall have been stimulated. In so far as these bodily
movements constitute the essence of the process there
is nothing to distinguish Curiosity from any one of
the ordinary list of instincts.

But the behaviour characteristic of Curiosity is normally (and not merely as the result of acquired habit)
accompanied by certain activities of our intellectual
powers. We are, when curious, conscious of a strong
effort of attention, which increases the fertility both of
memory and association; and both in the child and in
the adult Curiosity may be stimulated by an idea presented by memory or association as well as by an external fact. Sometimes the astronomer who sits at his
telescope watching, in a passion of Curiosity, a newly
flaming star, finds that all that is left of the impulse
towards cautious approach with a view to the stimulation of some bodily act, is a quickened pulse or a
slight and rather troublesome trembling of his hand.
The heightening of attention and memory acting on
his organised system of ideas and experience becomes

the essential element of the whole process. If, therefore, a distinction is to be drawn between Instinct and Intelligence, the disposition of Curiosity may in his case be classed as almost purely intelligent.

The disposition again, which students of animal behaviour call "Trial and Error," provides a process by which an animal can find a means of satisfying some strong instinctive desire, when the bodily acts characteristic of the simpler instincts have failed to do so. Under such circumstances the animal begins a succession of random movements, accompanied, apparently, by intense and often distressing nervous excitement. One of these movements may succeed in producing a useful result. If so, and if the same difficulty recurs again, the process will be gone through in a shortened form. Finally, the successful act will be repeated with no preliminary random movements, and a useful habit will have been formed.

The Trial and Error process may take place, even among mankind, with little or no accompaniment of intelligence. An absent-minded man, with a new pocket for his railway-ticket, may go through the whole ritual of random search every morning for a fortnight while he is reading his newspaper, and may finally acquire a new and useful habit of which he is completely unconscious. A stupid cook will attack the handles and valves of a new stove with no more intelligence than is used by a goldfish darting about a new tank. But normally the nervous excitement characteristic of Trial and Error brings memory and association into vigorous play, and the bodily acts are accompanied and in part controlled by a stream of

more or less conscious recollections and inferences.[1]
Many uneducated people, indeed, can only do intellectual work in the mental attitude of Trial and Error,
though the random muscular movements which accompany their efforts are worse than useless to them.
I remember that a railway porter once said to me,
"Jim Brown is working to pass his examination as a
signalman, and it has got so on his mind that he
jumped up in bed last night and blacked his wife's
eye."

In the case of Thought the essential functions of
the disposition are clearly intellectual. The word
"thought" is used in many senses. Sometimes, for
instance, it means the whole content of consciousness,
sometimes the act of logical inference. I mean here
by the disposition of Thought our tendency to carry
out the process of reflection or "thinking"—the process
to which we refer when we say that we stopped what
we were doing in order to "think."

The chief external sign of Thought in this sense is a
bodily inertia, which contrasts sharply with the tightened muscles of Curiosity, or the random movements
of Trial and Error. The thinker is either perfectly still

[1] Comparative psychologists are not agreed as to the extent to
which mental association accompanies or controls the "Trial and
Error" process among animals. Professor Hobhouse in his *Mind
and Evolution* (1901), chap. vii., explains clearly the difference
existing at that time between his own conclusions and those of Professor Thorndyke. But Thorndyke in his *Animal Intelligence* (1911),
especially in chap. v., seems to come nearer to Hobhouse's position.
In any case the experimental evidence shows a marked distinction
between the processes of learning in the monkeys and apes and
those in other mammals, the primates in that respect approaching
very much more closely to the human type. Gregarious hunting
animals, as every one knows who has watched a pack of hounds at
work, go through a process which may be called Collective Trial
and Error. The whole pack are then in the characteristic state of
restless excitement, and all follow the lead of any one of them who
hits on the scent.

or performs unconsciously some monotonous and instinctive movement like walking. Mr. H. P. Robinson describes this characteristic bodily condition in a book written after observing the behaviour of the apes and monkeys in the Zoological Gardens. "What is it that they think about so hard?" he asks. "That their thoughts have no relation to their actions is obvious; for not one of them but will sit for half an hour, graver than Confucius, only to break off suddenly to pick with intensity of concentration a straw to pieces." [1] Here we obviously see a transference from a condition of Thought to the completely different and less purely intellectual condition of Curiosity. Most people who have watched a good sheep-dog on a warm afternoon, as he lies motionless but open-eyed with his nose between his paws, will believe that he too falls from time to time into the state of Thought.

In the case of man, where alone we can get evidence by introspection, this bodily condition is strictly subordinate to a mental activity, consisting, in its simplest form, of an automatic succession of ideas and feelings, which, by a process not yet differentiated as memory, or imagination, or reasoning, arrange themselves into organised relations. When once started, the process may sink below the level of consciousness, and may continue during sleep, or when we are engaged on some other occupation, provided that that occupation makes no urgent call on our attention. If that which happens to us during such a state of Thought happens also to the sheep-dog, his memory, when the moment of action comes, will in consequence be better arranged and more available, his inferences more

[1] *Of Distinguished Animals,* H. Perry Robinson (1910), p. 155.

rapid, his "wits," as we say, "more about him" than if it had never occurred.

Thought is normally accompanied by a general feeling of quiet pleasantness, which is also in sharp contrast to the "excitement" of Curiosity or the "worry" of Trial and Error.

Of these three potentially or definitely intellectual dispositions it may have been Thought which was most helpful to primitive man in taking the first steps from a mainly instinctive to a largely intelligent life. Early man must have shared to the full the proverbial Curiosity of the monkey. His mobile hands and restless nervous system must have made the process of Trial and Error more effective in him than in any other animal. But he may have learnt most when, in periods of waking or dreaming reverie, he wove his random memories and associations into a more or less organised whole.

One may suppose that in the higher non-human animals Thought is always a quasi-automatic process. It comes on, that is to say, under favourable circumstances without an effort, and as long as it lasts is uncontrolled by any conscious purpose. It may be that in man, as far as his purely inherited nature is concerned, the same is true, and that the only continued and independent Thought "natural" to him is the deep, undirected meditation of the shepherd or the fisherman. If so, the essential fact which has made the Great Society possible is the discovery, handed down by tradition and instruction, that Thought can be fed by deliberately collected material, and stimulated, sustained, and, to a certain extent, controlled by an effort of the will. The "natural" boy begins to

turn into the civilised man when the schoolmaster tells
him to stop "dreaming" and to "think," though it is
often only after a period of painful confusion and misunderstanding that he discovers that the thinking
which he is told to attempt is a kind of controlled
dreaming.[1] Shepherds and fishermen make no such
effort, and sometimes acquire thereby a quality of mind
which the townsman, with his handier, more controlled
and, for most purposes, more effective cleverness, finds
himself envying.

But man would not have been able to create the
enormous intellectual gap between himself and the
other animals if he had not also evolved the disposition
of Language. By Language I here mean our inherited
inclination to express and to receive ideas by symbols,
i.e., not only by speech and writing, but also by drawing
and significant gestures. It is indeed only the fear of
neologism which prevents me from using some more
inclusive term such as "symbolism." This disposition
is apparently peculiar to man. Other animals, like
dogs, wolves, and certain species of birds, communicate
to each other by means of sounds and movements, or
even by the secretion of strong odours, the fact that
their instincts of fear, or hunger, or sex, or hunting
have been excited by some appropriate stimulus. But
the difference between such a communication of emotional states and the communication by man of ideas
which may be almost passionless is so great as to be
qualitative rather than quantitative.

The absence, indeed, of a close analogy in that respect between man and any of the other higher animals might create a presumption that Language (like

[1] See later, Chapter X.

the use of any one of the languages) is a habit, newly learnt by each generation, rather than a true inherited disposition.[1] The evidence, however, in favour of inheritance seems clear. It consists partly in the well-known physiological discovery of definite "speech" and "word-deafness" areas in the normal human brain, and partly in the behaviour of children and savages. No one who has closely watched a child "learning to speak" in his second year will doubt that, while his actual vocabulary is acquired, the inclination to use significant vocables is inherited. Even in drawing there is apparently a greater similarity in the way in which, for instance, children or savages symbolise the human figure than can be explained by the learning of a purely conventional art.

But it is worth while noting that the problems raised by the inclusion of Language as a true disposition offer a useful reminder that my distinctions, both between "simple" and "complex" dispositions, and between "inherited" dispositions and "acquired" powers, are apt, like almost all classifications, to produce conceptions

[1] Mr. McDougall, e.g., in his Social Psychology, p. 49, lays down the rule that: "If a similar emotion and impulse are clearly displayed in the instinctive activities of the higher animals, that fact will afford a strong presumption that the emotion and impulse are primary and simple; on the other hand, if no such instinctive activity occurs among the higher animals, we must suspect the affective state in question of being either a complex composite emotion or no true emotion." This rule should not, however, be adhered to as against actual evidence indicating the existence of a disposition in man which has not yet been demonstrated in other animals. Biologists now tell us that anthropoid apes are not very near collateral relations of man. The nearer types have died out. If the anthropoid apes had themselves died out, man would have had many dispositions peculiar to himself.

Mr. F. E. Beddard tells me, e.g., that experiments at the Zoological Gardens show that the instinctive fear of reptiles as such is confined to the young of man and of the higher apes, who perhaps shared with early man ancestors that were once nearly exterminated by tree-climbing snakes.

rather more definite than are the facts at the limits of each class. I might, for instance, have classified Language as a "simple" disposition, on the ground that the utterance of words is a much less prolonged process than is the behaviour, *e.g.*, characteristic of Mother-Love or Curiosity. And, again, the evolution (whether through Natural Selection or a succession of "sports") of our inherited disposition to use language must have needed (one might almost say, must have been parasitic upon) the simultaneous existence of a growing body of conventional forms of expression newly "acquired" by each generation.

We are now in a position to conclude the argument of the last two chapters. Man, I have said, inherits a nature, whether "material" or "vital," or "spiritual," containing many thousands of dispositions which incline him to react in various ways to appropriate stimuli. Many of these dispositions should be left rather to anatomy and physiology than to psychology. The psychological dispositions may be divided roughly into comparatively simple facts like the senses, memory, fatigue, etc., and the more complex facts of Instinct and Intelligence.

The instinctive and intelligent dispositions do not form a single continuum. Fear is a ˙different thing from Curiosity, and Trial and Error from Thought. But they do form a series across which it is very difficult to draw broad lines of demarcation. We may arrange that series in order of apparent evolutionary origin, beginning at the bottom with such facts as hunger and sex, which we share with the whole of the vertebrate, and almost the whole of the animal, kingdom, and ending at the top with those intellectual faculties which are either peculiar to man, or shared, in a more rudimentary form, by only a few of the higher mammals. That series will, if followed from bottom to top, be marked on the whole by increasing consciousness, and by decreasing fixity and driving power, or, what is the same thing, increasing plasticity. Our thinking is more easily modified by our environment than our appetite, just as our appetite is more easily modified than the way in which we walk or breathe.

If we look at the Instinctive and Intelligent dispositions as one series, we can also see that the various dispositions do not act in isolation, but that many of them are normally connected with each other. Obstructed Sex-Love, for instance, normally produces a violent outbreak of Pugnacity, and Fear is still more closely connected with Mother-Love. Sometimes two dispositions like Fear and Curiosity are, so to speak, rivals. They are normally set in action by closely similar stimuli and may be observed to alternate rapidly. Self-Assertion and Humility (the "Give a Lead" and "Take a Lead" instincts) alternate in the same way. Facts like these may, indeed, indicate that with increased knowledge we may ultimately come to look upon the separate human dispositions less as isolated facts ascertained by empirical observation than as the results of a wider causal relationship.

My two chapters, of course, give only the barest outline of the human psychological dispositions. They are rather a diagram than even a sketch. I shall describe in later chapters with more detail certain dispositions which are of special importance to the social

psychologist. But I shall not hope even to indicate
all those inherited psychological factors which, with
individual variations, go to make up the human moral
type, the factors which justify us in saying that a man's
"character" is like that of his mother or of his grandfather,[1] or that the "psychology" of a novel or play is
"all wrong," in that a character who did or said one
thing would not have done or said another. Such a
diagram, however, while it will not enable any one to
dispense with the help of experience and insight, may
at least be useful in affording centres of crystallisation for experience, and in warning us of certain gross
errors in social calculation.

Finally, it must always be remembered that social
psychology is a specialised science, dealing only with
a special group of the causes of human actions. The
statesman who wishes to organise mankind wisely, or
even the social psychologist when he takes it upon
himself to give direct advice to the statesman, must
know or estimate the results of many other sciences.
Before we know how any particular body of people will
be affected by any particular measure we must know
not only their nature but the environment, intellectual
and physical, which results from their history and their
surroundings.

And social psychology can never lead men to wise
practical conclusions unless it keeps in view its relation to that science of human breeding which Sir Francis Galton named Eugenics. Every change in social
organisation affects not only the harmony between the

[1] See, for instance, the persistence (greater, apparently, than
would be due to family tradition) with which a certain type of dry
conservative learning appeared among the nephews and great-
nephews of Wordsworth.

existing generation and its surroundings, but the conditions which affect the physical and mental inheritance of succeeding generations. I remember, during a debate at the London County Council Education Committee, hearing it seriously proposed by an experienced representative that we should attempt to prevent more than one child in any family from receiving a scholarship. The proposer of this regulation pointed out that there were certain families in which practically all the children got scholarships and that this was "unfair." It never occurred to him that he was trying to penalise the begetting of children in those few but all-important cases in which general mental ability appears as what the Mendelians call a "prepotent" biological factor. On the other hand, when Professor Bourne argues that "Hygiene, education, social institutions may improve the lot of the individual, but they cannot produce any permanent effect on the race," [1] one finds oneself wondering whether he seriously expects that eugenic science will progress, or eugenic motives and methods be effective in a society unhygienic, uneducated, and unorganised.

[1] Gilbert C. Bourne, *The Herbert Spencer Lecture* (1900), p. 36.

CHAPTER IV

DISPOSITION AND ENVIRONMENT

In the last two chapters I have referred only incidentally to those facts in our environment which constitute the "appropriate stimuli" of our dispositions. I have assumed that not only do we inherit the dispositions of Love and Fear and Curiosity, but that women and children also exist for men to love, dangerous things for men to fear, and unusual things for men to be curious about.

In this chapter I shall examine the general relation between our dispositions and the environment which stimulates them.

The first point brought out by such an examination is that dispositions which seem, when considered by themselves, to be homogeneous are found, when examined in relation to their stimuli, to consist of many independently varying tendencies. Fear, for instance, if its manifestations in the consciousness and bodily movements of different men are alone thought of, will appear to vary only in the degree of its intensity. But when the external causes which excite fear are examined it will be found that different men are not only afraid in different degrees, but are afraid of different things. Some men have an instinctive fear of precipitous heights, others of the sea or of a crowd,

and a well-known British general is said to have a fear
of cats. Nerve-doctors have invented a number of
Greek or semi-Greek words such as agoraphobia, och-
lophobia, claustrophobia to designate such special
fears when they reach a pathological intensity.[1]

Hunger, again, may be excited (apart from the effects of habit and training) in different men by very
different stimuli. The same is true of the intellectual
dispositions. In the case of "born" artists or "born"
musicians or scientists, Curiosity and Thought are
stimulated in one child by objects which leave another
child entirely uninterested.

The second point concerns that process of recognition (of "perception"—to use the technical psychological term) on which the stimulation of a disposition
in any given case depends. We do not desire to eat
an apple until we recognise (to use a somewhat intellectualist term) it as an apple. But this faculty of
recognition is (apart from experience) to a certain extent elastic. All the apples in the world, or all the
snakes, differ in some respects from each other; so that
if a man is born with a taste for "apples," or a fear of
"snakes," his taste or fear are stimulated by any one
of a number of somewhat different objects. It would
be extremely useful if an experimental·psychologist
would test this elasticity in the case of a strongly
marked human instinct, and would check his results
by experiments of the same kind on one of the higher
animals. Some one perhaps who is fortunate enough
to possess a highly specialised instinct of a kind not

[1] See the admirable analysis of various types of Fear (based
upon thousands of answers to a questionnaire) by Professor G.
Stanley Hall in the *American Journal of Psychology* (1897). See
also Note A on p. 68.

easily modified by experience, might submit himself to such a series of experiments. The test stimuli might, in a case of cat-fear, include a series of feline animals, more or less nearly related to the common cat, an animal which looks like a cat but belongs to a different genus, a recently dead cat, a living cat in a glass box, a stuffed cat unscented, a stuffed cat scented, the same with a mechanical purr, and finally a series of mental images of a cat, which might range from a strong induced belief that a cat was in the room (when, in fact, no cat was there) to the image produced by talking or thinking or dreaming (in a hypnotic trance) about a cat. Corresponding experiments might be made in a case of specialised animal fear, such as that which horses are said to have for camels.

One supposes that the process of recognition in these cases would not be found to be like a gun-lock, which delivers the same blow whether the pull on the trigger, provided that it is enough to release the spring, is heavy or light; but that its effect would be stronger or weaker according to the nearness of the particular stimulus to some type which would constitute the apex of a "polygon of variation," of which the ordinate was the degree of fear and the abscissa the degree of variation from that type. In the case of cat-fear, the most intense fear might be found to be created, not by the domestic cat, but by some feline from that part of the Malay Archipelago in which the remains of Pithecanthropus have been found. The domestic cat might be discovered to produce the same amount of fear (measured by pulse disturbance) as a carefully stuffed and scented specimen of the Malaysian animal. The fact that we in England never see that special kind of cat would not prevent, for hundreds of generations, men being born with that special kind of fear. A Londoner may be born with an abnormal fear of snakes, and may die an old man without discovering that fact. The whole human race, indeed, may still inherit a special fear of some extinct species of saurian or woolly elephant.[1]

But while the strength of the stimulation of any instinct in man or other animals may depend throughout on the degree of the external likeness of the stimulus to a mean type, the usefulness of the resulting action depends, not on the degree, but on the character of that likeness, whether, that is to say, it is *relevant* to the original advantage or danger which the disposition was evolved to secure or avoid. If a gull has a highly specialised instinct which enables it to catch pilchards, and if herrings take the place of pilchards in the seas to which the gulls of that species resort, the pilchard-instinct will still be useful, although it may be somewhat weakened and confused, and although every now and then a bird may choke itself by swallowing too large a fish. But the pilchard-instinct will be worse than useless to the gull if it is stimulated by a fisherman's bait made to look like a pilchard, or by the reflected light from a bit of wet seaweed.

Throughout the whole process of evolution there has indeed been a constant and enormous waste of life and effort due to the laying of eggs in the wrong places because they look rather like the right places, and

[1] A letter to the *Times* of March 25, 1914, describes a man with a special fear of a certain species of Australian spiders, large enough to be dangerous to a baby monkey. It is interesting that an imitation spider (used in a practical joke) did not affect him.

the capture of uneatable things because they are of the same size or colour as some eatable things. The process by which animals recognise harmful or useful objects has always been rough and inaccurate, and the queer ingenuity of natural selection has provided all sorts of means by which one living thing takes advantage of the mistakes of another. Flowers are fertilised because they smell like carrion, insects escape because they look like twigs or wasps, and a cruel little South American weasel has become almost exactly like the squirrels on which he preys.

But it is in civilised man that the relation between disposition and stimulus is most complex. Man is born with a set of dispositions related, clumsily enough but still intelligibly, to the world of tropical or sub-tropical wood and cave which he inhabited during millions of years of slow evolution, and whose main characteristics changed little over vast periods of time. The story of civilisation begins when he was driven by hunger or by insect-borne disease to go North and South into new climates. There his comparatively plastic intelligence enabled him to sustain life under new conditions, not in the main by evolving new dispositions, but by acquiring new habits, and by making clothes, houses, and other modifications of his material surroundings.

At no period was he, apparently, either in the old environment or the new, very successful in creating a harmony between himself and his world. Students of pre-history tell us, for instance, that the disposition of Fear, which originally gave man and his animal predecessors a rather inefficient protection from being killed by carnivorous beasts, tormented him all through the Stone Ages because it was stimulated by dreams and

omens and by the belief in malevolent supernatural
beings. There is evidence that perversions of the sex
instinct by inappropriate stimuli may have begun
among our ancestors before they could be called men.

In our time the coming of the Great Society has
created an environment in which, for most of us,
neither our instinctive nor our intelligent dispositions
find it easy to discover their most useful stimuli. Any
one who desires to appreciate this should visit one of
those "casual labour" quarters in London, where modern civilisation has so disastrously failed, and where
the facts of life are hidden neither by conventional
manners nor by the privacy which is possible in the
great half-empty houses of the well-to-do. Stay there,
walking and watching, from the afternoon closing of
the schools till the return home of the men. Look at
the windows of the newsagents and tobacconists, and
the frank display in the dingy little chemists' shops.
Listen to the women coming out of the "off-licence"
grocery, and the girls who are waiting to enter the
music-halls and the cinematograph theatres. Notice
what part of the evening paper the men are reading.

The people round you are of all ages from infancy
to dotage; and you can see what it is that here stimulates the instincts which one by one appear in the
growth of a human being. The babies are tugging at
dirty india-rubber teats. The sweet shops are selling
hundredweights of bright-coloured stuff, which excites
the appetite of the children without nourishing their
bodies. That pale-faced boy first knew love, not when
he looked at a girl whom later he might marry, but
when a dirty picture post-card caught his eye or he
watched a suggestive film. His dreams of heroism are

satisfied by halfpenny romances, half criminal and half absurd. Loyalty and comradeship mean sticking to his street gang; and the joy of constructive work means the money which he can get for riding behind a van or running messages.

The men are never far removed from the two great social forces of gambling and alcohol. If the desire of change, of risk, of achievement comes on, then the bookmaker is always round the corner; and the publican will give at any moment, for a few pence, that dreaming reverie, that sense of the tremendous significance of the world, which led their ancestors, sitting at the tent door or among the mountain sheep, to the beginnings of philosophy and science. And because the new facts by which our dispositions are now stimulated are only inexact substitutes for the old facts by which they were stimulated during the long process of evolution, the stimulation itself is weak and capricious. Even the enthusiasm of the group at the public-house door, who are discussing a glove-fight, seems, as you watch them, to be thin and half-hearted.

A little farther on the street widens, because a hundred years ago it used to cross a village green. You hear a tired and springless hymn-tune, and stop while a Salvation Army preacher shouts a quotation from St. Paul:

If ye live after the flesh, ye shall die; but if ye through the Spirit do mortify the deeds of the body, ye shall live.

He is imploring his scanty following of women and children, and the few inattentive passers-by, to strive and pray till all those instincts which can be put to such evil use have been killed out of their souls. You remember as you listen that in the tall tenement-building behind you, or in the new brick suburb a mile or two away, there are thousands of men and women who are making perhaps the most heroic effort to "mortify the deeds of the body" that ever has been attempted. They are mainly impelled, not by the theology of Blood and Fire, but by an intense longing to be "respectable," to have some meaning and dignity in their own lives and those of their children, to be rid of the hopeless yielding to temptation, the weak shame, the squalor and disease of the life from which they have so hardly escaped. Neither father nor mother spend a halfpenny or a half hour without calculation, the children are carefully dressed in clothes which they dare not spoil, and are strictly confined, except for occasional holidays, to house or school. And yet in a poor district the school medical officer may report that the children of the more respectable families are physically and nervously in a worse condition than the rest.[1]

For we cannot in St. Paul's sense "mortify" our dispositions. If they are not stimulated, they do not therefore die, nor is the human being what he would be if they had never existed. If we leave unstimulated, or, to use a shorter term, if we "baulk" any one

[1] See, e.g., Dr. Bishop Harman, quoted in the *Report of the Medical Officer to the London School Board for 1903*, p. 14. "The children are of a respectable class. They are well fed and well clothed, but are altogether a flabby and pappy lot. . . . The children are too respectable to play in the street. They have no near park or fields; their back gardens or house rooms are small, so that they do not compare favourably (save in cleanliness) with children in poorer quarters who play freely in the open air." On the whole question see Miss Jane Addams' admirable book, *The Spirit of Youth in the City Streets*.

of our main dispositions, Curiosity, Property, Trial and Error, Sex, and the rest, we produce in ourselves a state of nervous strain. It may be desirable in any particular case of conduct that we should do so, but we ought to know what we are doing.

The baulking of each disposition produces its own type of strain; but the distinctions between the types are, so far, unnamed and unrecognised, and a trained psychologist would do a real service to civilised life if he would carefully observe and describe them.

One peculiarity of the state of "baulked disposition" is that it is extremely difficult for the sufferer to find his own way out of it. The stimulus must come from outside. When once he is "dull" or "flat" or "sick of things" or whatever the name may be which he gives to his feelings, he cannot, unless he is a man of quite exceptional resource and nervous elasticity, invent anything to do which will "stimulate" him. Now, for instance, that the European nations keep hundreds of thousands of men under arms in time of peace, the colonels of regiments and the captains of warships know by experience that their men become "fidgetty" or "fed up" by a life which gives play only to a few dispositions; and when that occurs they prescribe in a haphazard way a smoking concert, or a route march, or a football match, or, on board ship, a dance, or clothes-mending, or gun drill, for them all alike. A skilled London hostess is more successful when she goes round a room full of bored celebrities, applying to each an appropriate stimulus: "Miss Jones *so* wants to know about your last voyage," or, "Here is a friend of Mr. Brown" (a scientific opponent), or, more simply, "I want to introduce you to that girl with the beautiful hair," until each is roused to that "energy of the soul" which is Aristotle's definition of happiness. If one looks at a respectable crowd in a London park on the afternoon of a Bank holiday, one feels an intense longing for the appearance of a thousand such hostesses and of a social system which would enable them to get to work.[1]

This want of harmony, in great things and in small,

[1] If, however, we are to learn how by deliberate contrivance to relax the nervous strain of "baulked disposition," we must first get an agreed answer to the question whether, or to what degree, the baulking of one disposition can be alleviated by the satisfaction of another. There is, for instance, a traditional body of ethical teaching (forming the staple material of religious addresses "to men only") which assumes that the strain of the sex instinct can be relaxed or abolished by any form of vigorous bodily and mental exercise. This assumption is rejected by some psychologists, and is probably not true in the absolute form in which it is often stated. Freud, again, and the other members of the new school of "psychoanalysts" use the term "sublimation" for "the deviation of the sexual motive-powers from sexual ·aims to new aims" (Freud, *Three Contributions to Sexual Theory*, translated by J. J. Putnam, p. 39). To this "sublimation" of the sexual motive they ascribe many of the higher activities of civilised man. But Freud himself does not seem to argue that the "sublimated" functions of the sex-instinct serve as a satisfaction of the instinct in its original form.

Very little has been written on the question of the vicarious satisfaction of other dispositions than that of sex. William James, however, raises that question in relation to the fighting instinct in the paper on "A Moral Equivalent for War," in his *Memories and Studies*, 1911. See also Chapter IX., pp. 179-184, of this book.

An extraordinarily interesting experimental approach to the physiological side of the whole problem has been made by Professor W. B. Cannon of the Harvard Medical School in two papers on "The Emotional Stimulation of Adrenal Secretion" (*American Journal of Physiology*, April, 1911), and "Emotional Glycosuria" (*ibid.*, December 1, 1911), which are to form part of a forthcoming book. His ·work suggests to me that some of the obscure conditions of "baulked disposition" (owing, *e.g.*, to the absence of stimulation of such dispositions as anger and fear) may be due physiologically to the non-discharge of its normal secretion by the adrenal or some other gland. If so, a new and more precise meaning will be seen in the celebrated passage (*Poetics*, vi. 2) in which Aristotle states that tragedy "achieves by pity and terror the purging of the passions of that kind" (τὴν τῶν τοιούτων παθημάτων κάθαρσιν), and the less-known passage (*Politics*, vii. 6) in which he refers to the psychologically "cathartic" effects of certain kinds of music.

between our race and its environment has been noticed ever since men, at the beginning of civilisation,
began consciously to reflect upon their way of living.
They dimly felt that their earliest instincts were related to an open-air life in which their ancestors had
supported themselves on the gifts of the untilled land.
Such a life was "natural," and poets, for thousands of
years, have longed to return to it, to recall the "golden
age" before the invention of fire, or the Garden of
Eden, whose inhabitants knew neither clothing nor
agriculture.

It was the supreme achievement of the Greek intellect to substitute for this vain longing a new conception of nature. To Aristotle, as to Hobbes, it was
evident that the old life in which man, without the
powers which civilisation gave him, faced an untamed
world, must have been "poor, nasty, brutish and
short." [1] It was true that man's nature and his environment were at war, but the remedy was not to go
back to the forests of the past, but to invent the city
of the future, the material and social organisation
which should contrive a new harmony, higher because
it was deliberate. When Aristotle said "Man is an
animal adapted for living in a city-state," [2] he meant,
not that man was living in such a state when Zeus
was born, but that the city-state stimulated his nature
to its noblest expression. "For what every being is
in its perfect condition, that certainly is the nature of
that being." [3] Even for Zeno's less confident philosophy "Follow Nature" meant not "Go back to the past"

[1] Hobbes, *Leviathan* (edition of 1839, p. 112).
[2] *Politics*, bk. i. chap. ii.   [3] *Ibid.*, bk. i. chap. ii.

but "Examine the conditions of a good life in the present."

This is the master-task of civilised mankind. They will fail in it again and again, partly for lack of inventive power, partly from sheer ignorance of the less obvious facts of their material surroundings and mental structure. But it is hardly possible for any one to endure life who does not believe that they will succeed in producing a harmony between themselves and their environment far deeper and wider than anything which we can see to-day.

NOTE A (see *ante*, p. 58, *n.*).—There are two types of special "fears." The first is the inherited instinctive type, which I discuss on pp. 58-60, and which may be illustrated by the special fear of snakes found among human beings and the apes. The second type is the life-long "phobia" which may result from a "forgotten experience" (usually some event in early childhood). See, *e.g.*, the description of a case of acquired cat-fear (due to a forgotten fright at five years of age, afterwards revealed under hypnotism) in Dr. Morton Prince's book on *The Unconscious* (1914), p. 17. Further enquiry may show the proportion in which the two types occur in actual life. Many of the facts collected by Dr. Prince, by Freud and his followers, and by others, as to "forgotten experiences," "coconsciousness," "dissociated personality," etc., though they have so far only been brought into the service of individual pathological psychology, may be ultimately found to be of importance in the study of social psychology.

CHAPTER V

HABIT

In the last three chapters I have given a rough outline, from the point of view of sociology, of the main human psychological dispositions, and a general discussion of their relation to those facts of our environment by which they are stimulated into activity.

In the next five chapters I shall discuss in greater detail certain dispositions, both "simple" and "complex," which are of special sociological importance. Those which I have selected are Habit, Fear, Pleasure-Pain, Thought, and the intricate psychological facts covered by the terms Imitation, Sympathy, and Love and Hatred.

Not only are these dispositions important in themselves, but each of them has been made the foundation of a complete sociological scheme by some school of thinkers. Indeed the few great writers who, mainly in England and France, dealt during the last two centuries with social psychology advanced in their methods little beyond the point reached by the early Greek natural philosophers. The first Greek thinkers had neither the vocabulary nor the logical nor mathematical apparatus which would have enabled them to treat material events as the resultant of a number of independently varying causes. Each philosopher therefore ascribed all events to one cause, Water, or Fire, or Number, or Flux. In modern Europe, while the progress of logic and mathematics was transforming the methods of the natural sciences, the classical sociologists were still attempting, either by distortion of the evidence, or by a vague and metaphorical use of language, to ascribe all social effects to some one psychological cause. Just as Thales took Water as his single all-sufficient cause, and Anaximenes took Air; so Hobbes took Fear; Bentham, Pleasure-Pain; Comte, Love; and Tarde, Imitation.

In order to guard against this traditional tendency it is perhaps worth while to warn my readers, once for all, that I shall be dealing in each of the following chapters with one only of a number of causes, which, in any practical problem, interact with each other. And in order to avoid the vague use of language which makes that tendency possible, I shall attempt to define each disposition with sufficient strictness to prevent its meaning from being pushed beyond its own province.

In this chapter I shall deal with Habit. It has not been made the basis of a complete scheme by any among the greater sociologists; but if one examines the arguments of that numerous class of writers who plead for "scientific" government in the monthly and quarterly reviews, one finds that they constantly assume its universal efficacy.

The "Habit-Philosophers" are generally men who have spent a great part of their life in the exercise of autocratic discipline or the application of fixed rules, soldiers, retired Anglo-Indians, lawyers, or those professors and school-masters whose pedagogic training has not involved any acquaintance with modern psychological enquiry.

Sir Henry Maine was a lawyer, a professor, and an Anglo-Indian, and his work on *Popular Government* (1885) may be taken as a good example of this point of view. He says:

> Obedience is rendered by the great bulk of civilised societies without an effort and quite unconsciously. But that is only because, in the course of countless ages, the stern discharge of their chief duty by States has created habits and sentiments which save the necessity of penal interference because nearly everybody shares them.[1]

The reference to "countless ages" indicates that Sir Henry Maine was a Lamarkian, who assumed that acquired characteristics are inherited. But the same position is held by men who would admit that social habits must be reacquired by each generation of mankind. When the Duke of Wellington, the greatest of Anglo-Indian soldiers, said: "Habit a second nature! Habit is ten times nature,"[2] he was referring to a process requiring not "countless ages" but only the military lifetime of a sepoy.

To a consistent "Habit-Philosopher," change, merely because it is change, must necessarily be dangerous. The Duke of Wellington strongly opposed in 1851 the substitution of rifles for smooth-bore muskets in the British Army.[3] He would probably have argued that if the habits of the Army had been formed by drill with a rifle, the rifle would have been better than the musket, but that the advantage of the better

---

[1] H. Maine, *Popular Government*, p. 63.
[2] Quoted, W. James, *Principles of Psychology*, vol. i. p. 120.
[3] Biddulph, *Lord Cardwell at the War Office*, p. 47.

weapon was less than the disadvantage of breaking what Walter Bagehot used to call "the cake of custom." [1] Some of the "Die-Hards" in the English constitutional struggle of 1910 would have admitted that a second chamber on a non-hereditary basis might have been quite as good as the English House of Lords; but the essence of their case was that the English people had formed the habit of obedience to the House of Lords and not to some different chamber.

The supreme danger, in the view of this type of thinker, arises when change is brought about, not by the deliberate action of a sovereign body which can in part carry over the habit of obedience in its subjects from the old to the new conditions, but through sporadic breaches of custom by individual citizens.

"If a democracy," says Maine, "were to allow a portion of the multitude of which it consists to set some law at defiance which it happens to dislike, it would be guilty of a crime which hardly any other virtue could redeem, and which century upon century might fail to repair." [2]

Before discussing to what degree the Habit-Philosophers are right, it is necessary to define Habit in terms which would be accepted by those experimental psychologists who have done so much to give it precise meaning. Habit, then, is constituted by the fact that if our nervous system is stimulated along certain lines of discharge, leading either to action or feeling or thought, the next stimulus of the same kind finds the nervous system to a certain extent prepared. The resulting act or feeling or thought then follows more certainly and requires a weaker stimulation. Finally

[1] *Physics and Politics,* p. 53.   [2] *Popular Government,* p. 64.

the habit becomes a definite tendency, which may be started with little or no external stimulus.

There is no evidence to show that habits are transmitted by biological inheritance, but the disposition of Habit varies enormously in individuals, and such variations may be transmitted. Different individuals may be born with a disposition to form habits in general, or particular habits, easily or with difficulty, and to lose them quickly or slowly. One man, for instance, may be born with, and transmit to his descendants, a marked facility in forming habits in respect of music, and another in respect of language.

The power of forming habits varies also greatly with age; children and young people finding it more easy both to form and to drop habits than their elders. It also varies with race. The Greeks, for instance, had little power of habituation, and were surprised to find that the North European people whom they called Kelts reached, when they were trained to fighting or sea-faring, an absolute indifference to danger which seemed to themselves to be a kind of insanity.[1]

Habit, I have said, may influence our bodily actions, or our feelings, or our trains of thought. But a habit of feeling or thought does not necessarily produce a habit of action, as moralists from Aristotle to William James have pointed out.[2]

Habit is perhaps the most important of the psychological causes which have made the organisation of the Great Society possible. The population of London

---

[1] Aristotle, *Ethics*, bk. iii. ch. vii.: "He would be a madman or inaccessible to pain if he feared nothing, neither earthquake nor the billows, as they tell of the Kelts."

[2] See on this point the beautiful chapter on Habit in James's *Principles of Psychology*.

would be starved in a week if the flywheel of Habit
were removed, if no signalman or clerk or policeman
ever did anything which was not suggested by a first-
hand impulse, or if no one were more honest or punctual or industrious than he was led to be by his conscious love, on that particular day, for his master or
his work, or by his religion, or by a conviction of
danger from the criminal law.

It is not, therefore, a mere accident that the Great
Society has been developed with most success among
those North European races whose power of blind
habituation excited the contempt of the Greeks. If
Aristotle could stand on London Bridge or at Liverpool Street Station on any week-day at 8.45 A.M., he
would think that the "Kelts" were more insane than
ever.

Mr. McDougall, in accordance with his unwillingness to admit the independent action of our intellectual
dispositions, says, "Habits are formed only in the service of the instincts." [1]   But, as a matter of fact, it is
through habit that the influence of intelligence has
most control over the lives of the majority of civilised
men.   Our instincts as compared with those of other
animals are weak and plastic.   From the beginning of
our lives our own intelligence or that of others directs
a process of habit-education, by which some instincts
are more or less successfully inhibited, and others, like
hunting, or music, or curiosity, which, without the aid
of deliberate purpose, might have died out in the
course of growth, become the master-passions of specialised lives.

Why, therefore, should not all those who desire the

[1] *Social Psychology*, p. 43.

continued existence of the Great Society become
"Habit-Philosophers" of Sir Henry Maine's type? If
Habit is truly "second nature," if it "becomes in a
manner part of our organisation," [1] so that it is indistinguishable from the facts which were there from
birth, the adaptation of man's nature to his new
environment is easy enough. All we have to do is to
discover what is wanting in our inherited dispositions
and to supply it by education. Education costs time
and effort, and so we should have to economise it,
choosing the most necessary habits, and perhaps modifying those environmental facts which make an ex-
cessive demand on habituation. But complete adaptation between man and his environment would, on that
assumption, be well within sight.

Habit, however, is not second nature. In the first
place, the facts in any man's nervous structure which
are there by habituation are less stable than those
which are there by inheritance. A nervous shock, for
instance, or any intense nervous excitement, seems to
have the power of abolishing settled habits, while inherited dispositions remain unchanged. We may believe that the "nature" of a race has been transformed
by custom and education. We may point out that
the deliberate infliction of torture on human beings has
become almost unthinkable to men whose ancestors,
ten generations ago, took it as a matter of course. But
when civilised American soldiers were submitted to
the strain of guerilla warfare in the Philippines, many
of them, who had inherited apparently no worse na-
tures than their comrades, inflicted day after day the

[1] Huxley, *Elementary Physiology* (2nd ed., 1885), p. 286.

most abominable tortures on the prisoners.[1] In the fury of the Reformation at Muenster, or the Revolution at Paris, the moral habits of whole populations disappeared.

Habit, again, lacks that breadth of stimulation which I have noted in the case of the inherited dispositions.[2] Fear or Hunger is excited by a large variety of dangerous or edible things, but the habit of military obedience may attach itself merely to the sound of a particular word of command, or to the sight of a particular uniform, and the habit of punctuality in business to the performance of a particular task. The moral catastrophes and confusions indeed, in revolutions or among religious converts, are due perhaps even more to the removal of the habitual stimuli of rites and ceremonies, old acquaintances, or the daily surroundings of life than to the actual nervous effect of excitement and shock. To an English private soldier who finds himself "East of Suez," says Rudyard Kipling, "there ain't no ten commandments."

If a habit is to have sufficient permanence to re-establish itself after a nervous shock, or sufficient generality to adapt itself to variations in its external stimuli, it must be combined with and supported by some organised body of ideas. On this point, if one turns from the mechanical treatment of Habit by the modern psychologists back to Plato and Aristotle, it is astonishing to see how much more deeply the Greek moralists entered into the real problems which the limitations of Habit present in times of change like our

[1] See documents quoted by Mr. Ralph Norman Angell Lane in his *Patriotism under Three Flags*, pp. 99-112.
[2] See Chapter IV. pp. 58-61.

own. Men who lived in the city-states of Hellas between 430 and 330 B.C. knew well how urgent was the
danger involved in the relation between Habit and
motive in a new environment. When Plato wishes to
describe the most unfortunate of all human beings, he
pictures a man, who, "having spent his former life in
a well-disciplined state, had become virtuous by habit
without philosophy," [1] and who, in the under-world,
was set to choose his own lot for a second life. He
chose "the most absolute despotism he could find" and
"failed to remark that he was fated therein, among
other calamities, to devour his own children."

"We can only," says Aristotle, "call a man's actions
just or virtuous when the man who does them knows
what he is doing; when he acts with deliberate choice,
and his choice is based on the real nature of his action;
and thirdly, when his tendency so to act is steady and
not easily changed." [2] The relation between Habit and
Thought in conduct could not be better expressed.
Virtue, for Aristotle, is not mere Habit, but a "condition of settled moral choice," which, while it includes
Habit, also includes what Plato calls philosophy.

The lines indeed on which the Great Society is now
developing make the need of "philosophy" as a support of Habit greater every year. The history of all
wars since the introduction of magazine rifles and
quick-firing guns shows that, while discipline is still
important, "philosophy" has become more important.
The soldier in South Africa, or Manchuria, or Tripoli,

---

[1] *Republic*, 619 ἐν τεταγμένῃ πολιτείᾳ ἐν τῷ προτέρῳ βίῳ βεβιωκότα ἔθει ἄνευ
φιλοσοφίας ἀρετῆς μετειληφότα.
[2] *Ethics*, bk. ii. chap. iv. τὰ δὲ κατὰ τὰς ἀρετὰς γινόμενα οὐκ ἐὰν αὐτά πως
ἔχῃ, δικαίως ἢ σωφρόνως πράττεται, ἀλλὰ καὶ ἐὰν ὁ πράττων πως ἔχων πράττῃ,
πρῶτον μὲν ἐὰν εἰδὼς, ἔπειτ᾽ ἐὰν προαιρούμενος, καὶ προαιρούμενος δι᾽ αὐτὰ, τὸ
δὲ τρίτον καὶ ἐὰν βεβαίως καὶ ἀμετακινήτως ἔχων πράττῃ.

or Thrace had to fight, ten feet from his nearest comrade, an individual battle, which was part of a vast
engagement on a front, perhaps, of a hundred miles.
Under these conditions the side which believed itself
to represent some moral ideal, of freedom or self-
defence, fought incomparably better than the side
which carried on, from the habit of obedience, a campaign of policy or conquest. Each man of the "philo-
sophic" army "knew what he was doing, and acted
with a deliberate choice . . . based on the real nature
of his action."

And the same is true of the recruit who enters the
wide complexities of modern industry. A member of
the London County Council Education Committee was
once explaining to me the truth about the education of
the working classes. I said, "You seem to desire that
popular education should consist solely of manual
training and elementary Bible lessons." "That," I
was answered, "is exactly what I do want." A boy
equipped with such an education would be as helpless
in a modern industrial community as was Plato's unhappy ghost before the heap of untried lots.

But there is a further cause which makes it unsafe
to treat Habit as second nature or as a self-sufficient
basis for social life. Not only are habits when produced more unstable than our inherited dispositions,
but the process of producing habits by mere repetition
is uncertain in its results. The stimulation of our
nervous system along any given line of discharge
makes, as I have already said, a further stimulation
along the same line more easy. It also "uses up"
something in the nervous structure which requires
time to repair. Every teacher knows that, if a boy

has to spend two hours in doing a succession of elementary sums of the same kind, he will do them with growing ease *quâ* habit and growing difficulty *quâ* fatigue.[1] After a period of rest the fatigue wears off and the habit remains; so that a boy may then prove to have been making most progress towards accuracy in sum-working when he was too tired to work his sums accurately. This is what James meant when he quoted the saying, "We learn to swim during the winter and to skate during the summer." [2]

The effects, however, of fatigue are not completely done with when they have, for the moment, been overcome by rest. If an habitual action is often repeated up to the point of fatigue, the nervous system is apt to lose its power of recovery. Just when the violin student or the typist is bringing her technique to absolute completion, violinist's or typist's "cramp" may come on, and the nervous system may refuse to repeat the habitual act. Something of the same kind seems to happen from time to time in the process of forming intellectual or emotional habits. When the monk has, by intense and continued effort, made himself able to realise at will the object of his adoration, something snaps, and he can do so no more. The English "public school" system constitutes one of the most tremendous instruments of habituation that has ever existed; but at the moment when a lad of eighteen seems on the point of becoming a perfect Etonian, he has been

---

[1] Cp., *e.g.*, Binet, *La Fatigue intellectuelle*, pt. ii. ch. vi., where it is shown on experimental evidence that in each successive period of a long morning's work at elementary arithmetic the scholars do more sums, but do them less accurately.

[2] *Principles of Psychology*, vol. i. p. 110.

known to turn suddenly and unaccountably into something worse or better.

It is this fact, in combination with the nervous
strain which inevitably results when important instincts are left unstimulated,[1] that explains why systems of social organisation founded on pure Habit are
apt to decay from within, even when they are not
overthrown from without. "Drive out Nature with a
pitchfork and she will always come back" is a proverb
whose truth was learnt by the Spartans in the fourth
century B.C., and by the successors of John Knox in
Scotland or of Frederick William I. in Prussia more
than two thousand years later.

The problem, therefore, of the adaptation of our
nature to our environment cannot be solved by merely
enforcing those habits which are most convenient under existing circumstances. A habit can neither be
formed without risk of failure in the process, nor permanently retained, when formed, unless it is adapted,
not only to the facts of the outer world, but also to
the whole of our inner nature. The teachers of the
arts have always, in their own way, known this. The
trainer of a racing crew may make mistakes. He may
teach his men movements which, when they have acquired them, they will find to be "unnatural" and
therefore destructive of nervous ease. He may work
them for too long hours, or may keep intelligent young
men too long in an atmosphere of stupid rowing
"shop." But he, like a teacher of painting or music,
knows that there are certain bodily and mental habits
which give good results because they are "natural,"
and others, perhaps less difficult to acquire at first,

[1] Cp. *ante*, pp. 64, 65.

which fail because they are "unnatural." And he
knows that neither the process of habituation nor the
life of formed habit is tolerable unless it is accompanied by a certain amount of variation. The violinist, even when he has acquired the best technique that
is possible, must not always play the same piece. The
oarsman must not always row over the same course or
at the same rate of striking.

Habits which are "natural" in themselves and are
carried out with a sufficient element of variety are accompanied by a feeling of energy and freedom. "Unnatural" habits are accompanied, long before the actual
breaking-point is reached, by a feeling of unreality and
dissatisfaction. It may however take many years in
the life of an individual before dissatisfaction even
begins; or a habit may only become "unnatural" when
some unobserved change in the conditions of its action
has taken place. The discipline of the French army
in 1814 may have seemed in all externals the same
as it was in 1796, the Franciscan Rule at the death of
Savonarola may have seemed the same as it was at
the death of St. Francis, and yet that free activity,
which gave to "custom, law, and statute," in the mind
of the young Wordsworth, "the attraction of a country
of romance," was present in each case under the earlier,
and wanting under the later, conditions.

The enlargement of scale, therefore, which makes
Habit increasingly necessary in the Great Society, increases also the necessity of criticising and, from time
to time, abandoning existing habits. Just as modern
horticulturalists, who propagate millions of fruit trees
or potatoes from cuttings, require the periodical production of new varieties from actual seeding, so in the

modern world of habit and repetition we have learnt
to attach a new value to the man who goes back to his
first-hand impulses. The controllers of the Great Industry are always on the lookout for that type of man
whom Americans call "a live wire." For such a man
secretaries and typists and foremen carry on all that
punctual performance of habitual acts which took up
so much of the time and labour of a merchant or manufacturer even fifty years ago. He is set to form a habit
of non-habituation, of picking up and acting on his
mental suggestions at the point when they first appear
as an uncomfortable and perhaps almost subconscious
interference with an easy train of thought. It is this
habit of overriding habit which was meant by Oliver
Cromwell when he said, "He goes furthest who knows
not whither he is going"; by Napoleon when he raged
against those who allowed their minds to form "pictures"; even by Mr. Spofforth, the cricketer, when he
said, "Show me the man who knows how he is going
to play the next ball and I will show you a man whom
I can bowl out." As Professor E. A. Ross of Wis-
consin says:

> In a dynamic society so many readjustments are neces-
> sary, such far-reaching transformations are experienced in
> half a lifetime, that the past is discredited. One forms a
> habit of breaking habits.[1]

In every art the power and responsibility of the man
who acquires, and by ever new efforts retains, the
habit of origination are now increasing. With eyes tired
by thousands of perfect mechanical reproductions, we
stand before the pictures of Raphael, and wonder how

[1] *Social Psychology*, p. 79.

our fathers could have been stirred to enthusiasm by the facile habitual lines of that prince among drawing-masters. It is in Rembrandt, with the infinity of surprise which vibrates along every scratch of his etching-needle or stroke of his brush, that we find refreshment and harmony.

In music, in literature, in the conduct of life, our fathers used to build the tombs of the prophets whom their fathers had stoned. Now, even if a stone is picked up, it drops from the half-hearted fingers of the critic, who does not know whether in a few days he will not have become a disciple. The originator is made to feel that for him that crystallisation of past habits and current opinions, which we call duty, does not exist. His business is to be perpetually and ever-freshly himself.

But Plato's warning against Habit without philosophy has perhaps its deepest meaning when applied to the habit of origination. Napoleon on the Imperial throne, the financial genius when he has overcome his rivals, the leader of young opinion when his books are read and his plays acted in twenty languages, may create nothing but confusion and weakness unless his power is related to some greater purpose, in whose service is liberty.

CHAPTER VI

FEAR

HABIT results from repetition, whether of acts or thoughts or feelings. But repetition must have a beginning, and the beginning must be due to something else than Habit. If, therefore, the subjects of any state obey a repeated order through Habit, there still remains the question why they obeyed the original order. A believer in "scientific government" of the Anglo-Indian type, if he is asked that question, will generally answer that the original obedience was due to Fear.

This view is supported by the high authority of Hobbes, the first, the ablest, and the most courageous of the English writers who have attempted to create a theory of society by means of introspective psychology. "He that is to govern a whole nation," he says, "must read in himself, not this or that particular man, but mankind." [1]

His *Leviathan* was written between 1641 and 1651, while he was a Royalist exile in Paris; and those who, like Hobbes or Marx, write and think in exile, while they often gain in a fierce concentration of purpose, lose by the absence of those daily and hourly hints of the working of other men's minds, which are necessary if analysis of motive is not to become over-

[1] *Leviathan* (edition of 1839), p. xii.

84

simplified and distorted. Though, therefore, the publication both of Marx's *Kapital* and of Hobbes' *Leviathan* was an important event in the history of the
world, yet each book produced a reaction which made
it doubtful whether its main effect was to forward or
to hinder the cause which it advocated. The *Kapital*
has gone far to divide modern Germany into two mutu-
ally intolerant camps, unable to understand each
other's thoughts and even the vocabulary in which
those thoughts are expressed; and it is the camp of
Bismarck and not that of Marx which has so far
gained thereby. The *Leviathan* encouraged the restored Stuarts and their advisers to attempt to found
a personal monarchy by military force. That attempt
not only brought about the Revolution of 1688, but
created the reasoned opposition to sovereign power,
either executive or legislative, which was developed
by Locke and Montesquieu and helped to give the
United States of America a constitution equally difficult to administer and to reform. To this day the
eloquence and lucidity of Hobbes—"the old hard-
hearted fellow, the father of them all," as Francis
Place called him [1]—are a real danger to those few
Englishmen who are prepared to follow science in
politics. Hobbes seems to make "hardness" a necessary condition of accuracy in social thought, and requires us to ignore or inhibit those vague feelings of
human kindness which do not fit into his system.
Huxley, who wrote ,"Read Hobbes if you want to get
hard sense in good English," [2] might have founded a
modern school of scientific politics, if he had not sub-

[1] Letter to James Mill, October 20, 1816.
[2] *Life*, vol. ii. p. 74.

mitted himself to a tradition which made the main political forces of his own time unintelligible to him.

Hobbes, like his fellow-exiles in Paris, lived among exaggerated rumours of the social confusion which the doctrines of Natural Equality and Natural Benevolence had produced in England. The guiding impulse of his life was at that time the hope that Charles the Second might return and reintroduce order by the wholesome discipline of Fear. Again and again he argues that to rely on any other motive is to trust to mere words in a world of hard realities.

> Men have no pleasure, but on the contrary a great deal of grief, in keeping company where there is no power able to overawe them all;[1]

and

> No man obeys them whom they think have no power to help or hurt them.[2]

If it is objected that the existence in other animals of instinctive social affection creates a presumption that such affection will also be found in man, Hobbes replies by denying the analogy, "The agreement of these creatures is natural; that of men is by covenant only, which is artificial." [3] The only natural human affection which he allowed was that which arises from sex-love and parenthood, the family concord which "dependeth on natural lust." [4]

He got over the psychological facts which told against him either by treating them as exceptional, or

---

[1] *Leviathan* (edition of 1839), p. 112.
[2] *Ibid.*, p. 76. [3] *Ibid.*, p. 157.
[4] *Ibid.* (edition of 1839), p. 114.

by classifying every disposition which can restrain men
from unsocial conduct as a form of Fear. "Pity . . .
ariseth from the imagination that the like calamity
may befall himself," [1] the "fear of things invisible is
the natural seed of that which every man in himself
calleth religion, and in them that worship, or fear that
power otherwise than they do, superstition." [2]

He is the more easily able to do this because he
constantly "intellectualises" all the human passions by
treating them as the result of a calculation of interest.
"Both to love and to fear is to value." [3] But if he
bases passion on calculation he also makes calculation passionate. Whenever a man, after thinking out
the probable results of any proposed act, decides not
to do it, Hobbes assumes that his motive is Fear, and
he is helped in this by his own magnificent power of
imagining and presenting the case in which Fear does
accompany calculation.

That man which looks too far before him in the care of
future time hath his heart all the day long gnawed on by
fear of death, poverty, or other calamity; and has no repose,
no pause of his anxiety, but in sleep.[4]

Modern social psychologists cannot hope to equal
Hobbes' eloquence and force. But they can avoid
some of his mistakes by adopting a definition of Fear
which will at least distinguish it from other dissuasive
motives. Such a definition might describe Fear as an
instinct which, when excited by one of its appropriate
stimuli, inclines us to experience a nervous shock extending from a slight thrill up to convulsions and in-

[1] *Ibid.*, p. 47.   [2] *Ibid.*, p. 93.
[3] *Ibid.*, p. 77.   [4] *Ibid.*, p. 95.

sensibility. This shock is accompanied or preceded by an impulse either to remain perfectly still or to run away and hide.

In its origin Fear tended to preserve life by preventing animals from doing certain dangerous things. It varies greatly among individuals and races, but must always have been a rather clumsy instinct. It protected each species against a few of its most frequent dangers and left it unprotected against others. Its symptoms not infrequently are a cause of death, even among the lower animals. Snakes, for instance, exploit the paralysing terror which protects small birds from being seen by hawks.

From a very early stage, therefore, in his social development man has learnt the necessity of recognising and, if possible, controlling Fear. Every savage would understand the point of the story about the officer at Waterloo who said, "Yes, I am afraid, and if you had been half as much afraid as I am, you would have run away an hour ago."

In modern civilisation many of the original stimuli of Fear have disappeared [1] or have been so modified that they are no longer dangerous, while we have become intellectually aware of new dangers of which we have no instinctive dread. A man will turn dizzy as he looks down, in perfect safety, from the leaning tower at Pisa, or moves a vote of thanks at a charity dinner; and will find the greatest difficulty in making himself afraid to drink water in his hotel bedroom, which he believes to be very probably infected with typhoid. Indeed, if an intelligent married citizen were now to find himself as completely divested of the dis-

[1] See *ante*, p. 59.

position of Fear as was the boy who married the princess in Grimm's fairy tale, that fact would in all probability make little change in his way of life. Affection for his family, public spirit, religion, and the reasonable expectation of personal happiness would still be sufficient to create and maintain the habit of avoiding unnecessary danger to health and life.

But the mere absence of the original stimuli, instead of destroying the disposition of Fear among the sedentary inhabitants of a commercial city, merely leaves it existing but unstimulated, and so creates a condition of "baulked disposition," [1] in which a limited but not inconsiderable degree of Fear may be desired for its own sake. Small boys in city streets run in front of motor-cars to enjoy the resulting sensation. Hundreds of people may be seen at any great Exhibition, waiting in long lines to be allowed to pay sixpence each for a few moments of Fear on the "wiggle-woggle" or the "aerial-railway"; and some of the best and ablest individuals among the urban brain-workers of England and Germany take infinite pains year after year to spend weeks or months upon the Alps in pursuits whose most valued product is in their case the sensation of Fear. Perhaps, indeed, it is this desire for Fear rather than the impulse of Curiosity which has been the most important single cause of those dangerous journeys of discovery, by which the whole earth has been mapped out during the last four hundred years.

The clumsiness and uncertainty of Fear, its imperfect adaptation even to the environment of aboriginal life, and its constant irrelevance to the environment of civilisation, make it, of all human dispositions, the

[1] See *ante,* p. 64.

least suitable as a general basis for modern government and education. Not many decades ago the schoolmaster who deliberately aimed at producing and maintaining a state of terror among his scholars was still common. But as men began, under the influence of Rousseau and his successors, to think of the psychology of education, they recognised both that insensitive children were not terrified by their methods, and that terror brought to the point of "breaking the will" had a peculiarly injurious effect upon the brains of sensitive children. In the English "public" and "preparatory" schools the "bracing" effect of a mild degree of Fear is aimed at in compulsory cricket and football. Certain flogging customs still survive, which are only intelligible as relics of a period when education by extreme Fear was attempted in earnest. But there is now a general understanding among masters and boys that Fear is to have no part in that process, and that discipline is to be maintained by a cool calculation of the advantages and disadvantages of disobedience and punishment. If, once in a while, a severe flogging helps to silence for life a lad who might have been a poet, the sufferer and not the system is apt to be blamed.

I can remember, when I was seven or eight years old, that a deservedly respected churchwarden joined my father and myself, as we walked by a point in the street which I could still identify, and told, for my benefit, how a friend of his, who had heard his son swear, lit a bundle of matches and put them, as a foretaste of hell-fire, on the boy's tongue. Such actions, as well as books like a certain *Persuasives to Early Piety*, which aimed at producing the same result upon

me by cold print, must now be rare, and one of the
chief reasons for their disuse was practical experience
of the extreme uncertainty of their effect both upon
conduct and belief.

Even in the punishment of criminals we have (if
one ignores occasional panics) reached a point where
Sir William Dyott's statement from the bench during
the era of the Reform Bill that "nothing but the terror
of human suffering can avail to prevent crime" [1] sounds
old fashioned and ineffective; and to most of us it
seemed that the leaders of the militant suffragists in
England made a serious mistake in psychological tac-
tics when they attempted to substitute real Fear for
the advertisement and annoyance which resulted from
their earlier methods.

The attempt to govern whole populations by the
political use of Fear is not yet abandoned. But evidence is accumulating that the measures adopted with
that purpose, torture, flogging, massacres, pillage, public executions, blowing from guns, etc., are apt to produce, not only widespread Fear, but dogged obstinacy
among some of the older members of the populations
concerned, and a positive delight in danger among some
of the younger; while the blind panic which prevents
efficient action may at any moment strike the ruling
minority instead of the subject majority. In the past
indeed, the governments which used such means have
fallen, or have adopted a new policy either of con-
ciliation or of extermination.

The tradition of government by Fear still hangs
about some of the details of Prussian administration.

[1] Quoted by J. L. and B. Hammond, *The Village Labourer*, p.
201.

In Berlin one may hear a policeman addressing a group at a street corner in that "schnarrend" tone which is intended to produce a physical thrill. But the great majority of the Berliners apparently consider the tradition a little absurd, and in the stern calculation of the Social-Democrats as to whether a general strike, or even a civil war, may not some day be worth while, the element of actual Fear seems to have little part.

The Turks no longer rule in Europe, though a policy of government by Fear survives, with appropriate results, in Russia. But it is outside Europe, where the representatives of the Great Powers exercise military control over alien races, that government by Fear is habitually defended as a necessary and permanent condition. Lieutenant-Colonel G. de S. Barrow, for instance, in a lecture reported in the *Journal of the United Service Institution of India,* says:

Fear is an elemental, perhaps the most elemental, of the factors which go to make up our moral nature. . . . It is with us now just as strong and ruling an influence in our lives, whether as individuals or nations, as ever it was in the days of primeval man. . . . The crude desire of fighting for food becomes developed into the virtues of patriotism, love of liberty, and country, but always with the same origin—Fear.[1]

The form of this may be due to Hobbes' eloquence, filtered through eight generations of smoking-room talk, but the spirit of it, daily repeated in half-a-dozen

[1] September, 1912. I owe my introduction to this interesting lecture to an article in the *Daily News* by my friend, Mr. William Archer. It is noteworthy that Colonel Barrow, like Hobbes, combines an exaggerated statement of the instinctive nature of fear with "intellectualism" in his explanation of its working. "Fear," he says, "springs from the desire of life."

languages, runs through many of the reported utterances of the representatives of European civilisation in Africa, Persia, and the islands and peninsulas of the East.

CHAPTER VII

PLEASURE-PAIN AND HAPPINESS

FOR more than a century after the publication of the *Leviathan,* the English defenders of constitutional liberty opposed Hobbes' psychological plea for absolutism with arguments drawn not from psychology but from the metaphysical conception of Natural Right. By 1776, however—the "Annus Mirabilis" in which Bentham's *Fragment on Government,* Adam Smith's *Wealth of Nations,* and the American Declaration of Independence all appeared,—a new psychological theory of society, based, not on Fear, but on the attractive and repulsive influence of Pleasure and Pain, was already becoming influential.

The Declaration of Independence includes "the pursuit of happiness" among the "inalienable rights" of mankind, but Jefferson must have found the chief evidence for the existence of men's metaphysical right to pursue happiness in the psychological fact that they did pursue it. From Bentham's mind the conception of Natural Right had already disappeared. His *Introduction to the Principles of Morals and Legislation* (1789) opens with the strictly psychological statement, "Nature has placed mankind under the governance of two sovereign masters, pain and pleasure." [1] Two

[1] Bentham, *Works.* The sentence, as M. Halévy points out in his masterly treatise, is taken almost unchanged from Helvetius (Halévy, *La Formation du Radicalisme Philosophique,* vol. i. p. 298).

years later he tells the revolutionists in France that "Natural Rights is simple nonsense, natural and imprescriptable Rights rhetorical nonsense—nonsense upon stilts." [1]

Bentham did not die till 1832, and before he died his doctrines, partly through their direct influence upon the few readers of his manuscripts and printed works, but more generally through their effect on Paley's theology, Whately's ethics and economics, Romilly's legal reforms, and the economic and political theories of Ricardo and James Mill, had attained an authority over English thought which increased during the next thirty years and has not yet quite disappeared. The conscious intellectual life of the average Englishman is still often spent among the ruins of Utilitarianism. His favourite journalists still use phrases like "the laws of political economy," and "the facts of human nature," in senses which assume the whole Benthamite psychology; though they do so with that slightly irritable emphasis which results from a feeling that criticism in a slipshod and sentimental age has weakened the authority of principle.

Bentham's psychology was based upon three propositions, asserted or implied. The first was the "intellectualist" assumption that all human action was the result of a conscious search for the means of attaining some "end" or "good" other than the action itself. The second was "Hedonism"—the proposition that all human goods could be shown to consist of the one good of Pleasure (or Happiness, which was treated as the sum of Pleasures), and the avoidance of Pain. The third was the Greatest Happiness Principle, the

[1] Bentham, "Anarchical Fallacies" (1791), *Works,* vol. ii. p. 501.

proposition that the end of all action by men in society
was the production of the greatest quantity of Pleasure for the greatest number of the members of the
society concerned.

With Utilitarian Intellectualism I have already
dealt.[1] With the difficulties and contradictions of
Bentham's Greatest Happiness Principle I shall deal
later in this chapter. For the moment I confine myself to his Hedonism.

The Hedonist doctrine itself, as stated or assumed
by Bentham, involves three separate propositions: that
the only effective human motive is the desire for
Pleasure and for the avoidance of Pain; that Pain and
Pleasure are the negative and positive ends of a simple
gradation of feeling; and that the state of consciousness called Happiness is the same as that called
Pleasure.[2]

On the first of these propositions—that ideas of
Pleasure-Pain are the universal and only motive—I
shall not spend much time. In order to arrive at it
Bentham had to strain the meaning of words almost
as seriously as did Hobbes. If Hobbes defined pity
as a kind of fear, Bentham declared that men are
moved not directly by curiosity, but indirectly by the
pleasure of curiosity, not directly by anger but indirectly by a calculation as to the means of avoiding the
"pains of unsatisfied vindictiveness."[3] Even in the
eighteenth century a man of Bentham's genius and

---

[1] See *ante,* p. 38, and my *Human Nature in Politics,* pt. i. ch. i.
[2] Bentham, *Works,* vol. iii. p. 214 ("Pannomian Fragments").
"Happiness is a word employed to denote the sum of the pleasures
experienced during that quantity of time which is under consideration, deduction made or not made of the quantity of pain experienced during the same quantity of time."
[3] *Works,* vol. i., "Table of the Springs of Action," pp. 197-203.

sincerity could hardly have adhered to this position if he had not been a shy and sedentary bachelor, living among ideas of action and ideas of pleasure rather than real acts and real pleasures.

The second and third Hedonist propositions—that Pain is the negation of Pleasure, and Happiness the extension of Pleasure in time—the propositions which Bentham summed up in the statement, "What happiness is every man knows, because what pleasure is every man knows, and what pain is every man knows," [1] present greater difficulties. Against them I shall argue, firstly that the sensations called Pains are not the mere negation of the sensations called Pleasures, secondly that the "feeling-tones" of Pleasantness and Unpleasantness are not the same as the sensations called Pains and Pleasures, and thirdly that these feeling-tones of Pleasantness and Unpleasantness are not the same as the states of consciousness called Happiness and Unhappiness.

There is perhaps no point on which modern experimental psychology has been more successful than in the examination of the "Pain" sensations, and the differentiation of them from the feeling-tone of Unpleasantness. It has been shown that mankind, like many other animals, possess a system of nerves ending in those "pain-spots" which lie scattered, sometimes closely and sometimes widely, among the "cold-spots," "heat-spots," and "touch-spots" on our skin. The stimulation of these nerves produces the "pain" sensations of pricking, smarting, burning, and the like. Other nerves situated more deeply in our tissues pro-

[1] *Ibid.*, vol. ix. p. 123.

duce on stimulation the "pain" sensation of aching.[1]
A doctor may find it advisable to distinguish carefully
between the smarting and aching sensations, but a
social psychologist may be allowed to speak of both as
instances of the one sensation of Pain.

The evolutionary origin of both the superficial and
the deeper pain-nerves is obviously to be found in the
fact that they, by giving rise to their appropriate
sensations, inclined animals to avoid certain conditions
dangerous to life.

In the same way, we and other animals have in
certain parts of our bodies other nerves producing
"Pleasure" sensations, whose evolutionary origin obviously was the useful fact that those who felt them
were inclined to seek for their continuance by performing acts likely to preserve the species. These
nerves are particularly connected with the functions
of nutrition (including tasting and smelling) and sex.
A Pain sensation can coexist with a Pleasure sensation, and is obviously not its mere opposite.

These special Pain or Pleasure *sensations* are found
by almost all modern psychologists to be different
from the *feeling-tones* of Pleasantness and Unpleasantness. As Professor Titchener (who has done much
experimental work on the subject) says: "Pain . . .
is a sensation, and it is a sensation which at different
times and under different circumstances may be pleasant, indifferent, or unpleasant." [2] And in the same

[1] See, *e.g.*, Myers' *Text-Book of Experimental Psychology*, pp.
14-16 (Bibliography, p. 19), and Titchener, *Text-Book of Psychology*,
pp. 152-159 (Bibliography, p. 159), and pp. 183-193 (Bibliography,
p. 193).

[2] *Text-Book of Psychology*, vol. i. p. 227. See Bibliography on
pp. 263-264. Max Meyer, *Psychological Review* (New York), July,
1908, pp. 202-216, gives a long list of psychological opinions on the

way some of the Pleasure sensations may, under certain circumstances, be indifferent or unpleasant in feeling-tone.

Professor Max Meyer says "Pleasantness and unpleasantness are the highest product of mental evolution." [1] Feeling-tone, that is to say, is a more highly evolved form of consciousness than mere sensation, and must from its beginning have been a much safer guide than mere sensation to the preservation of life and health. It was, for instance, a useful fact in the psychology of our ape-ancestors that the not inconsiderable amount of pain involved in scratching parasites off one's skin was pleasant, and that eating the most delicious food to absolute repletion was unpleasant. Feeling-tone indicated not the mere stimulation of certain special sensations, but excess or defect in the stimulation, not only of those sensations, but of any of our dispositions.[2]

The æsthetic feelings of Beauty and Ugliness constitute a special case of Pleasant or Unpleasant feeling-tone, due to the fact that the simple intellectual disposition of Perception (or Recognition) has been stimulated normally or abnormally. The whole existence of self-directed living beings depends on their power

---

subject, most of which agree more or less closely with the view taken by me above. By exception, Professors H. R. Marshall and Lagerborg "fail to distinguish between unpleasantness and the sensation of pain" (p. 204), and Stumpf "regards pleasantness and unpleasantness as sensations" (p. 205).

[1] *Psychological Review* (New York), July, 1908, p. 320.

[2] Professor Bawdon, *Psychological Review* (New York), September 1910, p. 337, puts this fact into the very specialised language of technical psychology: "Agreeable emotion is connected with such massing of stimuli as leads to a response within the normal limits of the functional capacity of the organism, while pain accompanies the piling up of stimuli and the subsequent discharge when these exceed the limits of such normal functioning."

of recognising objects in the world around them as identical with, or belonging to, the same class as objects seen or heard before; and, in the higher animals, Pleasantness results from the normal and unimpeded performance of that intellectual function. In man Pleasantness increases up to a certain point with the repetition of recognition, provided that that repetition has the slight degree of variation which prevents the fatigue of absolute monotony. A whole audience at a farce will yell with delight when they recognise that a comedian is for the twentieth time, under slightly varied circumstances, saying "Do you know-w?" A dog is apparently affected in the same way by picking up the lost scent of a fox, or by recognising his master's step. It is not only the prospect of catching the fox or meeting his master, but also the process of recognition itself which seems to delight him.

Certain pure colours and harmonious sounds are in nature sometimes precisely reproduced, and therefore can be precisely and without effort recognised. Man, for instance, and some birds have apparently an æsthetic delight in seeing or collecting objects of pure colour,[1] or in hearing or producing pure sounds.

Form as well as colour and sound may be recognised, and man finds a very high degree of pleasantness in following, consciously or subconsciously, the rhythm of that unbroken but unmonotonous form-relation which constitutes "pattern." If one offers a child or savage the choice of two necklaces, both composed of shells of various sizes belonging to the same species; and if one necklace is arranged in a

---

[1] Cf. the behaviour of the gardener bower-bird (Lloyd Morgan, *Animal Behaviour*, 1900, p. 273).

graded pattern of ascending and descending size, and the other consists of shells threaded haphazard, he will always choose the first. The pattern, he will say, is "pretty." And if the pattern is made more complex, so as to involve a double rhythm of form and form, or of colour and form, he will probably find it (provided it is not too elaborate for his recognition) even more pretty. The civilised man, whose power of recognition has been specially trained, experiences a more subtle and more intense delight in the intricate pattern of a chorus of Æschylus, or of an overture of Wagner, or of the nave of a Gothic cathedral, where perspective turns monotony into rhythm.

And, by one of the few splendid accidents of evolution, this complex rhythm of unmonotonous repetition corresponds, not only to the specific resemblances among things immediately useful or hurtful to man, but to the ultimate pattern which the finest effort of man's mind is able to detect in the universe as a whole. Kosmos, the name which the early Greek philosophers gave to the universe, means simply "pattern," and the intellectual lives of Plato or Dante or Spinoza or Newton were largely guided and sustained by their delight in the sheer beauty of the rhythmic relation between law and instance, species and individual, or cause and effect.[1]

[1] I confine myself above to the special æsthetic feeling of "pattern" beauty. There are, of course, other "pleasant" feelings which are closely allied to it, but of different origin. Our delight, for instance, in a beautiful woman's form is largely the result of the valuable evolutionary fact that the instincts of sex are most strongly stimulated by indications of perfect health; though the "pattern" feeling often enters into it as well. A climber's delight, again, at the prospect from a Swiss summit may include very little of the "pattern feeling," and may be caused almost entirely by the sense of achievement and novelty.

In the complex and "unnatural" world of modern civilisation a felt contrast between the feeling tone of Pleasantness and Unpleasantness and the Pain and Pleasure sensations is extremely common, especially when the pain-nerves have been for a long time unstimulated, and the condition of "baulked disposition" has arisen. A man or boy, living a sheltered life, may find a rather high degree of the sensation of pain (as he also may find the sensation of fear) actually pleasant. I can myself remember being one of a group of boys who, one evening, varied the intolerable monotony of boarding-school "prep" by running needles through the lobes of our ears in order to enjoy the sensation; and most people can understand how monks and nuns come to long for the smart of the scourge.

In the civilised world, Feeling-Tone, though it is a better guide than Sensation, may still be misleading. The man who, while resisting the gross temptations of his uncontrolled senses, spends his days in a carefully measured epicureanism, in which art, science, bodily exercise, and social intercourse are all pursued up to and not beyond the point of greatest pleasantness, is apt to find, as the years go on, that some of the deeper and more permanent needs of his nature are unsatisfied. And if an epicurean loses to the slightest degree his own nervous health, exquisite pleasantness may attach itself to actions and states of mind which are obviously dangerous. James, for instance, quotes Saint Pierre, who says: "For myself I find that the feelings of melancholy are the most voluptuous of all sensations," and Marie Bashkirtseff: "I enjoy weeping, I enjoy my despair." [1]

Now the testimony of language indicates that there are a third pair of states of consciousness, Happiness and Unhappiness, which stand in something like the same relation to the Feeling-Tones of Pleasantness and Unpleasantness as those do to the "Pleasure" and "Pain" Sensations. The word for Happiness is different from that for Pleasantness, or for any pleasure, in Greek and Latin, in the modern European languages, and, I am told, in Sanscrit and Hebrew.

Is this indication psychologically sound? I am myself inclined to answer, Yes. It is very difficult in such matters to be sure that one is not confusing a difference in degree with one of kind, but the difference between Happiness and Pleasantness, and between Unhappiness and Unpleasantness does seem to me to be best described as one of kind. One may illustrate it by the story in *Punch* (probably a transcript from fact), in which a little boy, listening to a regimental band, says: "Mother, how is it that soldiers' music always makes me feel so much happier than I really am?" [2]

Man, from the commencement of fully-conscious childhood, lives not only consciously but subconsciously in the past of memory and the future of expectation, as well as in the experience of the present. He can therefore often choose to spend any moment, either in the mere consciousness of that moment, or in the more solid, and, as he feels, more permanent, type of consciousness which represents, as the little boy

[1] James, *Varieties of Religious Experience*, p. 83 (note).
[2] *Punch*, March 24, 1909.

said, what he *really* is. If he chooses always to live in the pleasantness of the moment he will become half aware of the dissatisfaction of his more permanent self. This is a situation with which modern psychological novelists often deal. The heroine of Mrs. Edith Wharton's *House of Mirth,* and the hero of Turgenev's *Spring Floods* are aware of the pleasantness of refined luxury and clever talk, and resolutely live in that pleasantness till they can no longer ignore the dissatisfaction beneath it. If they had been "happy" their consciousness and their subconsciousness, the novelist preaches, would have been at one.

"Happiness" in this sense is the subject-matter of Aristotle's *Ethics,* and the foundation of his whole social philosophy. He believed that it could only be attained by the ever-fresh activity of a will trained in the tradition of virtue, and acting in a duly ordered material environment.[1] To him therefore Happiness was not only good in itself but an absolutely safe guide for social life. The course of individual conduct, or the form of civic organisation which made Happiness most possible must be the best.

If Bentham had drawn this distinction between Pleasantness and Happiness, between the consciousness of the moment and the consciousness which, even during the moment, includes the past and the future, not only would Carlyle's criticism of the "pig-philosophy" have been turned aside, but the best of Bentham's disciples would have been spared much of that bewilderment and disappointment which shows itself in their letters and autobiographies. John Stuart Mill would have had words by which he could have ex-

[1] Ψυχῆς ἐνέργεια κατ' ἀρετὴν ἐν βίῳ τελείῳ (*Ethics,* bk. i. ch. vii.).

plained the relation of the deeper purposes of his life to the weary discomfort which followed the overwork of his boyhood. And Francis Place need not have felt, as he felt in the months after his wife's death, that life without a resolute attempt to escape from grief involved an abandonment of his principles.[1]

But the world is not, it would seem, so made that even the state of Happiness must necessarily coincide with that "judgment of the wise" on the whole facts of social life which was Aristotle's final Court of Appeal. The identity of the world as it is and the world as we would wish it to be does not go so far. Aristotle, indeed, himself, when he tried to realise what Happiness meant to him without reference to its causes or consequences, found it, not in that vigorous combination of civic and intellectual activity towards which the main body of his teaching tended, but in the state of Contemplation which alone, he says, is "desired for its own sake, since nothing results from it but the fact of having contemplated."[2]

Aristotle's distinction between Pleasure and Happiness, and his belief that Happiness could exist only in a man whose will had been trained by the environment of a well-ordered state, made his identification of Happiness and Social Good at least arguable. But

---

[1] The distinction would, I think, also have helped Professor Titchener in the difficulty which he obviously feels in the following passage: "Is it really true that the pleasure of a good dinner is identical with the pleasure of a good action?

"Well! remember always that affective psychology is in the trial stage, and that no one can dogmatise on the question. But in the writer's belief it is true. A good dinner and a good action seem to him to differ—not in their pleasantness: that is precisely where they are alike; but in practically everything else" (*Text-Book of Psychology*, 1910, p. 257).

[2] οὐδὲν γὰρ ἀπ' αὐτῆς γίνεται παρὰ τὸ θεωρῆσαι (*Ethics*, bk. x. chap. vii.)

as soon as the Utilitarians identified Pleasure and Happiness they created a logical gulf, which they never succeeded in filling, between their rigid psychological Hedonism and their adoption of the "principle" of "The Greatest Happiness of the Greatest Number" as the basis of social organisation. Individual Pleasure has no obvious dependence on social good. If, therefore, one accepts the propositions that Happiness is Pleasure, and Pleasure the only good, the Greatest Happiness Principle immediately raises the question whether we have any right to expect that every man will be guided in his social action by a desire for the good of the majority of his fellows.

Bentham himself, in the course of his long life, solved this problem in several, sometimes inconsistent, ways, and it is not possible to draw from the mass of his writings and rewritings a perfectly clear account even of the successive changes in his position. At first he seems to have been unconscious of the existence of any difficulty. The discovery that Pleasure was the only human good, and the passionate desire to spread the knowledge of his discovery, and so to increase the amount of Pleasure in the world, all seemed to him part of one revelation. Looking back, in 1822, at the age of seventy-four, upon his childhood and youth, he wrote:

The reader cannot have gone through the first sentence in the Fragment [on Government, 1776] without having seen the passion that gave rise to it, the passion for improvement . . . in every line, but particularly in the line of government. At an age a few months before or after seven years the first embers of it were kindled by Telemachus [Fenelon's *Télémaque*, 1699]. By an early pamphlet of

Priestley's [1] . . . light was added to the warmth. In the phrase "the greatest happiness of the greatest number," I then saw delineated for the first time a plain as well as a true standard for whatever is right or wrong, useful, useless or mischievous in human conduct whether in the field of morals or of politics. . . . No sooner had my candle been taken out of the bushel than I looked for the descent of torches to it from the highest regions. [2]

As long as Bentham thought and felt in this way, it was possible for him to hold that no one could act without regard to the sum of happiness resulting from his action unless he were stupid or perverted.

In other moods Bentham used, like Plato, the analogy of the arts. The statesman and the school-master were artists who practised "the art of direct-ing men's actions to the production of the greatest possible quantity of happiness." [3] It might be taken for granted that the true artist would desire to do his work well. Just as Plato says, "Have the arts any other interest than their own highest perfection," [4] so Bentham held to the end of his life that

. . . in the eyes of every impartial arbiter, writing in the character of legislator, and having exactly the same regard for the happiness of every member of the community in question as for that of every other, the greatest happiness

---

[1] Priestley, *An Essay on the First Principles of Government* (1768).
[2] *Works*, vol. x. p. 79.
[3] Introduction, *Works,* vol. i. p. 142. Cf. Halévy, vol. i. note 124, p. 298.
[4] *Republic* (Golden Treasury Series, p. 21). The essence of Plato's argument from the arts sometimes reappears in the modern use of the word "science." For instance, my friend, Professor Gustaf Steffen of Gotenburg, in his *Lebensbedingungen Moderner Kultur* (pp. 6 and 7), speaks of the "slavery of the will and the intellect to the separate interests of Nation, Districts, Professions, Classes, Fam-ilies, and Individuals," as "This unscientific treatment of a purely scientific problem."

of the greatest number of the members of that same community cannot but be recognised in the character of the right and proper and sole right and proper end of government. [1]

But experience of the English statesmen of his day slowly convinced Bentham both that an imperfect devotion to the Greatest Happiness of the Greatest Number was not an abnormal fact in human nature, and that a man might be skilled and successful in government without making the interest of those whom he governed his sole object.

When the *Fragment on Government* appeared in 1776, somebody asked Sir Alexander Wedderburn, the Solicitor-General, what he thought of "the principle of utility." He answered, Bentham was told, "It is a dangerous one." "Till within a few years," wrote Bentham in a passage first published in 1828, "I am ashamed to think how few, did this same response remain a mystery to me. The principle of utility a dangerous principle! Dangerous to endeavour to do what is most useful! The proposition (said I to myself) is a self-contradictory one. Confusion of ideas on his part (for I could find no other cause) was the cause to which I attributed it. The confusion was in mine. The man was a shrewd man, and knew well enough what he meant, though at that time I did not." [2]

Bentham was deeply affected by John Howard's discovery of the horrors of the English prisons, and

[1] *Works,* vol. ix. p. 6, Introduction to the "Constitutional Code," written apparently between 1820 and 1830 (see notes to pp. 2 and 3 of the Introduction).

[2] *Works,* vol. i. (Historical Preface to the *Fragment on Government*), pp. 245, 246.

later by the reports of new horrors in the hulks and the Australian penal settlements. He attempted to introduce a system of scientific prison management, and was encouraged both by Government promises and the passage of an enabling Act of Parliament. After his father's death in 1792 he sank practically the whole of his fortune in purchasing a site for a new model Prison on his "Panopticon" plan. But the Government grew tired of him; the prison was not built, nor Bentham's expenditure, till 1813, repaid. Wearied, apparently ruined and almost heart-broken, but still industrious, he met James Mill in 1808.

Bentham, who in 1808 was sixty years of age, had hitherto been, if anything, a Tory. Mill was a Whig, who was soon drawn by Francis Place into the Radical group which had won the Westminster election of 1807. The policy of Place and Mill was based upon a belief in the complete selfishness of the English governing minority, and a determination to oppose to it the organised selfishness of the governed majority. In a few years' time Bentham had adopted whole-heartedly both their belief and the policy of radical democracy which followed from it. "Now," he writes in 1822, "for some years past all inconsistencies, all surprises, have vanished. . . . A clue to the interior of the labyrinth has been found; it is the principle of self-preference. Man, from the very constitution of his nature, prefers his own happiness to that of all other sensitive beings put together." [1]

Henceforward, for Bentham, representative democ-

---

[1] *Works,* vol. x. p. 80. He put the self-preference principle in another passage with even greater precision: "On the occasion of every act he exercises, every human being is led to pursue that line of conduct which, according to his view of the case, taken by him

racy was an ingenious machine for extracting, as was afterwards said, "golden conduct from leaden instincts." The voter, like the flea which a showman harnesses to a tiny carriage, is, while struggling to go his own way, to achieve a result which he does not necessarily contemplate or desire.

Sometimes, at this period of his life, it even seemed to Bentham an actual advantage that the citizens of a democracy should neither profess nor feel any regard for the general good. In a passage which reads rather grimly now, he rejoices over the description which his friends gave him of the hard material-ism which was then showing itself in the politics of the United States:

As to professions and boasts of purity of motives; in the debates and discussions that have taken place in the United States, little or nothing of this sort of talk is heard. Why? Because, in the first place, there is no such demand for it; in the next place, there would be no use for it, for there would be no prospect of its gaining credence.[1]

The defects of such a view did not fully show themselves as long as Benthamism was confined to Bentham and his first friends. He never, till his extreme old age, admitted to his intimacy a man he did not believe to share his own "passion for improve-ment," or retained any one as a friend after he thought him to have lost it. His correspondence, for instance, shows him upbraiding Brougham because huge fees

---

at the moment, will be in the highest degree contributory to his own greatest happiness." Introduction to the "Constitutional Code," *Works,* vol. ix. p. 5.

[1] "Constitutional Code" (*Works,* vol. ix. p. 63).

for legal work were choking the passion which should have led him to the unpaid service of law reform.[1]

James Mill and his son, Romilly, Place, Grote, and Parkes were possessed by a determination to lessen the misery of the world, which was not seriously diminished even when they believed that it was a kind of selfishness. But as time went on, the "principle of self-preference" was adopted as a speculative opinion by men who had no real share in the passion of its founder. When Macaulay, for instance, published his *Edinburgh Review* attacks on Utilitarianism in 1829, the only reply was Bowring's editorial statement in the Westminster Review that honesty was the best policy, and that utilitarianism meant nothing but the "plain imperative proposition—Pursue the rule which is best for the general happiness; because, in the long run and taking all the chances that are before you together, it is the mostly likely to increase your own."[2] In 1849 Bowring went to China, and soon illustrated the doctrine of the "greatest happiness of the greatest number" by levying a particularly scandalous war upon one-fifth of the human race.

When Benthamism became popularised, the theory that society was, or could be, so constructed, either by divine purpose or human contrivance, that every one

---

[1] *E.g.,* Bentham writes (in the little-known collection of his letters in the British Museum) to Brougham signing himself "your still loving though so badly offended Grandpapa." "I hear you, screaming like mad in the middle of the nursery, throat hoarse, eyes running. Pray Nurse, dear Nurse! Fees for Henry—More Fees—More Fees. These words you can speak plain enough already. When will you have learnt your Primer? When will you be able to spell *'Greatest Happiness Principle'? Non-Disappointment Principle?* Ends of Justice . . . avoidance of delay expense and vexation?" March 30, 1830. (British Museum, Add. MS., 33,546 f. 386).

[2] *Westminster Review,* October 1829, p. 535.

by following his own interest best served the interest of the whole, had hardly any results which were not evil. Bentham's true followers in that respect were not John Mill and the Neo-Utilitarians but the philistine political economists, who found their flea-carriage not in the machinery of democracy but in that of commercial exchange. In 1831, the year before Bentham's death, Whately was professor of political economy at Oxford, and in his lectures for that year he says, with reference to the action of corn-dealers in raising prices during a scarcity:

> Various parts of man's conduct as a member of society are often attributed to human forethought and design, which might with greater truth be referred to a kind of instinct, or something analogous to it; which leads him, while pursuing some immediate personal gratification, to further an object not contemplated by him. In many cases we are liable to mistake for the wisdom of Man what is in truth the wisdom of God.[1]

Factory owners, whom Whately's teaching reached at third-hand through the newspapers and magazines, did, in fact, try to ignore any kindness which they might feel for their operatives, because they honestly believed that such feelings were "against the laws of political economy."

And Whately did not confine his teaching to the rich. With no prescience of Marx, he urged the same doctrine on the poor. The British Museum has a copy of the sixth edition (1842) of his *Easy Letters on Money Matters for the use of young people*, published by the Society for the Promotion of Christian Know-

---

[1] *Introductory Lectures on Political Economy* (1831), pp. 100-101.

ledge, and used largely in the National Society's schools at the time. In it (p. 62) Whately says to boys who would soon be working men:

It is curious to observe how through the wise and beneficent arrangement of Providence men thus do the greatest service to the public when they are thinking of nothing but their own gain.

Perhaps some of the Sheffield saw-grinders, whose "rattening" was exposed in 1867, had used this book at school, and had applied its lessons in the interest of their own, and not of the archbishop's class.

When the last third of the nineteenth century began, John Mill was still alive, and in economics and sociology was the accepted leader both of the universities and of the newspapers. But Utilitarianism was plainly dying, and dying because its central problem of human motive was still unsolved. The pathetic candour of Henry Sidgwick shows us Mill's best disciple at the stage of thought when he could only reconcile Hedonism and the Greatest Happiness principle by assuming an effort of will which had no relation to his psychological scheme:

My first adhesion to a definite ethical system was to the Utilitarianism of Mill. . . . The two elements of Mill's view which I am accustomed to distinguish as Psychological Hedonism (that each man does seek his own happiness) and Ethical Hedonism (that each man ought to seek the general happiness) both attracted me, and I did not at first perceive their incoherence.

Psychological Hedonism—the law of universal pleasure-seeking—attracted me by its frank naturalness. Ethical Hedonism, as expounded by Mill, was morally inspiring by its dictate of readiness for absolute self-sacrifice. They appealed to different elements of my nature, but they brought these into apparent harmony: they both used the same words "pleasure," and "happiness," and the persuasiveness of Mill's exposition veiled for a time the profound discrepancy between the natural end of action—private happiness, and the end of duty—general happiness. Or if a doubt assailed me as to the coincidence of private and general happiness, I was inclined to hold that it ought to be cast to the winds by a generous resolution.[1]

[1] *The Methods of Ethics,* 6th ed. p. xv.

CHAPTER VIII

THE PSYCHOLOGY OF THE CROWD

WHEN Bentham's psychology, like that of Hobbes, proved to be an insufficient basis for social theory, the main current of English thought turned once more to metaphysics. It was the Catholic Revival in religion, and the Idealism of Hegel, as expounded by Caird and Green, which mainly profited by the failure of Utilitarianism.

But there are always a few thinkers who, even in times of disappointment, feel the need of a positive science of man and society; and when, in 1845, Auguste Comte's writings first reached England it seemed for a moment that this need might be satisfied by his system.

For English readers of that generation the main significance of Comte's Positivism was its denial of Bentham's psychological principle that "man from the very structure of his nature prefers his own happiness to that of all sensitive beings put together." [1] The most important fact of man's nature was, according to Comte, not his indifference to the good of other men, but his disinterested love for them. Comte, like Bentham, was an "intellectualist" in the sense that he made every human action result from an intel-

[1] *Ante*, p. 109.

115

lectual enquiry as to the means of satisfying some end. But the choice of the social end, the original driving force, which Bentham ascribed to the desire for Pleasure, Comte ascribed to Love. "The necessity," he said, "of assigning with exact truth the place occupied by the intellect and by the heart in the organisation of human nature and of society, leads to the decision that Affection must be the central point of the synthesis. . . . The only position for which the intellect is permanently adapted is to be the servant of the social sympathies." [1] "It is for the heart to suggest our problems, it is for the intellect to solve them." [2]

George Eliot and Harriet Martineau, for instance, had known in their own personal experience the intense moral discomfort involved in the choice between Benthamism, which seemed to leave no scientific justification for Love, and Supernaturalism, which only restored Love by rejecting science. To them Comte's doctrine that the reality of instinctive Love could be established by the most rigorously scientific examination, either of the history of civilisation or of individual psychology, came like water into a thirsty land.

Positivism, however, never succeeded in gaining anything like the influence which Utilitarianism had exercised. Its weakness was chiefly due to the thoroughly unpositive character of Comte's own mind. When he is historical one is never sure whether his "laws" are generalisations from recorded facts or statements of assumed moral necessities. What, for

[1] *Positive Polity* (Eng. trans., 1875), vol. i. p. II.
[2] *Ibid.* p. 14.

instance, does he exactly mean when he says: "The social instinct had to be [dut être] purely civic in antiquity, collective in the Middle Age, and universal in the Final State, as its modern aspirations indicate"? [1] When he is psychological one also feels that he never sufficiently distinguishes between that which ought to be and that which is. He says, for instance, "We tire of thinking and even of acting; we never tire of loving." [2] It would be pleasant if it were so, but most candidates, when they creep away for a few days' rest after an election, would say that they are more tired of loving than either of thinking or of acting.

Comte died the year before Darwin published his theory of evolution, and his own biology is based on the Lamarkian doctrine of the inheritance of acquired characteristics, pushed to a point where it almost avowedly represents rather an ideal principle than a statement of fact. "We can," he says, "even conceive that, on the biological principles of inheritance, a few generations would succeed in modifying the cerebral organisation itself in a society so constituted, the volume of the organs of feeling becoming augmented or diminished by continual exercise or disuse." [3]

In 1859 the *Origin of Species* appeared, and within

---

[1] *Positive Polity* (Eng. trans., 1876), vol. iii. (*Social Dynamics*), p. 57.

[2] *Ibid.* vol. i. p. 1.

[3] *Ibid.* (Eng. trans.), vol. ii. p. 123. The same confusion of ideal and fact is seen even more clearly when Comte treats of the anatomy of the brain. "The principles on which we have been proceeding would seem to leave little doubt, in minds penetrated with the true spirit of our subjective theory as to where [the instinct of self-preservation] should be placed. The nutritive instinct would occupy the lowest portion in the brain, as near as possible to the motor apparatus and to the vegetative viscera. I would place it, therefore, in the median portion of the cerebellum. . . ." *Loc. cit.* vol. i. pp. 561, 562. Comte's brain-anatomy was much influenced by Gall (1758-1828), the founder of phrenology. I refer above, not

a few years the Positivist as well as the Utilitarian
view of human nature seemed old-fashioned. The
proved continuity of human and non-human life
demanded a biological outlook which should study
mankind, not in isolation, but as one of a number of
related species.

The first effect, however, of Darwinism upon social
science was curiously unsatisfactory. The early evolutionary sociologists knew very little about the psychology of even the highest non-human animals, and
were tempted to adopt superficial and mechanical
explanations of animal conduct, which in turn reacted
upon their conceptions of human conduct. To observe
from outside (as one observes an ants' nest through
a magnifying glass) the "struggle for life" or the
working of the "gregarious instincts" in human
society seemed to the contemporaries of Darwin to
be a much more "scientific" method than to analyse
the minutiæ of one's own feelings.

Walter Bagehot brought out his *Physics and
Politics* in 1873, and it was at once widely accepted,
both in England and abroad, as indicating the course
which sociology was likely to take under the influence
of the Darwinian discoveries. He treats man throughout as a gregarious animal, to be examined (as the
title of his book implies) by the method of the physical sciences. Now, gregarious species only survive
because in certain emergencies each individual can be
trusted to act much in the same way as the rest.
The shortest and easiest way to explain this fact was to

---

to its accuracy or inaccuracy, but to Comte's vague use of "would
occupy" [doit ainsi occuper] and "I would place it therefore." He
clearly draws, in this case again, no sharp distinction between what
is and what ought to be.

infer the existence of a general instinct of Imitation, which inclines any animal possessed of that instinct to copy all those actions by members of its own species which catch its attention. The assumption of such an instinct made it easy to apply the methods of "physics" to "politics," and to measure imitative attraction as the physicist measures gravitation. It is accordingly on Imitation that Bagehot bases the greater part of his social analysis. "The propensity," he says, "of man to imitate what is before him is one of the strongest parts of his nature." [1] This analogy between man and the other animals can be made to appear complete if we hide the fact that we are ignorant of the degree to which animal consciousness resembles human consciousness, by assuming, as Bagehot assumes in the teeth of all the evidence, that Imitation is always unconscious. "This unconscious imitation," he says, "and encouragement of appreciated character, and this equally unconscious shrinking from and persecution of disliked character is the main force which moulds and fashions men in society as we now see it." [2]

In 1896 Gabriel Tarde brought out *Les Lois de l'Imitation,* a book whose influence on sociological speculation in Europe, and still more in America, has been extremely important. Tarde held that "the general laws governing imitative repetition . . . are to sociology what the laws of habit and heredity are

[1] *Physics and Politics* (edition of 1906), p. 92.
[2] *Loc. cit.* p. 97. Bagehot's derivation of social organisation from instinctive imitation is helped by the fact that he, like Comte and Maine, accepted the Lamarkian doctrine of the biological inheritance of acquired characteristics. What was at first a "cake of custom" becomes an inherited instinct. "The frame" of man's "morals is set by long ages of transmitted discipline" (p. 40).

to biology, the laws of gravitation to astronomy and the laws of vibration to physics," [1] and again: "Any act of any one of our fellows inspires us who are lookers-on with the more or less irrational idea of imitation." [2] I myself find it difficult to understand how Tarde's book, even with the advantage of its air of scientific modernity, ever acquired so great an influence. He is not content with treating every case where the sight or hearing of any action results in the performance of a similar action as an instance of a general instinct of Imitation, but groups, under the name of Imitation, acts which are in no sense results of the observation of similar acts. Two men who have never seen each other may walk in much the same way because, being men, they have legs of much the same shape, or they may both use safety matches because they each find them the most convenient way of getting fire, and in either case Tarde ascribes their action to Imitation. Even if a woman buys a hat at the same shop where she herself bought one before, he declares that she acts from Memory and that Memory is a kind of Imitation. Tarde uses indeed the word Imitation in so many different senses, and so runs the various senses into each other that I have found the *Lois de l'Imitation* one of the most baffling and unsatisfactory books that I have ever read. As Durkheim says, the idea of Imitation becomes in Tarde "d'une ambiguité qui défie la discussion." [3]

[1] *Social Laws* (trans. Warren), p. 61.
[2] *Laws of Imitation* (Eng. trans. by Parsons), p. 79.
[3] *Le Suicide*, chap. iv. p. 108. See also an admirable monograph on Tarde in *Psychological Interpretations of Society,* by Michael M. Davis (Longmans, 1909).

Tarde's views have been widely popularised, especially by M. Le Bon in his well-known *Psychologie de la Foule* and other books, and by Professor E. A. Ross in his *Social Psychology,* so that the "Psychology of the Crowd" now enjoys in the social philosophy of the newspapers some of the old authority of the Laws of Political Economy.

The late Professor William James was, in temperament and method, far removed both from the externalism and from the hasty psychological assumptions which are characteristic of Tarde and the other "Crowd-Psychologists," but I have before me a letter from him, written in 1908, in which he says, "I myself see things à la Tarde, perhaps too exclusively"; and in his great *Principles of Psychology* (1890) he had already adopted from Bagehot that view of instinctive Imitation which Tarde systematised in 1896. "From childhood onward," says James, "man is essentially *the* imitative animal. His whole educability, and in fact the whole history of civilisation, depend on this trait. . . . " [1]

On the other hand, during the last five or six years the very existence of such an "instinct of Imitation" has been denied by leading psychologists. Mr. McDougall, for instance, says, "Careful consideration of the nature of imitative actions shows that they are of many kinds, that they issue from mental processes of a number of different types, and that none are attributable to a specific instinct of imitation. . . . " [2] And Professor Pillsbury of Michigan says, "Imitation does not play the important part in social selec-

---

[1] James, *Principles of Psychology,* vol. ii. p. 408.
[2] *Social Psychology,* p. 91.

tion or in any other form of learning that has been supposed." [1]

The facts which underlie this contradiction are very complex, and to explain my view of them I must begin by referring back to the statement of the relation between our dispositions and their environment contained in Chapter IV. I there argued that the occurrence of such external events as were, in the long evolutionary period which preceded civilisation, frequent, important, and recognisable, tends to stimulate us to those actions which were then, on the whole, likely to preserve the species. A child, on seeing a snake or a lion, goes through the actions—running away, screaming, or cowering—appropriate to the Fear instinct, though, because his distant ancestors had not invented firearms, he does not instinctively fear a revolver.

Now, under certain circumstances and with regard to certain instincts, it was an advantage to our ancestors that the instinct in question should be stimulated by the perception that other members of the species were already acting in the manner appropriate to it. If, for instance, a group of animals were constantly being attacked by beasts of prey, those individuals would be most likely to survive who did not wait to see the enemy themselves, but tried to escape as soon as they saw one of their fellows running away or heard it screaming; and it would probably be an advantage to the whole group that their flight should take the form of a simultaneous stampede. In the same way it would be an advantage to the whole

[1] *Popular Science Monthly*, March, 1906. Article on "Trial and Error as a Factor in Evolution," p. 279.

group that any individual who noticed conduct among his fellows which indicated danger should warn the rest by screaming.

Bagehot or Tarde would simplify all this by saying, not that the perception of the stimulation of the Fear instinct in others may be an appropriate stimulus of the Fear instinct in the perceiver, but that, owing to a general instinct of Imitation, the sight of running causes the desire to run and the sound of screaming the desire to scream—in spite of the fact that the sight of running may equally cause a desire to scream, or the sound of screaming a desire to run.

Other instincts among gregarious or semi-gregarious animals whose appropriate stimulation may, under certain circumstances, look like evidence of a general instinct of Imitation, are those of "Collective Defence," and "Following a Lead." In case of danger, for instance, men and, after a more elaborate fashion, horned cattle gather together for mutual protection. This instinct may be stimulated by the sight of an enemy, in which case no one would call it Imitation; or it may be stimulated by the sight of other animals gathering together, in which case it looks like Imitation but is not.

The behaviour of a flock of sheep is constantly adduced as proving that sheep are "imitative" animals. When it is necessary to change pasture or to escape from danger, they instinctively "follow the lead" of any of their number who "takes the lead." But if a sheep, being bitten by a fly, scratches its ear with one foot, the sheep feeding beside it does not do the same, as it would if sheep had a general instinct to imitate each other's actions.

The imitation by children of their elders in the process of learning to speak is an instance of a special instinct whose normal function may involve acts of real imitation, but which still does not constitute evidence of a general instinct to imitate. And if we exclude all these types of specific stimulation, nothing is left of the alleged general instinct of Imitation except a few instances of physiological reflexes such as yawning, laughing, and hiccoughing, which affect, in a way still little understood, certain special lower nerve centres.

The second main element in "Crowd-Psychology" is an alleged general instinct of Sympathy—in the literal sense of a mechanical reproduction in the observer of emotions manifested by any other member of his species. There is more evidence for this than for a general instinct of Imitation. Though, for instance, the indication of Fear given by the act of running away may or may not stimulate in the observer a desire to run away, it does normally stimulate in him the whole fear-process, of which (while running away is only one of its possible manifestations) the *emotion* of Fear is a constant element.

Psychologists have, indeed, had considerable difficulty in distinguishing between Imitation and Sympathy, since instinctive processes generally involve both action and emotion. The phenomena of panic are given by them as an instance sometimes of Imitation and sometimes of Sympathy. If the writer thinks of the reproduction of the act of running away, it is Imitation; if he thinks of the reproduction of the emotion of Fear, it is Sympathy.[1]

And yet, here too, it is important to distinguish between the statement that indications of some particular emotion are, under circumstances fixed by the history of our evolution, a normal stimulus to the experience of the same emotion in the observer, and the statement that all emotions tend so to reproduce themselves under all circumstances. It may be just as normal for indications of any emotion to stimulate, under other appropriate circumstances, a quite different emotion in the observer. Indications of sex-love in the male may stimulate sex-love in the female, but they may, under other circumstances, stimulate fear or disgust.

Pain is not an emotion, but Sympathy is often defined by the psychologists so as to include the reproduction of sensation and feeling-tone as well as of emotion, and the effect on the observer of indications of pain in another human being is often given as an instance of the general instinct of Sympathy. Indications of pain in others undoubtedly do almost invariably produce important effects on the observer. But there is no simple law that the effect produced is the mere reproduction of the pain. The effect may be fear, or anger, or an impulse to help, or all three. Nor is there a simple law that induced painful feelings

[1] McDougall (*Social Psychology*, p. 92) gives "the spread of fear and the flight impulse" as "one of the clearest and commonest examples" of "sympathetic induction of emotion." Ross (*Social Psychology*, p. 126) gives "the rapid spread of . . . terror" as an instance of Imitation. James (*Principles of Psychology*, vol. ii. p. 408) ascribes "panics" to "the imitative tendency." Ribot (*Psychology of the Emotions*, p. 231) says that "sympathy everywhere marks the passive receptive side of the phenomenon, imitation its active and motor side."

are normally due to indications of pain. The sight of a mutilated dead, and therefore painless, body may produce results indistinguishable from those arising from the sight of a mutilated living body. In any Parliamentary assembly the sight or sound of a genuinely angry man—of Mr. Plimsoll, for instance, during the debate on the Merchant Shipping Bill in 1876—always produces a marked emotional effect, but here, again, the effect is not a mere reproduction of his anger among the other members. It may be a vague shock akin to fear, or a sort of "follow the lead" feeling, which expresses itself in shouts of "Hear! Hear!"

Mr. McDougall, therefore, seems to me to over-simplify a complex body of fact when, in spite of his denial of a general instinct of Imitation, he affirms the existence of a general instinct of Sympathy. "By" 'sympathy' we mean," he says, "the tendency to experience, in face of the same object, the same emotions and impulses that are revealed by the behavior of our fellows." [1] And he seems to go still further from the evidence in the boldly anatomical statement: "I think the facts compel us to assume that in the gregarious animals each of the principal instincts has a special perceptual inlet (or recipient afferent part) that is adapted to receive and to elaborate the sense-impressions made by the expression of the same instinct in other animals of the same species." [2] An instance which he gives is derived from his own experience while watching a thunderstorm with a child in his arms :

[1] *Psychology* (Home University Library), p. 235.
[2] *Social Psychology,* p. 93.

> The child . . . screamed in terror; immediately on hear-
> ing the scream I experienced, during a fraction of a second,
> a pang of fear that could not have been more horrible had I
> been threatened with all the terrors of hell.[1]

Here undoubtedly the signs of fear in the child
immediately stimulated fear in the father. But the
father's fear might have been also normally stimulated by the sight of danger to the child of which the
child itself was unconscious, and the sight of the
child's fear might have normally stimulated a rush of
affection in the father instead of fear.

The third main element in the Psychology of the
Crowd," is Suggestion. This term is, as a rule,
defined by psychologists in rather loose descriptive
phrases. Mr. McDougall calls it "a process of communication resulting in the acceptance with conviction of the communicated proposition in the absence
of logically adequate grounds for its acceptance";[2]
Professor Baldwin—"the abrupt entrance from
without into consciousness of an idea or image which
becomes part of the stream of thought, and tends to
produce the muscular and volitional effects which
ordinarily follow upon its presence";[3] Professor
James—"that mental susceptibility which we all
to some degree possess of yielding assent to outward
suggestion, of affirming what we strongly conceive,
and of acting in accordance with what we are made
to expect." [4] Professor Titchener so defines it as to
include almost any case of the appropriate stimula-

[1] *Ibid.*, p. 95.
[2] *Social Psychology*, p. 97.
[3] *Handbook of Psychology*, vol. ii. p. 297.
[4] *Principles of Psychology*, vol. ii. p. 598.

tion of any instinctive disposition. "A suggestion," he says, "is any stimulus, external or internal, accompanied or unaccompanied by consciousness, which touches off a determining tendency." [1]

If one seeks for the meaning of suggestion by examining the instances which are given to illustrate these definitions, one finds that they include the causation of acts, beliefs, or feelings by many different processes, which are alike only in the negative fact that they are not fully conscious. Now, almost any relation between a stimulus and its resulting act or emotion or thought may be unconscious, incompletely conscious, or fully conscious. An unconscious or partially conscious relation may be one of Habit, as when the fact that we are in our bedroom unconsciously stimulates us to the acts of undressing and going to bed, normally with convenient but occasionally (if we have gone into the bedroom to dress for dinner) with inconvenient results. Or the fact that we have heard some one ask a riddle may arouse Curiosity without our being aware of it, and may cause us to go through an elaborate though unconscious mental search ending in our suddenly guessing the answer during family prayers. At a late general election I received a card asking for my vote. It represented a Yorkshire manufacturer in the uniform of a Territorial Colonel, and was surrounded by a border of red, blue, and white lines which accurately represented the "aura" which might surround one's visual memory of a man intimately associated with the British Flag. This card undoubtedly had some influence on the motives of many voters. If they

[1] *Text-Book of Psychology* (edition of 1910), p. 450.

were fully conscious of that influence it apparently would not, and if they were unconscious or only partially conscious of it, it would be called Suggestion.

Every newspaper and magazine now contains evidence that advertising-writing has become a profession suitable (as a *Standard* advertisement put it) for the "sons of gentlemen." Young men of good education, naturally warm feelings, and that delicate sense of the emotional effect of words which, under different circumstances, might have made them poets, are now being trained as convincing liars, as makers, that is to say, of statements, to whose truth they are indifferent, in such a form that readers shall subconsciously assume the personal sincerity of the writer. According to the *Daily News* of January 29, 1913, all employees of a well-known firm of drapers are instructed in "voice-magnetism." Voice-magnetism apparently means the art of producing, apart from any personal belief in the salesman as to the excellence of the goods offered, the tone which the customers consciously or unconsciously associate with sincerity. It is the oral form of lying, as advertisement-writing is the written form.

Now if, after reading a "heart-to-heart" advertisement, or listening to one of the young "voice-magnetisers," I should buy a box of tooth-powder solely on the conscious calculation that no one would spend so much money and ingenuity on advertising or selling it if it were very bad, a psychologist would say that my action is not due to Suggestion. If I am unconsciously influenced to the least degree by the advertisement or the voice, I so far act, according to the current definition, from Suggestion.

But there is no difference, except in degree of consciousness, between my unconscious inference and the quite conscious, though silly, inference drawn by the lady in *Punch* who said that she was going to buy Jones's soap "because it was so well spoken of in the advertisements."

It pays people to spend thousands a year on such placards as that which urges me to buy "Double Diamond" port because the passage in *Nicholas Nickleby* from which the title is borrowed proves it to have been "The Favourite Wine of the Brothers Cheeryble." The inference here is so obviously fallacious that one is inclined to assume it can only affect readers who are unconscious that they are drawing any inference at all. But a Free Trader or a Protectionist might contend that it is no more fallacious than the inference which may be quite consciously drawn from a poster with the words "Protect your Home and your Trade," or from another with the words "A Free Nation must have Free Trade." And even if the mental process which is set in action be as strictly logical as that which occurs when we correctly solve a mathematical problem during sleep, it would still apparently, if it is unconscious, be ascribed to Suggestion.

It would, therefore, I am convinced, tend to clearness in psychological statement if the use of the substantive "Suggestion" were abandoned, and if the adjectives "unconscious," "subconscious," or "incompletely conscious" took its place.

Just as it has been found almost impossible to distinguish between the current definitions of Imitation (the alleged general reproduction of action) and Sympathy (the alleged general reproduction of emotion), so it has been equally difficult to distinguish either of them from Suggestion. Professor E. A. Ross, for instance, says, "Suggestion and imitation are merely two aspects of the same thing, the one being cause, the other effect." [1] Tarde, who uses the term Hypnotism in the same sense in which the others use Suggestion, says "Society is imitation and imitation is a kind of hypnotism." [2]

In these passages, as in so much of what is written on the "Psychology of the Crowd," both Ross and Tarde seem to fall into the fallacy of the "undistributed middle." They state particular propositions in such a way that they can, and do, afterwards use them as universals. Ross gives evidence tending to show that some actions may be unconsciously stimulated by the sight of the same action performed by others (we may, for instance, go to bed at 3 P. M. because we are, without knowing it, in a "rest-cure" hotel, and are unconsciously affected by the sight of our fellow-guests going sleepily to their rooms), and then argues as if he had proved that "All actions performed by others unconsciously stimulate the same action in the observer." And yet, curiously enough, the very instance which he gives of his statement that "suggestion and imitation are merely two aspects of the same thing" is not even a case of stimulation by similar action. After describing the quasi-hypnotic condition which the Malays call *lâtah*, he quotes Sir F. A. Swettenham: "Once you have the attention

[1] *Social Psychology* (1908), p. 13.
[2] *Laws of Imitation* (trans.), p. 87; the passage is printed by Tarde himself in italics.

of lâtah-struck persons, by merely looking them hard in the face, they will fall helpless into the hands of the operator, instantly lose all self-control, and go passively through any performance, whether verbally imposed or merely suggested by a sign."[1] Obviously the "performance" is not an *imitation* of the verbal or other "sign."

Tarde's proposition is even looser and wider. His statement that "Society is imitation and imitation is a kind of hypnotism" means, in plain language, that every co-operative act done by any human being is always due to Imitation and is always unconscious.

The phenomena loosely grouped under the term Suggestion may be found to include the communication of thought by that process of "telepathy," of whose existence much evidence is being accumulated, but of whose origin and limitations we are still ignorant. Telepathy, however, as such, contains, apparently, no element akin to "Imitation" or "Sympathy," and none of the peculiar emotional qualities ascribed to Suggestion by the Crowd-Psychologists. It may be found to play a very important part in the collective action and thought of mankind, but it will probably be classified as a new sense rather than a new instinct.

The Crowd-Psychologists often imply that in modern civilised society the unconscious causation of action, feeling, and thought, through fashion, prestige, party spirit, and other forms of Suggestion, plays a much larger part than in simpler and earlier forms of social organisation. On the whole I believe that this

[1] *Social Psychology,* p. 13.

is not true. The inhabitant of a modern city is more fully conscious, "has his wits about him" for a larger proportion of the twenty-four hours than the peasant, and acts much less under the subconscious influence of routine. What the Crowd-Psychologists see is that the defects and the limitations of all human consciousness are much better understood and more cleverly exploited in the city.

Perhaps the nervous fatigue caused by an "unnatural" and constantly changing environment, and the state of "baulked disposition" [1] due to the want of satisfaction for important inherited dispositions, may be more common in the city than in the village. The villager has his own outbursts and his own revolts. But the bored "society" man and woman, the factory hand who has just finished a long day of well-paid but monotonous labour, or the artisan's childless wife in a new suburb, are liable to sudden breaks of habit after either conscious or unconscious contact with some new idea, which seem to those who watch them from without to be due, more obviously than the villagers' "sprees," to the blind and inexplicable mentality of "the Crowd."

The whole subject-matter, indeed, of the "Psychology of the Crowd" requires restatement and re-examination. We must first get rid of the verbal ambiguities which are due merely to the employment of collective terms. Nothing is more annoying or useless than the constant implication in books and articles about "Crowds" and "Groups" that such a statement as "Crowds display a singularly inferior mentality" [2]

---

[1] See Chapter IV. p. 57.   [2] Le Bon, *The Crowd* (Eng. trans.), p. 9.

means anything different from the statement that individual human beings when brought into close relation to numerous other individual human beings display such a mentality. Sometimes the use of collective terms results in statements loosely made in one sense being afterwards used as part of an argument in another sense. M. Le Bon, for instance, whose book on *The Crowd* has had, perhaps, a larger circulation than any other professedly psychological treatise of our time, says, "Crowds doubtless are always unconscious," without apparently being himself clear whether he means that crowds have no collective consciousness, or that every individual in a crowd is always completely unconscious, and then goes on to use his own statement as an illustration of the fact that "The part played by the unconscious in all our [sc. individual] acts is immense, and that played by reason is very small." [1]

After getting rid of merely verbal difficulties, we can then attempt to sum up as a whole those facts as to human nature which the Crowd-Psychologists noticed, and tried to explain by the terms Imitation, Sympathy, and Suggestion.

Broadly speaking, they were dealing with the ways (excluding the simple facts of sex and parenthood) in which man instinctively reacts to the presence of his fellows. Nothing which man perceives his fellows to be doing or feeling is, as Terence long ago pointed out, indifferent to him. But, as I have argued in the earlier pages of this chapter, his perception does not result in a uniform and mechanical impulse either to imitate the perceived action, or reproduce in himself

[1] *The Crowd,* pp. 9, 10.

the perceived emotion. The acts or feelings of his fellows affect the whole of his nature, and produce in each case (apart from the influence of the habits and knowledge of civilisation) the varied results—Fear, and Love, and Jealousy, and Thought, and a hundred others—which were advantageous in such cases to the race in the long process of evolution, and are felt to be "natural" now.

Even when the effect on us of what we perceive in our fellows is unconscious, it is not due to simple imitation or reproduction. Unconsciousness may be that of the whole person, as in hypnotism or sleep, or partial, as when a man intently occupied in thought reacts to the stimulus of his environment in dressing or eating. But in each case the reaction is that of his pre-existing dispositions, although the "narrowing" of reaction characteristic of unconsciousness may bring only one or a few of them into play. If a hypnotised man acts as the hypnotist orders him, or accepts without hesitation the hypnotist's statements of fact, it is because he has a disposition (the Follow the Lead instinct) which inclines him to obey an authoritative command. If he wrinkles his face in disgust on being told that his hand is dirty, or kneels in adoration on being told that he is in the presence of divine power, he does so because such reactions are "natural" to him.

The question which is really raised by the Crowd-Psychologists is how far these reactions, conscious or unconscious, to the stimulus of our fellow-men are different in character when those who affect us are numerous, from what they are when we are affected by a few or by single individuals. The answer to that question I believe to be that, in some cases, where we are in immediate contact through our senses with large numbers of our fellows engaged in the same action or influenced by the same emotion as ourselves, the difference in degree of stimulation is so great as to approach a difference of kind. If a thousand men are close together in the presence of danger (as in a theatre fire) and some of them show signs of fear, the others are apt to be more afraid than they would be if each of them had to face the danger alone or with two or three others. The same is perhaps true in the case of anger and the instincts of Giving and Taking the Lead. The nervous "exaltation" so produced may be the effect of the rapid repetition of the stimulus, acting as repetition acts, for instance, when it produces sea-sickness or tickling. It may be due to a specialised "herd instinct" because of which a vague excitement is stimulated, I have sometimes thought, through some ill analysed sense akin to smell. If the exaltation is extreme, conscious control of feeling and action is diminished, reaction is "narrowed," and men may behave, as they behave in dreams, less rationally and morally than they do if the whole of their nature is brought into play.

In the Great Society, however, the collection of large masses of excited men in physical contact with each other is (except during war) comparatively rare, and in any case the number of persons in the largest crowd is insignificant as compared with the number of members of a great nation or inhabitants of a great city. The most important point, therefore, for us in the Crowd problem is whether the peculiar exaltation of feeling and action which is caused by the sensible presence of large numbers of our fellows, is also caused by the existence of the still larger numbers of whom we read and are told, but who do not directly stimulate us through our senses. M. Le Bon throughout his book assumes that this is the case. He constantly identifies the "Crowd" with the "Masses" of a modern nation or the voters in a modern democratic election.[1] M. Tarde saw the difficulty and distinguishes (in *L'Opinion et La Foule*) between the Crowd and what he calls the Public. My own conclusion from the available evidence is that in times of great general excitement, or in the case of individuals who are very easily influenced or have unusual powers of visual imagination, the picture formed in our mind (with the help of descriptive reporting and newspaper photographs) of our distant fellows may produce to a considerable degree the same effects of exaltation as would be produced by their presence. But the degree to which this actually occurs is, I believe, habitually and grossly exaggerated by the Crowd-Psychologists.

Bagehot was a Whig who took a very pessimistic view of the great step towards democracy made by the English Reform Act of 1867. Tarde and Le Bon were Frenchmen brought up on vivid descriptions of the Revolution and themselves apprehensive of the spread of Socialism. Political movements which were in fact carried out, in large part, by men conscious and thoughtful though necessarily ill-informed, seemed therefore to them, as they watched them from outside, to be due to the blind and unconscious impulses of masses "incapable both of reflection and reasoning."[2]

The inhabitants of a modern state, whether they are

[1] See, *e.g.*, pp. 15, 35, and 42.
[2] *The Crowd*, p. 75.

officials or journalists or working men, are indeed ignorant of much which it would be well for them to
know, and unmoved by much which it would be well
for them to feel. That they are so is due not to the
fact that "individually" they are thoughtful and temperate and "collectively" blind and ferocious, but to
the fact that they are human beings, whose intellectual
and emotional nature was evolved in contact with the
restricted environment of the primitive world, and who
have not yet learnt, if ever they will, either to educate
in each generation their faculties to fit their environment, or to change their environment so as to fit their
faculties.

CHAPTER IX

LOVE AND HATRED

In the preceding chapter I argued that the co-operative action of men in society is due, not (as the early Darwinian sociologists supposed) to simple and mechanical instincts of Imitation, or Sympathy, or Suggestion, but to the stimulation in each human being, by his relation to his fellow-men, of many varied and interacting dispositions, for the observation of which introspection as well as external evidence is required.

If this is true, we are brought back at once to the problem which tormented Sidgwick and the later Utilitarians, and for which Comte's Positivism was offered as a solution. Was Bentham right in saying that each "man from the very structure of his nature" prefers his own good (whether it be happiness or something else) to that of all other men? Or was Bishop Butler right (if we ignore the teleological form in which he put it) when he said, "There are as real and the same kind of indications in human nature, that we were made for society and to do good to our fellow-creatures, as that we were intended to take care of our own life and health and private good?" [1]

The answer to a question on which able men have for so long disputed is not likely to be either easy or

[1] "Upon Human Nature," Sermon I. (Cassell, 1887, p. 12).

simple; and it is best, in seeking it, to proceed from the known to the unknown, or rather from the agreed to the doubtful.

Every one admits that, when the young, either of man or of any of the other higher mammals, are still unable to protect themselves, the mother normally attempts, even at serious risk to herself, to protect and cherish them. The evidence of big-game hunters all over the world, or the records in a London police court of the behaviour of women with babies and drunken husbands, or, still better, the observation of an average day spent by a decent working-class mother with four or five young children, will establish this. Introspective evidence shows further that this behaviour is accompanied by the warm emotion of Love, and by waves of an intense and fully conscious, though sometimes an ill-informed, desire for the health, the happiness, the "good" in every sense, of the child.

Some modern psychologists, being determined to claim nothing as a human disposition for whose existence both in man and in other related species there is not the clearest and most ample proof, have affirmed that this Mother-Love is the only true altruistic disposition. Mr. McDougall, for instance, uses the term "The Tender Emotion" for the "affective aspect" of that "Parental Instinct," which he identifies with the "Maternal Instinct." [1] He says:

From this emotion and its impulse to cherish and protect spring generosity, gratitude, love, pity, true benevolence, and altruistic conduct of every kind; in it they have their main and absolutely essential root, without which they would not be. Any seemingly altruistic action in which it

[1] *Social Psychology*, p. 66.

plays no part is but a sham, the issue of cold calculation
or of habits formed under the influence of rewards and punishments.[1]

But such a simplification of a complex problem has
its own dangers. Just as Hobbes and Bentham first
explained all social impulses as cases of the single disposition of Fear or Pain, and then found themselves
compelled, in order to account for the facts, to extend
their own definition by using words in a strained and
non-natural sense, so Mr. McDougall has to twist his
definition of Mother-Love in order to make it cover
facts which he himself admits. Fathers have, he acknowledges, a disinterested love for their children,
though it is not as strong as that felt by mothers. He
therefore declares that Father-Love is a kind of
Mother-Love. "How can we account," he says, "for
the fact that men are at all capable of this emotion
and of this disinterested protective impulse? For in
its racial origin the instinct was undoubtedly primarily
maternal. The answer is that it is very common to
see a character acquired by one sex to meet its special
needs, transmitted, generally imperfectly and with
large individual variations, to the members of the other
sex. Familiar examples of such transmission of sexual
characters are afforded by the horns and antlers of
some species of sheep and deer." [2]

[1] *Social Psychology,* p. 71.
[2] *Ibid.* p. 69. In the same way some members of the new school
of psychologists founded on Freud's "Psycho-analysis" say that all
Love between human beings is sex-feeling. Ferenczi, for instance,
states, "Everything points to the conclusion that an unconscious
sexual element is the basis of every sympathetic emotion" (dass
jedem Sympathiegefühl eine unbewusste sexuelle Stellungnahme zu-
grunde liegt) (*Introjektion und Uebertragung,* p. 451, quoted by Er-
nest Jones, *Papers on Psycho-Analysis,* p. 280).

To myself it seems more satisfactory to begin with a complex statement than to introduce complexity in the application of a simple statement. The evidence, then, seems to me to indicate that in the loosely organised groups to which our ancestors—human and pre-human—belonged, several dispositions were evolved, each of which, in varying degrees, produced distinterested Love as part of its normal process. The Love which accompanied Motherhood was by far the strongest, but Love and a conscious desire for the safety and good of the loved person also arose, though to a less degree, from the sex-relation between men and women, the relation during youth of brotherhood and sisterhood, and that between the adult males and the children (whether they were the result of monogamous, polygamous, or group intercourse) in whose defence the males fought and to whom they brought food.[1] It is largely a point of convenience whether Love in each of those cases be spoken of as part of a separate disposition, or whether it be spoken of as a single disposition, brought into action in each case by a different stimulus.

Much less clear, but of vital importance in the analysis of the Great Society, is the question whether disinterested Love was also evolved in the relation between fellow-members of the tribe or species. Aristotle thought that such Love existed "not only among men but among birds and most of the animals," [2] and Prince Kropotkin has collected many facts indicating the existence, among non-human animals, of a desire

---

[1] See Malinowski, *The Family among the Australian Aborigines* (University of London Press, 1913), p. 191 *et seq.*, for "the emotional characteristics of kinship."

[2] *Ethics*, bk. viii. chap. iii.

to help other members of the same species.[1] In the
case of man, the evidence still awaits further collection
and analysis, but my opinion is that a certain degree
of Love is stimulated by our perception of other human beings, both generally and particularly when we
feel that it is in our power to injure or benefit them.
In its origin such Love may have been one factor in
a disposition inclining us to aid our tribal comrades in
hunting or fighting or flight. Introspectively it pre-
sents itself as an emotion which may either be so weak
and vague as only just to reach consciousness, or so
intense as to create an almost intoxicating exaltation,
and it is accompanied by a conscious desire for the
good, either of mankind or a nation or class, or of some
individual whose only relation to us is that of membership of our species. In the last case Love shades into
the deep personal emotion of Friendship.

Love for our fellow-man may take the negative form
of disinterested Pity for suffering and an unwillingness
to inflict harm. Mr. McDougall says that this negative form of Love exists, and that "the distress of any
adult (towards whom we harbour no hostile sentiment)
evokes the emotion," [2] though his theory makes it
necessary for him to point out that this is another
instance of "the vast extension of the field of application of the maternal instinct." [3]

Of Pity for a fellow human being as such, the best
account I know is that given by Professor Gilbert
Murray (whose evidence is the more valuable because
he is rather a first-hand student of literature and life
than a systematic psychologist) in his *Rise of the*

[1] *Mutual Aid, a Factor of Evolution* (1902).
[2] *Social Psychology,* p. 74.
[3] *Loc. cit.* p. 73.

Greek Epic. He calls it by the Greek name Aidos. I cannot refrain from quoting part of his description:

If you take people . . . who have broken away from all their old sanctions, and select among them some strong and turbulent chief who fears no one, you will first think that such a man is free to do whatever enters his head. And then, as a matter of fact, you find that among his lawlessness there will crop up some possible action which somehow makes him feel uncomfortable. If he has done it he "rues" the deed and is haunted by it. If he has not done it he refrains from doing it. And this not because any one forces him, nor yet because any particular result will accrue to him afterwards. But simply because he feels Aidos. No one can tell where the exact point of honour will arise. When Achilles fought against Eëtion's city, "he sacked all the happy city of the Cilician men, high-gated Thebe, and slew Eëtion; but he spoiled him not of his armour. He had Aidos in his heart for that; but he burned him there as he lay in his rich-wrought armour, and heaped a mound above him. And all around him there grew elm-trees planted by the mountain spirits, daughters of Aegis-bearing Zeus." That is Aidos pure and clean, and the later lines ring with the peculiar tenderness of it. Achilles had nothing to gain, nothing to lose. Nobody would have said a word if he had taken Eëtion's richly wrought armour. It would have been quite the natural thing to do. But he happened to feel Aidos about it.[1]

Later on Professor Murray shows how easily such a primitive and incalculable disposition may be ignored or rejected by the systematic philosophers who analyse a highly organised society. "If you look," he says, "at the history of later Greek ethics, it is rather a surprise to find how small a place is occupied by Aidos. . . . Plato and Aristotle are both perhaps too much inclined

[1] *Rise of the Greek Epic,* p. 80.

to despise those emotions which appeal to men's simplest instincts and have a touch of the animal about them." [1]

The disposition of Philanthropy (if one may use the term in its original sense of the Love of one's fellows as such) varies very widely among individuals. In each individual it is apt to vary with age, and perhaps, in its simplest form, to be strongest during the years of early manhood and womanhood between eighteen and twenty-five. Different races of mankind possess the disposition in varying degrees, and also vary in the degree in which they stimulate it among other races. Its weakness and uncertainty suggest that it is a late and half-finished product of evolution, and those who have to use the dispositions of men for their own purposes constantly tend to rely, as a substitute for, or aid to it, on the stronger and earlier instincts of Loyalty (Following the Lead) for a party or a chief, or the still earlier affections of sex or parenthood. The English Trade Unionists who were engaged during the middle of the nineteenth century in the long agitation for the reduction of the hours of factory labour, knew that the "Aidos" of the average member of Parliament and the vague sense of human solidarity in their fellow working men counted for something. But they knew also that it was only by constantly emphasising the fact that children and women were concerned that the cupidity of some employers and the confidence of others in the theory of economic individualism could be overcome. The Ten Hours Bill was carried in the name of the children, and the "battle of the Nine Hours Bill" was, as one of their own leaders declared

[1] *Rise of the Greek Epic*, p. 87.

in 1878, fought "from behind the women's petti-
coats." [1] Even in the manifesto of the South African
Uitlanders in 1895, it was not so much for the many
male owners and brokers of mining shares as for the
few women and children on the Rand that invasion
was urged,[2] and it was of the "girls in the Gold-Reef
City" that the Poet Laureate sang.

But there is one extremely important type of our
Love for our fellows in which I believe the substituted
action of Parent-Love or Loyalty plays little or no part.
The very existence of the Great Society requires that
there should be found in each generation a certain
number of men and women whose desire for the good
of others is sufficiently reliable and continuous to ensure that they will carry out the duty of originating
leadership (mere dexterous self-advancement does not
originate) either in administration or thought.

Whoever has known any such men will accept the
statement, which they themselves constantly make,
that no ambition, however lofty, would be sufficient
to carry them through the unexciting toil, the constant
disappointments, the ever-present uncertainty of result, which are involved in the intellectual organisation
of a modern community. Peel, the greatest of English
political leaders, was expressing his most intimate conviction when he wrote, "You will believe . . . that
office and power may be anything but an object of
ambition, and that I must be insane if I could have
been induced by anything but a sense of public duty

[1] Webb, *History of Trade Unionism,* p. 297.
[2] *Times,* January 1, 1896.

to undertake what I have undertaken this session." [1]

"Public Spirit" is perhaps a better (because a less intellectualised) name for that which Peel recognised in himself than his own phrase "a sense of public duty."

It is of course impossible to draw a clear line between the Public Spirit of Peel or Stein, and the lesser altruism which makes a dull citizen just willing to vote on a question in which he is not personally concerned. But the study of the exceptional cases will help us to understand the cases which are more common and less clear. If one asked a dozen of these modern leaders for an introspective account of the emotion of Public Spirit, most of them (if they were able accurately to observe their own consciousness) would, I believe, come back to that original Love and Pity for their fellow human beings as such which I have just been attempting, without either exaggerating its efficiency or denying its existence, to describe.

In enquiring how anything so primitive, so weak, so intermittent, or "touched with the animal" as instinctive Philanthropy can have such a strong and continuous result as the more important manifestations of Public Spirit, I find myself helped by an analogy which I heard used in an Oxford discussion club. One of the speakers pointed out that the whole system of modern music, all the overwhelming course of feeling and thought which is roused by a Beethoven Sonata, depends upon the existence in mankind of that primitive and simple preference for rhythmically related sounds which may be observed in some of the

[1] Sir R. Peel to Richard Cobden, June 24, 1846 (Morley's *Life of Cobden,* edition of 1906, p. 397).

higher non-human animals, and which is directly appealed to by the crooning chants or throbbing drums of a West African tribe. Without that "touch of the animal" a modern concert would be as unintelligible to us as a picture gallery to a blind man. But the original rhythmic instinct is made astonishingly wider, more powerful, and more lasting by training, by many-sided intellectual and emotional associations, and by our general æsthetic interest in elaborated form.

On the same lines one can attempt to separate out the psychological elements which enable our intermittent natural interest in our fellow-men to become the Public Spirit of a life-long servant of society.

In the first place, just as a professed musician will normally require an unusually good "ear" to start with, so a man conspicuous for Public Spirit will normally start with an unusually sensitive disposition of Love. Bentham was perhaps the most typically "public-spirited" man of his time, though his work consisted not in administration but in the direction and inspiration of a school of thinkers and reformers. He, writing at the age of eighty-two, said:

Never has it happened to me to witness suffering on the part of any creature, whether of my own species or any other, without experiencing, in some degree or other, a sensation of the like nature in my own nerves.[1]

If Bentham had been a modern psychologist he would probably have recognised that the effect caused in him by the sight of suffering was rather the stimulation of Pity than a mere reproduction of the suffer-

[1] Bentham, "Official Aptitude maximised" (Preface written 1830, ætat. 82), *Works*, vol. v. p. 266.

ing itself. But the description of an unusual degree of original sensitiveness is unmistakable.

It will be observed that Bentham speaks of the effect on him of the suffering of creatures not belonging to his own species. If our examination of the stronger and more continuous types of Philanthropy included the saints and the great exemplars of personal morality, a fact would become clear which I think is often overlaid by the specialised activity of modern public-spirited men and women. The love for mankind felt by Gautama or St. Francis clearly extended itself into love for non-human forms of life.[1] This extension of Love beyond the human species may of course be due merely to acquired intellectual associations; but it may also be due (as I am inclined to think it is) to a true disposition, even if its origin is not yet explained by what we know of our own past evolution. Perhaps, indeed, the most important mistake made by Comte when he founded the Religion of Humanity was his failure to realise that for one, and perhaps the highest, type of religious genius man as part of a living universe may excite more Love and Reverence than Man as an isolated species.

Next to a high degree of original Love, the most important of the factors by which our primitive Philanthropy becomes effective Public Spirit is an Imagination, presenting to its possessor the existence of his fellow-men with sufficient vividness. No one can love that which is not real to him. Now the simplest form of reality is that which results from the direct testi-

[1] "I once saw a botanist most tenderly replace a plant which he had inadvertently uprooted, though we were on a bleak hillside in Tibet where no human being was likely to see the flower again" (Sir Francis Younghusband, *Within*, p. 103).

mony of our senses, and many sociologists have contended that outside the range of our senses strong social emotion is impossible. "Love," says Mr. Warner Fite in his interesting book on *Individualism*, "may be quite real within a relatively narrow circle; and toward our fellow-men in the world at large we may cultivate an attitude of open-mindedness and goodwill. We may, and ought, to find a generous pleasure in every enlargement of our sympathies. But to claim that we love our fellow-man simply as our fellow-man is to assert a measure of actual sympathy and comprehension which is absurdly far from real." [1] "It is impossible," said Leslie Stephen, "that men should be moral simply by a desire for the greatest happiness of the greatest number. What does and always must guide men is their personal relation to the little circle which they actually influence." [2]

This is clearly a mistake. It is true that the firsthand testimony of our senses has a peculiar quality in its power of psychological stimulus which is not shared by the second-hand testimony of imagination or memory; but nevertheless Love for those whose existence is presented to us only through our Imagination may act with enormous force. When Schiller wrote:

> Seid umschlungen, Millionen!
> Diesen Kuss der ganzen Welt! [3]

he was certainly not making-believe.

This imaginative reality of our neighbours whom

[1] *Individualism*, p. 205.
[2] *The English Utilitarians*, vol. ii. p. 329.
[3] "Be ye embraced, ye Millions. I send this kiss to the whole world" ("Hymn to Joy," 1785).

we have not seen may take one of two forms. When
Schiller made his "Hymn to Joy," he was twenty-
five years old. His experience of his fellow-men outside the Military Academy and the barracks was
mainly confined to the reading of much bad eighteenth-
century poetry and worse eighteenth-century romance.
The "Millions" whom he so vividly conceived were the
romantic figures at which we smile in the German
drawings of that period, and they were thought of as
one step in a glorious ladder of life stretching from
the "worm" to the "cherub."

Few people, however, of active public spirit retain
after their adolescence that kind of conception of
mankind which inspires Schiller's poem. The picture
by which experience soon explains their instinctive
recognition of their species [1] is a generalisation largely
subconscious, drawn not from books and drawings, but
from the individuals and classes for whom public men
work, and whom they can only help if they see them
without illusion. Has this realist conception the same
power of stimulating Love as Schiller's romantic conception? [2] I am inclined to answer that as soon as
our conception of mankind starts on the path from
romance to realism, its power of stimulating Love depends on the completion of its journey. Cynicism is
often the result of half-knowledge. Most of the great

---

[1] See, later, Chapter X. p. 176 *et seq.,* for the intellectual implications of instinctive recognition.

[2] I have dealt in another book (*Human Nature in Politics,* p.
155) with the destruction by experience, *e.g.,* in the case of Wordsworth, of a romantic and oversimplified conception of mankind. I
was there, however, dealing with the question of the conditions
under which new and more complex conceptions could be made the
material of effective thought. Here I am dealing with the cognate
but different question of the conditions under which the more complex conception can stimulate emotion.

artistic interpreters of mankind have added to the permanent sum of human goodwill just in proportion to the force and detachment with which they have told the truth. It is largely due to Sir Walter Scott that Englishmen can love Scotchmen much more easily than, for instance, they can love Irishmen. But if we now think with affection of the Scotch national type, it is because we remember, not the heroes and heroines whom Sir Walter deliberately tried to make sympathetic, but the dour Cameronians, the canny peasants, the unashamed lads and maidens, in describing whom he had no purpose except to make a recognisable picture. The least touch of romantic idealisation would have made so typical and lovable a Greek as Homer's Odysseus into a figure as detestable as Tennyson's Lancelot. Modern reproductions of Rembrandt and Millet have enabled thousands of young people to look with genuine kindliness upon the quiet self-satisfaction of an unintellectual old woman, or the heavy walk of a sweat-drenched labourer. But Rembrandt and Millet worked with such detachment that they were denounced by their contemporaries as libellers of the human race. The people of the United States have before them the task of creating an emotional solidarity between the descendants of the original settlers and the South European immigrants who join them at the rate of a million a year. The best work in their admirable magazines is aimed at making this solidarity possible by describing twenty races to each other. But one feels that it will only succeed in so far as the interpreters forget their aim in the one purpose of austere truth.

And in this respect that which is true of the few

leaders is true also in its degree of the weaker and more limited Love which guides ordinary men. I have already said that permanent and elastic social Habits are not likely to be created among an industrial population without so much "philosophy" as is given by school-instruction in such elements of the Humanities as history and geography—that a curriculum of "Cowper-Temple religion and manual training" would make citizens whose moral habits could not be relied on.[1] In the same way the minimum of Love which is necessary to hold together the cities and nations of the Great Society may be found to require that what school children learn of the unseen millions of their fellows shall be, as far as the writers of books and the trainers of teachers can make it, the truth. In Prussia the avowed use of the schools, not for the spread of truth but for the "War against social-democracy" may be in part responsible for that absence of Love between members of different classes, that class-war of which the growth of social-democracy is only one symptom. And as the scale and complexity of social organisation extend, the need of clear-sighted Love will extend with it. If a hereditary monarchy with the power of dismissing professors or censoring plays, or a church whose property is secured to the holders of an unchanging creed, or an endowed and entrenched party system, is found to require for its continued existence a deliberate make-believe as to the human type, that fact must be considered in the light of its probable effects, not only on the progress of social science, but also on the emotional coherence of society.

Psychology has the same detached purpose as liter-

[1] See *ante,* p. 78.

ature, though it is the inherited human type, rather than that type overlaid with all the variations of individuality and place and tradition, with which it is mainly concerned; and I find myself sometimes wondering what may be the effect of the growth of Psychology on the efficiency of Love. In the past those psychological generalisations which called themselves the Science of Political Economy undoubtedly stood in the way of Love. The employer saw his operatives with their weary eyes and half-open mouths at the end of a twelve hours' day only as "free agents," and their poverty only as the "stimulus of competition." But the more complex and, as one hopes, the truer description of mankind which the psychology of the twentieth century is slowly building up may help Love rather than hinder it. If, after a period of psychological reading, one stands on a railway platform or at a window, looking at that unknown crowd which makes the solitude of London, the faces which one will never see again seem less indifferent than they did before. Those men who are innocent of psychology, but have an exceptional gift of reading physiognomy, may see more than the less gifted in spite of their book-learning. But book-learning and the habit of attention which it produces does seem to make it easier to interpret the less obvious signs of psychological states, and more probable that those states will stimulate a certain degree of Love. The tired mother snapping at her tired child, the weak smile of the dreamy youth, the intense self-consciousness of the two talkers who are "showing off" to the other inmates of the omnibus, all seem intelligible and kindly. And if formal psychology lends a measure of reality to those whom one sees only for a moment, it can also sharpen and make more poignant the mental picture, which every member of the Great Society forms, of that larger multitude of his contemporaries whom he will never see, but whose lives he must necessarily influence.

The majority, however, of those who will be affected by the action of any inhabitant of a Great City or State are separated from him, not by space and multitude only, but also by time. Every ton of coal that we burn, every scar on the face of nature that we help to make, every new custom which we start or old custom which we modify, above all every act or refusal to act which affects the procreation of children, will influence the uncounted millions who do not yet exist. And perhaps the most important emotional effect of the growth and spread of psychological science may consist in such an extension of our imagination as may make more real to our feelings those in whom our type, with slow developments, must persist, even though nearly everything which now influences us after birth may change beyond our power of prophecy.

And since psychology aims at the discovery of causal relationships as well as the true description of isolated facts, it may increase Public Spirit, not only by creating a sharper and more stimulating vision of the human type, but by enabling the public-spirited man to realise more clearly those effects on human consciousness which he desires to produce, and to believe more firmly that he can play his part in producing them. "We cannot," said Aristotle, "form a purpose

the fulfilment of which we believe to be impossible
. . . however strong our desire for it may be." [1]

Again, besides the original sensitiveness of his Love
and that sharpening of its stimulation which is due
to Imagination and Knowledge, the exceptionally
public-spirited man will generally find that his motive
power is increased by the satisfaction which his daily
work may give to the "intellectual" or semi-intellec-
tual dispositions of Curiosity, Craftmanship, and the
Æsthetic Instinct.[2]   In the intervals when the conscious desire for the good of his fellows grows cold,
his work may be carried on for its own sake; or work
commenced under the impulse of intellectual interest
may be carried on under the impulse of Love; or all
three motives may be intermingled at the same time.

John Stuart Mill, for instance, gives in his *Autobiography* a description of his feelings at the moment
when, at the age of sixteen, he ceased to be a mere
student of Benthamism and became its devotee.   The
early vividness of his passion for knowledge, his intoxicating sense of the beauty of an ordered universe, and
his dawning love for mankind all crowd into his memory:

When I laid down the last volume of the *Traité* [*de Lég-
islation*], I had become a different being.   The "principle of
utility" . . . fell exactly into its place as the keystone

---

[1] *Ethics*, bk. iii. 2. 7, προαίρεσις μὲν γάρ οὔκ ἐστι τῶν ἀδυνάτων . . .
βούλησις δύ ἐστὶ τῶν ἀδυνάτων, οἷον ἀθανασίας.

An English cabinet minister once told me that he could separate the statesmen whom he had known into those whose vision
of the future consisted of themselves and their "careers," and those
whose vision consisted of the results on their fellow-men of the
policy for which they were working.   It is this second type of mind
which would be normally characteristic of "Public Spirit."

[2] Cf. *ante*, Chapter III. p. 45, and Chapter VII. p. 107.

which held together the detached and fragmentary com-
ponent parts of my knowledge and beliefs. It gave unity
to my conceptions of things. I now had opinions; a creed,
a doctrine, a philosophy; in one of the best senses of the
word, a religion; the inculcation and diffusion of which
could be made the principal outward purpose of a life. And
I had a grand conception laid before me of changes to be
effected in the condition of mankind through that doctrine.[1]

Intellectual interest and the love of physical and
intellectual beauty may of course co-exist with an
exceptionally cold and self-centred character. But I
believe that Mr. Shaw stated a real though not a
universal truth when he contended that neither Art
for Art's sake nor Art for the Artist's sake is normally
sufficient to ensure the greatest even of purely artistic
achievements. "Great Art is never produced for its
own sake. It is too difficult to be worth the effort.
All the great artists enter into a terrible struggle with
the public, often involving bitter poverty and personal
humiliation, and always involving calumny and persecution, because they believe they are apostles doing
what used to be called the Will of God, and is now
called by many prosaic names, of which 'public work'
is the least controversial." [2]

In some happy instances the æsthetic emotion of
the artist is especially stimulated by the beauty of a
particular kind of human excellence, and the passion
for beauty is almost indistinguishable from the passion
for that excellence. This was peculiarly the case with
William Morris, both in his own whole life and talk,
and in such a passage as this from his *Dream of John
Ball*:

[1] J. S. Mill, *Autobiography,* p. 66.
[2] *Three Plays,* by Brieux; Preface, pp. xxi and xxii.

One [of the girls] came straight up to Will Green, and I could see at once that she was his daughter. She was tall and strongly made, with black hair like her father, somewhat comely though no great beauty; but as they met, her eyes smiled even more than her mouth, and made her face look very sweet and kind, and the smile was answered back in a way so quaintly like on her father's face that I too smiled for goodwill and pleasure.[1]

Morris does not stop to analyse, and never stopped to analyse, the relation between his "goodwill" and his "pleasure." When, in his last social romance, he tried to describe the form which his own deepest motives took in consciousness, he wrote again of the "vague hope, that was now become a pleasure, for days of peace and rest, and clearness and smiling goodwill." [2]

Mr. McDougall, in the passage which I have already quoted, speaks of the "sham" altruism, which is "the issue of cold calculation, or of habits formed under the influence of rewards and punishments." [3] This sham altruism so far exists that even the most public-spirited of men may be carried through work which he would otherwise have abandoned, by mere habit, or by the calculation of the effect of failure upon his career or his livelihood. But the habits which are most useful to him are not those which are formed "under the influence of rewards and punishments"; they are rather habits of answering, both in feeling and action, to stimuli whose original force would otherwise only be effective in moments of exceptionally vivid imagination or exceptionally exalted feeling. The

---

[1] *A Dream of John Ball* (Reeves and Turner, 1890), p. 55.
[2] Morris, *News from Nowhere* (Longmans, 1912), p. 3.
[3] *Ante*, p. 141.

ideally trained servant of the community is the man who, when during the indifferent reading of a Blue Book his eye is attracted by some numerical total of disease or unemployment, is in a moment both alive to its significance and already started on the work of remedy.[1]

If the various dispositions, parental, sexual, and general, which have distinterested Love as their common factor were opposed by no contrary dispositions, they would necessarily direct the whole conduct of society.

But men, from the first beginning of their reflection

[1] Mr. G. M. Trevelyan, in his admirable *Life of John Bright,* quotes several passages in which Bright tries to set out truthfully his own motives. Writing, for instance, in 1853 to Cobden, who was hanging back from a meeting on Parliamentary Reform, he says:

"*Personally* I would wish to have no meeting; but personally I would not be in public life. I would rather see more after my own interests and the interests of my children. But we are on the rails and must move on. We have work and must do it" (Bright to Cobden, January 14, 1853. Trevelyan, *Life of Bright,* p. 211).

And four years later he writes in his diary:

"I have worked *in earnest* in the political field, and if any meaner motive has ever stimulated or guided me, if ambition, or any love of display or of popularity, has at any time led me on, of which I am little conscious, I think I can honestly say that a love of what I have believed to be the truth, a strong desire for the good and true greatness of my country, and an unchangeable hostility to the selfishness and fraud which distinguish the government of the English oligarchy, have been the mainspring of my public and political conduct" (entry in diary, January 28, 1857. G. M. Trevelyan's *Life of John Bright,* p. 256).

These passages might be quoted as showing that Bright was influenced by habit, by the love of truth, by loyalty to his country and hatred of his opponents, but not by what I have called Love. And yet, in some introspective passages, Love makes itself clear. In writing, for instance, to Sumner during the danger of war between England and America he says:

"You know that I write to you with as much earnest wish for your national welfare as if I were a native and citizen of your country. I dread the consequences of war quite as much for your sakes as for our own. So great will be my horror of such a strife that I believe I shall retire from public life entirely . . . should war take place between your country and mine" (p. 314, Letter to Sumner, December 5, 1861).

upon their own nature, have noticed in themselves a recurring conflict between Love and Hatred, in which Love sometimes wins and is sometimes defeated. Under appropriate stimuli, that is to say, we are naturally inclined not only to love but also to hate each other, and to desire not only the safety and happiness of our fellows but their suffering and death.

That conflict is often spoken of as one between Altruism and Egoism, or between the Selfish and Unselfish groups of instincts. This distinction seems to me to be misleadingly "intellectual." A mother dashes into the fire to save her child's life, a lover gives his dearest possession to his mistress, or a statesman struggles all night against sleep while striving to make more effectual the clauses of a Bill, not because in each case they prefer the "interests" of others to their own but because they love. And in the same way men try to slay one another in battle, or to injure a rival wooer, or to destroy those of another race or religion, not because they prefer "their own interest" to that of others, but simply because they hate; because, that is to say, a disposition has been stimulated in them of which the emotion of hatred and the doing of injurious acts are normal manifestations.

Egoism and Altruism or "Selfishness" and "Unselfishness" have, it is true, real meanings, as descriptions either of the characters of individual men in whom certain dispositions normally leading to Love or Hatred are strong or weak, or of the ideals which are inculcated by different types of moral or religious discipline. But they do not fit the original dispositions themselves. A man who has just committed murder in a passion of jealousy, or saved life in a passion of pity, is puzzled if he is told that his motives were "selfish" or "unselfish."

Instead, therefore, of the terms Egoism or Selfishness, with their intellectualist associations, I shall use the word Hatred for the common conscious factor in those dispositions which incline us under appropriate stimuli to hate and injure, just as I have used the word Love for the common factor in those which incline us to love and benefit our fellows.

The normal stimulation of Hatred is less simple than that of Love. I have already argued that the bare fact that the mother perceives the existence of her child, or the husband the existence of his wife, or even any one human being the existence of another, tends to excite a stronger or weaker degree of Love. But the normal cause of Hatred is the fact that our perception of some other human being indicates, not his bare existence, but the fact that some strong desire of ours is about to be obstructed by him, that he is preventing us or about to prevent us from acquiring or keeping or consuming something which we value, from seeing something as to which we are curious, from meeting our beloved or cherishing our child, or from leading our fellows. It is in such cases of obstructed instinct that Anger, Jealousy, Rivalry, and the other states whose common quality is Hatred most commonly arise.

Hatred like Love can be made more continuous by Habit and by intellectual associations. It can be buttressed by the instincts of Giving or Taking the Lead (Ambition or Loyalty). It may, like Love, extend to non-human objects, so that the angry or disappointed man hates his home or the whole world.

In its evolutionary origin Hatred helped men to survive because it was a means of securing that the useful acts of acquisition, nutrition, sex, leadership, and the rest should take place. If any member of the tribe obstructed any other in that respect, friction and discomfort arose until the obstruction was removed.

And Hatred had also a more direct biological advantage. When two males fought for a female, the fittest to win became the father of her child. The stronger tribe in a quarrel about property might kill out the weaker, or by appropriating the safest cave or the best hunting-ground might become more numerous.

At the dawn, therefore, of civilisation those races of mankind seem to have been coming to the front among whom both Love and Hatred were most easily and intensely excited; who loved their wives, rejoiced in the number and health and beauty of their children, and were warm and devoted friends and comrades; but who were also quickly moved to implacable anger, and gave and received death with equal readiness.

This temper, and the traditional customs and ideals which naturally sprang from it, can be traced in those North European tribes who, from the Dorian invasion onwards, have worshipped the fighting gods of Valhalla and Olympus, have turned the cross into a sword, and have conquered other races with a greater natural interest in ideas or beauty, or with a greater natural liking for peace and goodwill. It was the possession of this temper which enabled a handful of imported Barbadian negroes the other day to exterminate with untiring gusto five-sixths of the gentle Putumayo Indians.

This quality of being "a good hater" has, in the modern civilised world, no longer so high a survival value as it had two or three thousand years ago, and perhaps, by the ordinary biological process of degeneration, it is tending to lose among us some of its original keenness. But it exists, and has to be allowed for at every point of social organisation. The degree of collectivism which is possible in any community, the practicability of Federal Government, the laws which regulate marriage and family life, the very way in which our houses should be built and our gardens fenced, are all necessarily influenced by the fact that the Great Society has nowhere been formed by the descendants of men as peaceful as the Putumayo Indians.

But while the psychological question of the relative strength of Love and Hatred enters into every social problem, there is one problem which is dominated by it, and whose importance at this moment of the world's history overshadows all others. Every frontier dispute between the Great Powers or their dependents, every new proposal to add to expenditure on armies and navies, renews the controversy whether the policy of the Powers should be directed to the settling of international disputes by such machinery as that of The Hague Court or the European Concert, or whether wars, on the tremendous scale which is now inevitable, should be taken as a normal incident of civilisation. In this controversy, the War Party (if I may use the term without offence for those who do not think it advisable for any nation to allow its present policy to be influenced by a belief in the possibility of permanent peace) occupy a position of great authority.

Probably many more than half of the professed historians and psychologists in Europe support it, and they base their arguments upon imposing biological and psychological generalisations.

These are in the main three: first, the biological statement that War is necessary for the improvement of the race by the survival of the fit, and for the prevention of regression by the extinction of the unfit: second, the psychological statement that War is, owing to the existence in Man of the warlike dispositions, inevitable, and that wise nations should concentrate all their resources on preparing for it: and, third, the further psychological statement that peace, even if it could be secured, would leave the warlike dispositions permanently unstimulated, and would therefore produce the nervous condition which I have called baulked disposition, and that man in such a condition cannot live a life which any one would call good.

The first argument possesses, I believe, little validity when it is applied to wars between the existing Great Powers. Nations do not adopt those ways of fighting that are most likely to improve the human race, but those which are most likely to secure success; and modern methods of warfare neither kill out the obviously unfit (who are excused from conscription and are not slaughtered after a victory) nor select the less fit fighting men for death. Where missile weapons have superseded thrusting or cutting weapons this has always been the case. The Spartan prisoner from Sphakteria protested that his own survival was no indication of his personal fitness nor unfitness. The arrow, as he said, "selects" neither the brave man nor the coward.[1] Shrapnel fired from behind a hill five miles off is even more indiscriminating.

Nor, if one of the existing Great Powers conquers another, is there any reason to expect that after the war is over the conquering population will increase faster than the conquered. A decisive victory in South Eastern Europe of the Germans and Magyars over the Slavs would not mean that a hundred years hence there would be more Germans alive and fewer Slavs than if the war had not taken place. It only means that the Slavs would be less free and less self-respecting.

There would seem therefore to be no biological advantage in that kind of war for which the Great Society is now organised, to set against the clear biological disadvantage involved in the slaughter of so many of the "fittest" males, and the clear biological dangers resulting from the spread of disease and the waste of that capital which might have produced permanently healthier conditions. If we merely desire to improve our breeding-stock it is obviously better to do so directly by the adoption of some form of "eugenic" policy rather than indirectly by making war. Lamb's Chinaman, when he burnt his house down as an indirect method of roasting a pig, did at least get the pig roasted, whereas a thirty-years' war between the Triple Alliance and the Triple Entente, waged for the purpose of improving the European type, would leave that type worse and not better.

As an instance of the second argument, that War is psychologically inevitable unless a revolution is brought about by means not yet invented, either in

[1] *Thucydides*, iv. 40.

human nature or the structure of world-society, I
propose to quote, not General Bernhardi or any other
professional soldier, but the serious and careful little
book (*A New Way of Life*) published in 1909 by Mr.
St. Loe Strachey, the editor of the *Spectator*. The
book is written to induce his countrymen "to face
the real facts" instead of living "in an unreal world
of sentiment and emotion" (p. 34), to see "that War
is the law of the civilised world quite as much as of
the uncivilised, and that mankind has as yet found no
other way of settling which will is to prevail, when
what we have termed a clash of wills takes place between communities who believe themselves to be equal
in physical force. Such clash of nations is as certain
to take place from time to time in the future as in the
past" (pp. 47-48). "We have got," he says, "in future
to face the world, not as we should like it to be, but
as it is—the world of blood and iron controlled by
men who are not humanitarians and philanthropists
. . . who do not take what they would call a Sunday-
school view of the world, but rather the view that man
is still a wild beast, that the race is to the strong and
not to the well-intentioned" (p. 12).

To preparation therefore for war it is the duty of
all states to devote the enormous powers, both over
the production of wealth and over the training of the
individual citizens, which have been developed by modern civilisation. In particular, it is the duty of the
British nation "with a single heart" to "determine"
that, "no matter what the sacrifice, she will retain the
command of the sea" (p. 3). It is, one gathers, equally
the duty of the Germans to challenge that command,
"to make Britain feel supremely uncomfortable on the

score of invasion." "Indeed, it may be said that a part of our determination to maintain the command of the sea resides in these very [German] arguments reversed or applied to our own case" (p. 122). Mr. Strachey therefore sketches, with prim satisfaction, a conversation (in the style of Touchstone) between two European nations; from the Retort Courteous, "We desire that you will refrain from taking such and such a course of action"; to the Countercheck Quarrelsome, "We have a right to take it and mean to take it," and the conclusion: "There is no way but War, and may God defend the right."

It is true that the sacrifice which Mr. Strachey proposes for the moment (the introduction of the Swiss system of military training into Great Britain and possibly Ireland) is not a very severe one; but I am dealing with his arguments and not with his proposals, and his arguments require that a nation which has determined to carry out a certain policy, "no matter what the sacrifice," must be willing to go beyond the Swiss and even beyond the German system of compulsory service. Nor of course do his arguments lead only to service for home defence. While pointing out that we have created in India a Pax Britannica, which he himself gives as an instance of a method of government "which the freemen of Europe reject instinctively as bringing greater evils in its train even than the reign of war" (pp. 39, 41), he says that "If we were faced with another Indian Mutiny, we might have to ask for half a million volunteers" (p. 23); and here, too, we must, if we are to be consistent, adopt the principle of "no matter what sacrifice," and be ready to send, if the military position requires it, our whole conscript army to India. The words "no matter what sacrifice" are easy to write, but they lead straight to that state of social organisation of which Professor Cannan says that:

A world composed of territorial socialist societies in which the whole surplus income over bare necessaries was spent in war and preparations for war, would obviously be a more miserable place than the world as we know it.[1]

Many men keep in their minds some particular piece of possible expenditure which they think to be needed, and against which as a "margin" they balance alternative expenditure. I sometimes use for this purpose the 5000 children who, in the poorer parts of London, are at any given moment kept away from school and confined to their frowsy living-rooms by ringworm. If the State were willing to incur the necessary expense ringworm could be completely stamped out in England, and the present reason why it is not stamped out is that we have preferred to spend on Dreadnoughts the money which might have been given in subsidies for local medical treatment. Other men may use as instances of such "marginal" expenditure the number of babies who could be saved in any year from life-long disease, the number of girls who are working overtime in badly paid trades, or the possible provision of skilled nurses in workhouse infirmaries. If we and the Germans both adopt Mr. Strachey's psychological generalisations, and both draw from them the principle of "no matter what sacrifice," then, in these and a thousand other respects, the "standard of comfort," both in England

[1] *The Economic Outlook*, pp. 292-293.

and in Germany, must not only be prevented from rising but must actually be lowered.

That does not of course prove that Mr. Strachey's generalisation is wrong; but it does make it desirable that we should examine the evidence for and against it with some care.   It is, for instance, often contended by members of the Peace party that the fact that individuals in several European countries now habitually use the law-courts instead of the duel as a means of settling disputes, indicates that a corresponding practice among nations is at least not psychologically impossible.   To this Mr. Strachey answers: "Why do men have recourse to a Court of Law in private quarrels, however heated they become and however convinced each may be that he is morally and legally in the right?   Because they are forced to do so and are allowed to use no other arbitrament" (p. 38).   He then argues that such an irresistible power to enforce the decisions of a European Court cannot and ought not to be set up.

But, as a matter of historical fact, the irresistible force by which men are now compelled to resort to the law-courts in their private quarrels is the result of custom arising from thousands of free decisions to do so.   In the growth of every European nation there was a stage when each head of a free family was in the position of a modern state.   He could choose either to bring his quarrel to an assembly of heads of families or to levy private war; and if he appealed to the assembly and the decision went against him, he could still ignore that decision and take his chance in a fight.

The Icelandic Family Sagas may be taken, for instance, as a laboratory experiment on Mr. Strachey's proposition, tried under conditions as favourable as possible to Mr. Strachey. The free Icelandic families formed of course a community incredibly smaller than a modern nation. But Mr. Strachey does not rely on that exaggerated "Crowd-Psychology" which contends that the larger a nation is the more irrational must be the behaviour of its individual citizens. He argues that individuals, whether in small or large communities, will not settle their disputes by law unless they are irresistibly compelled to do so; and in the Sagas we can watch men gradually forming the custom of resort to the law when they were just as free as are modern European nations to fight instead.

Njal and Gunnar, the heroes of the Njals Saga,[1] were certainly men with fighting instincts not less originally strong or more weakened by education and habit than those of an average modern European voter or statesman. Yet both of them, again and again, after some undeniable *casus belli* committed by their relations, go of their own choice to the Ting and accept the judgment of their neighbours. Gunnar, the fiercer of the two, does so largely because he is not ashamed to recognise in himself that primitive indisposition to inflict suffering wantonly which the Greeks called Aidos. "I would like to know," said he, "whether I am so much the less brisk and bold than other men because I think more of killing men than they." [2]

But they are also influenced by the danger to the whole community, the incalculable element of what

[1] Translated by G. W. Dasent (1861), now republished, in Dent's Everyman Series, as *The Story of Burnt Njal.*
[2] *Ibid.* p. 98.

Aristotle calls "infinity" involved in feuds carried out on Mr. Strachey's principle of "no matter what sacrifice." "For with law," says Njal, "shall our land be built up and settled, and with lawlessness wasted and spoiled." [1]

Their wives, Bergthora and Hallgerda, play Mr. Strachey's part in the story, and are always urging that the world is ruled by blood and iron, and not by Sunday-school maxims, and that fighting is much more logical and satisfactory than negotiating. But Njal and Gunnar held on to their purpose of showing that private resort to law without compulsion is psychologically possible sufficiently long to help in building up a custom which has since acquired the irresistible sanction of the modern state.

The third argument, that permanent peace, even though it may be psychologically possible, is inconsistent with a good life, has, I believe, in spite of its apparent paradox, more stuff in it than either of the other two arguments, that war is now required to improve our breeding-stock, and that peace is psychologically impossible.

This third argument is often combined with a statement of extreme Lamarkianism. Mankind, it is said, will "degenerate" during "the long canker of peace," not because the unfit survive, but because peace is a bad habit and bad habits are biologically transmitted. Mr. Strachey seems to mean something of this kind when he says:

Again, take Italy from 1715 to the outbreak of the Napoleonic Wars. The peninsula was lapped in peace, but

[1] *The Story of Burnt Njal,* p. 123.

men degenerated instead of improved. . . . In truth universal peace . . . does not breed worthier men and women. This is not a pleasant fact. On the contrary, it is a very sad fact, but it is one which we are bound to face, for if we do not face it we shall delude ourselves with shams and shadows (pp. 45-46).

If a few generations of peace would really bring it about that we were born peaceful, most men would consider that an important argument in favour of resort to The Hague Court for the settlement of international disputes. But Mr. Strachey's argument is really stronger without its Lamarkian support. It would then run that, since acquired habits are not transmitted, each generation will be born with fighting instincts which must be kept under by Habit. But a Habit which ignores a strong instinct produces, as I have said, the condition of "baulked disposition," and the character and nervous system of a man in that condition are apt to degenerate. Mr. Strachey's meaning is quite clear when he says:

If men are once taught that come what may they can eat, drink, and be merry, and go about the world in swinish equanimity, secure that their sty will never be disturbed, they will become the most hateful and demoralised of human beings (p. 82).

A man of independent fortune, who is uninterruptedly prosperous in his affairs, and whose wife and children and servants never oppose his will, misses the normal stimuli of anger. He will be for a time, perhaps for some years, the happier for it. But sooner or later he will become restless, unreliable, and probably unhappy. If he is a reservist and is called upon

to serve in an actual campaign he may, in the Aristotelian sense, be "purged," he may fight with exhilara-
tion and inner contentment, and come back to his
home an immensely better man. Military and Naval
professional officers always feel the truth of this. They
see their men "running to seed" in the endless preparations for a war which never takes place, and suspect
perhaps that they themselves are suffering in the same
way. A little of "the real thing," they are quite sure,
leaves every one who is not killed the better for it.

The argument is perhaps complicated by the fact
that modern war may provide a very insufficient satisfaction to the fighting instincts. Battle-fury and blood-
lust were evolved among our ancestors under conditions where you felt and saw the wounds you inflicted. Under modern conditions a man may come
back from a campaign in much the same state of
"baulked disposition" as that in which he entered on
it. "I was right through the Afridi War," an officer
once said wearily to me, "but I never saw a dead
Afridi." The gods in Valhalla would hardly choose
the organisation of modern lines of military communication, as they chose the play of sword and spear, to
be the most exquisite employment of eternity.

Hate, again, like Love, requires for its full stimulation a vivid realisation of its object, and in the sort
of European wars which threaten nowadays that realisation may be difficult to create. In the days when
the great Macdermott sang that "the Russians shall
not have Constantin-o-o-ple" we all had a clear though
mendacious picture both of the Russians and of Con-
stantinople in our minds. As I now write all good
Europeans are watching the controversy about Ser-

via's "window on the Adriatic" with the same feeling
of helpless apprehension with which a man lying bound
in a hay-barn might watch a child in the opposite
corner playing with matches. If war takes place we
shall certainly make some entity to hate, but for the
moment the cry that "the Austro-Hungarian Monarchy shall not have Durazzo" leaves even the Music
Halls cold and puzzled. We should get much more
satisfaction per thousand of violent deaths out of a
war between Manchester and Liverpool.

But the fact does remain that a rather large proportion of the members of the Great Society honestly
feel from time to time that they would be improved
by a war, and are only restrained by the fear of "the
infinite"—by the strong probability that they may get
more war than is necessary to improve their digestions.
It is not merely the fighting instinct which, they feel,
will be purged by a campaign, but the desire for
change, for fear nobly resisted, for the intense stimulation of those instincts which tell us to lead and follow.
Tennyson in March, 1854, stood on the "giant deck"
of one of Admiral Napier's ships (before they started
on their most unsatisfying expedition to the Baltic)
and "mixed his breath with a loyal people shouting a
battle-cry."

"Many a darkness," he wrote, "into the light shall leap,
And shine in the sudden making of splendid names,
And noble thought be freer under the sun,
And the heart of a people beat with one desire."

If the life of men is not to lose its savour their
powers must be exercised, and the secrets of their
nature searched by a way of living more varied, more

coloured, more exhilarating than that which most of the present English governing class seems to contemplate in its legislative plans for improving the condition of the governed. It may be that this may involve arrangements which shall require, in Mr. Strachey's words, that "Every man should some time in his life make a definite renunciation of ease and comfort for his country's good . . ." (p. 5), and that "the young barbarians of the residential quarters" should get some of the "wholesome discipline" now enjoyed by "the superior artisans and the clerks" (pp. 74-75).

But meanwhile I would plead that it would be not only more effective but more economical if we aimed at these results directly, instead of trusting that we may find them among the accidents and uncertainties, the fatigue and monotony of modern warfare.

"The custom of firing houses continued," says the "Dissertation on Roast Pig," "till, in process of time, a sage arose, like our Locke, who made a discovery that the flesh of swine might be cooked without the necessity of consuming a whole house to dress it. Then first began the rude form of a gridiron. Roasting by the string or spit came in a century or two later, I forget in whose dynasty. By such slow degrees, concludes the manuscript, do the most useful and seemingly the most obvious arts make their way among mankind."

We have now made our national houses so vast and complex that the custom of firing them in order to warm our souls is yearly becoming more dangerous and expensive, and the necessity of inventing some other nervous tonic more urgent.

CHAPTER X

THOUGHT

In each of the preceding five chapters I have tried to keep the practical purpose of my analysis constantly before me. I have asked, not only what is the present state of our knowledge about Habit, Fear, Pleasure, Love, and the rest, but whether an art exists which enables us to use that knowledge for improving the conditions of life in the Great Society.

I now propose to consider Thought with the same practical end in view.

In Chapter III. I argued that Thought is a true natural disposition. Under appropriate conditions, that is to say, we are naturally disposed to enter into a state of reverie, during which our ideas are so combined and arranged as to produce new mental results. I there also argued that Thought may be independently stimulated, and that it is not, as Mr. McDougall says, a merely subordinate mechanism acting only in obedience to the previous stimulation of one of the simpler instincts.

In this chapter I shall ask whether there is an art by which the efficiency of Thought can be improved.

Five hundred years ago no one would have had any hesitation in answering, "Yes, such an art of Thought exists; its name is Logic; it was invented by Aristotle; and it is the most important element in the curriculum of the schools and Universities." This belief in formal Aristotelian Logic as an art of thought died hard. During the years of the American and French Revolution Oxford students were still required, in order to receive their official certificates as trained thinkers, to repeat long Latin "strings" of syllogistic affirmations and denials on some question in moral or natural philosophy. Here is a translation of part of such a "string":

Opponent. What think you of this question, whether universal ideas are formed by abstraction?

Respondent. I affirm it.

Opponent. Universal ideas are not formed by abstraction: therefore you are deceived.

Respondent. I deny the antecedent.

Opponent. I prove the antecedent. Whatever is formed by sensation alone is not formed by abstraction: but universal ideas are formed by sensation alone: therefore universal ideas are not formed by abstraction.

Respondent. I deny the minor.

Opponent. I prove the minor. The idea of solidity is a universal idea: but the idea of solidity is formed by sensation alone: therefore universal ideas are formed by sensation alone, etc. etc.[1]

It was the custom by that time for the undergraduate to read his "strings" from a written paper hidden in his square cap, and it is safe to assert that Gibbon and Bentham left Oxford better prepared, if they followed that custom, to think about History or Law, than would have been the case if they had attempted, as students in the Middle Ages did seriously attempt,

---

[1] Godley, *Oxford in the Eighteenth Century*, p. 177.

to learn from Aristotle's rules how to acquire Aristotle's intellectual fertility.

Nowadays, the majority, perhaps, of educated men, if asked whether an art of Thought exists, would answer, "No: thoughts come of themselves by a process of whose character we are ignorant, and of which we are always unconscious at the time. No drilling either in Aristotle's syllogism or in any other logical method ever gave a man a new thought which he would not have had without it. All that we know is that some men think abundantly and consecutively, and other men scantily and at haphazard."

Some of the statements made by important modern psychologists would seem to support this view. They insist that the primary and essential process of Thought is unconscious, and therefore, at the moment of thinking, involuntary. Professor James said:

From the guessing of newspaper enigmas to the plotting of the policy of an empire there is no other process than this. We trust to the laws of cerebral nature to present us spontaneously with the appropriate idea.[1]

Many of the newer psychologists also declare that this process is in essence identical in ways of thinking which ordinary language suggests to be entirely separate. The "spontaneous presentation of the appropriate idea" (to repeat James' phrase) is, they say, the same thing whether we are remembering, or imagining, or reasoning. Professor Pillsbury says: "Neither the materials nor medium of reasoning, nor the laws of connection, are distinctive of reasoning as opposed

[1] *Principles of Psychology,* vol. i. p. 589.

to recall or imagination," [1] and again, "If one will but follow through a chain of reasoning, it will be observed that the elements are connected by the same laws of association that are operative in the simplest recall." [2] If it is objected that Memory reproduces impressions in the accidental order and form in which they reach us from outside, while Imagination or Reasoning arranges them in an order chosen by the mind itself, and transforms them into something different from the original, some of the experimentalists answer that Memory does in fact rearrange and transform the results of experience, and Imagination and Reasoning do no more.

The real differences between Memory, and Imagination, and Reasoning are to be found, they say, not in the primary process of thinking, but in our subsequent attitude towards our thoughts. If "the result is regarded as untrue to reality," the process is Imagination; "if it be regarded as a true combination even

---

[1] *Psychology of Reasoning,* by Professor W. B. Pillsbury of Michigan (1910), p. 4. The analysis of the thought-process by systematic introspective experiments carried on mainly within special laboratories is a branch of scientific enquiry in which, as in astronomy, the Americans have taken the lead. Any one who wishes to follow their work can do so in the specialist psychological journals, or may begin with the book just quoted and go on with *How We Think* (1901), and *Studies in Logical Theory* (1903), by Professor Dewey of Chicago, and *The Experimental Psychology of the Thought Process,* by Professor E. B. Titchener of Cornell (1909). In this last book there is summed up much recent work by American and German experimentalists at Würzburg and elsewhere. The records of that work are a pattern of scientific patience and candour, and have produced a conviction in at least one inexpert reader that from it will ultimately develop a great and fertile art of thinking. But the work itself is still confessedly tentative, and there seems as yet to be very incomplete agreement among the students in different laboratories as to many details both of terminology and of results.

[2] *Ibid.* p. 3. Professor Pillsbury uses the word "recall" as equivalent to Memory.

when new," it is Reasoning. "What is recognised is said to be remembered; what is not recognised is said to be the result of reasoning or imagination." [1] When I try to realise this I find myself recalling an afternoon in the early eighteen nineties when the late Lord Russell of Killowen (before his peerage) was parliamentary candidate for Hackney. He asked me one Saturday to do a round of open-air speaking with him. We drove from "pitch" to "pitch," climbed at each on to a waiting cart, and drew verbal pictures of the results of a victory for our side, which, at each repetition, grew more splendid and more convincing. When it was all over we stepped back into our cab, and the great man stretched his broad shoulders, took a long breath, and suddenly said in a new voice: "Do you know, I daresay a good deal could be done." In an instant our afternoon's work, which might perhaps up to that point have been classed as creative Imagination, became for him part of a process of Reasoning.

The view that Thought, even in its most complex form, bloweth as it listeth, and that no effort of ours can hope to control or improve it, might also be supported by the records of actual intellectual achievement. Thought-processes of astonishing length and complexity can, these show, take place with almost complete unconsciousness. Wagner, for instance, describes how, after a sleepless night followed by an uninteresting walk:

I stretched myself dead tired on a hard couch awaiting the long-desired hour of sleep. It did not come; but I fell into a kind of somnolent state in which I suddenly felt as though I were sinking in swiftly flowing water. The rush-

[1] Pillsbury, *Psychology of Reasoning*, p. 4.

ing sound formed itself in my brain into a musical sound, the chord of E flat major, which continually re-echoed in broken forms; these broken chords seemed to be melodic passages of increasing motion, yet the pure triad of E flat major never changed, but seemed by its continuance to impart infinite significance to the element in which I was sinking. I awoke in sudden terror from my doze, feeling as though the waves were rushing high above my head. I at once recognised that the orchestral overture to the *Rheingold*, which must long have lain latent within me, though it had been unable to find definite form, had at last been revealed to me.[1]

Dickens once told Forster: "As to the way in which these characters [in Martin Chuzzlewit] have opened out, that is, to me, one of the most surprising processes of the mind in this sort of invention. Given what one knows, what one does not know springs up"; [2] and again, "I don't invent it—really do not—but *see* it and write it down." [3]

The great French mathematician Henri Poincaré was once working at a difficult problem about Fuchsian functions. "Somehow or other he found that these investigations were leading to nothing, went off for a few days to the seaside and banished mathematics, as he supposed, from his thoughts. But suddenly one day when walking on the beach, he was 'stung by the splendour of a sudden thought' that the arithmetical transformations of indefinite ternary quadratic forms are identical with those of non-Euclidean Geometry." [4]

If this were, all, if we could never hope to know

[1] *My Life*, Wagner (Eng. trans.), vol. ii. p. 603.
[2] Forster's *Life of Dickens*, vol. ii. p. 58.
[3] *Ibid.* vol. iii. p. 308.
[4] From an admirable article on Poincaré in the *Westminster Gazette* of July 22, 1912.

anything about Thought except that it is unconscious and therefore involuntary, and if no means could be discovered of increasing the efficacy of Thought, then the outlook for the Great Society would be dark indeed. The whole of our analysis up to this point goes to prove that, as the scale of social organisation extends, the merely instinctive guidance of Fear, or Love, or Pleasure, or Habit becomes more and more unsafe; and that not only is a clearer consciousness of his actions and a stronger habit of forecasting their result needed by the ordinary man, but Thought in the great sense, the long-continued concentration of the professed thinker in which new knowledge is made available for the guidance of human life, is required as it has never been required before.

Fortunately for us, there are certain conditions accompanying or influencing the unconscious and involuntary processes of Thought which can be brought under our conscious control, and improvements in which do produce improvements in our thinking. These conditions, if we take the natural powers of any individual thinker for granted, may be classified as his material circumstances at the moment of Thought; the general mental "attitude" which more or less consciously accompanies his Thought; and his relation to the particular subject matter of his Thought. This last relation can again be divided into the content and arrangement of his Memory or of the external Record which takes its place, and his "Logic" in the stricter sense, that is to say, any system of methodically directing attention and criticising results which he may have adopted, either deliberately or in the process of acquir-

ing language, and which he may use either consciously
or by unconscious habit.

Let us begin with the material circumstances of the
thinker. I have already said (in Chapter III.) that,
although the satisfaction of Curiosity or the adaptation
of means to ends by the process of Trial and Error
may take place while the subject is in a condition of
restless excitement and movement, the reverie in which
our ideas arrange themselves for higher intellectual
purposes normally requires that the thinker should be
free from external interference and should be either
at rest or in a state of monotonous and unconscious
movement. No man is likely to produce creative
thoughts (either consciously or subconsciously) if he
is constantly interrupted by irregular noises, or if he
is very cold or hot, or very hungry.

Perhaps when we know more exactly than we do
now the history of the beginnings of European civilisation, we shall be able to trace the slow shifting of the
external conditions most favourable to Thought from
the climate of the southern Mediterranean to that of
North-West Europe. At first men seem to have thought
most successfully in the open air, during the cool hours
which follow sunset in a hot climate, when they could
escape from the noise of children and dogs in the
crowded cave or tent. Thousands of years later, and a
little farther north, permanent shaded places, temple
porticoes, or still later the Academe or the Stoa, were
built and kept quiet. Here men could fall into a condition of absorbed Thought by daylight without the
risk of sunstroke. Then came the monastery cell of
North Europe, dry and quiet, but in winter abomi-

nable cold.[1] The monasteries were followed by the
pleasant rooms with their big glazed windows and open
fireplaces which Erasmus found in the Tudor country
houses and Cambridge colleges. Jane Austen's Mans-
field Park marks the later point when the physical
possibility of Thought was just beginning to be extended, even in winter, to the housekeeping sex, and
when a girl below the rank of a noblewoman might
here and there hope for solitude and "a fire in the East
Room." Now the claim for the material possibility of
Thought is moving farther down the social scale, and
the Inspectors of the Board of Education point out as
a case of genuine hardship that an artisan student of
the Workers' Education Association "in order to get
a time when the house was quiet for working in, went
to bed at seven, got up at midnight, worked for two
hours, and then went to bed again." [2]

In the Great Society, however, side by side with the
growing recognition of the need for a larger proportion
of the population of thinking-places kept quiet and at
a fairly even temperature, has come the growing im-
possibility of thinking outside them. The modern Londoner cannot stroll in obedience to his mood into the
fields on a summer evening. He must first take a tram

[1] Ordericus Vitalis (Bohn's *Antiquarian Library,* vol. iii. pp. 40-
45) describes the controversy at the Benedictine Monastery of
Molême at the end of the eleventh century between the Abbot, who
wished to require all monks to dress and live like the primitive
Egyptian anchorites, and the monks, who argued that "the French,
who often shudder in the frosts of winter," required special privileges if they were to do their work of reading and meditation.
[2] Special Report on certain Tutorial Classes (*Board of Education Special Reports,* No. 2). Tolstoy can hardly have realised how
completely he abandoned his ideal of living a peasant's life when
he said, "There is one thing I cannot do without: I must have a
quiet room to work in" (*Life of Tolstoy,* by A. Maude, vol. ii. p.
528).

or railway journey, during which the mood of Thought will probably evaporate. The London or Manchester schoolmaster cannot, like Eugene Aram, sit in a field and brood "remote from all." If the London County Council desires that its schoolmasters and mistresses should think, it has to place "teachers-rooms" on the original plans of those great school buildings which take years to build; and the Progressives on the old School Board never felt more near to the actual problem of the intellectual vitality of education than when we were pleading that it was a wise economy to provide two separate rooms in every new school for the head-teacher and his or her assistants.

Thought again requires not only quiet and an even temperature, but food, and, in our climate, boots and woollen clothing. Another history of civilisation might be written showing the changes in the means by which thinkers have been so provided. A man who gives the best strength of each day to dreaming about the nature of God or of the State, or the shape of the earth, or the relation of the sides of a triangle to its hypotenuse, produces nothing which at the end of the day he can easily sell. Since the actual process of inference is unconscious, and his voluntary control over it indirect and uncertain, he is not even sure that he will produce any result at all, whether salable or unsalable, by months of effort. How then shall he live?

Perhaps most of the severe and continued thinking that has been done during the last ten thousand years has been a by-product of magic or religion. The medicine man or the priest did not spend his whole time in rain-making or sacrificing, and during his leisure was rather expected to fall into fits of abstraction.

In climates, again, where neither thick clothing nor artificial heat nor animal food is absolutely necessary, a thinker has sometimes been able to keep himself alive by begging from door to door, especially if, though not a priest, he is a holy man, giving alms to whom is a religious duty. Wagner's way of life, like Erasmus', was a modern adaptation of this system, in which begging letters are substituted for the begging bowl, and which is apt to involve a good deal of wasted effort and impaired morale.

Sometimes Thought has been a by-product of government. Kings and statesmen have almost everywhere except in modern America [1] been permitted to live under conditions which made leisure for reflection possible.

Sometimes a thinker like St. Paul or Spinoza has determined to live by the practice of a manual art, tent-making or lens-grinding. But St. Paul must have found small time for making tents when the churches founded by him began to grow, and Spinoza died of the effects of privation at forty-five.

More often the thinker has lived by teaching, and modern University organisation is deliberately aimed at creating such a relation between teacher and student as shall both stimulate the teacher and train the

[1] "All previous records at hand-shaking were broken by Governor and Mrs. Draper yesterday during the first hour of the Washington's birthday reception at the State House. They exchanged hand-clasps with 49 persons a minute from 10.30 o'clock until 11.30 o'clock" (*Boston Herald*, Feb. 23, 1910). One of the most valuable services done by President Wilson to the cause of political thought in America is his recent abandonment of such heroic attempts to ignore the change of scale in American life since 1783.

student. In the moral sciences this arrangement is the main source of modern Thought. But it is not wholly successful. There are hundreds of cases in which a professor's teaching spoils his thinking, and these are balanced by hundreds of others in which his thinking spoils his teaching.

Sometimes the thinker has supported himself as an artist. He has put part of his thoughts into acceptable artistic form and has sold the result. If in ancient times he was a musician, he made poems and chanted them to those who would pay for the right to listen. A thinker who is also an orator could in Greece recite, like Herodotus, prose compositions to the crowd at Olympia, and in modern Europe he can become a popular lecturer. The invention of printing and copyright has made it possible for an unusually fertile thinker in some cases to support himself by writing, though it may be doubted whether the life of the professional writer without other resources has not destroyed as much thought as it has produced. For the thinker requires not only food and clothing and quiet, but leisure, in the sense of absence of extreme nervous fatigue. His working day must in most cases be shorter than that of the manual worker or routine organiser, but the hours during which he is not thinking cannot be spent in other forms of hard intellectual labour. Hardly any man, for instance, can give six hours a day to journalism and follow it with four hours of concentrated thinking.

In modern times, as Mr. Lester F. Ward showed, a large proportion of the most important intellectual achievements have been the by-product of the institution of private property. He concluded, for instance, from the facts collected by Odin (*Genèse des grands hommes,* 1895), that about a third of the European writers of acknowledged genius have sprung from the small class of the land-owning nobility.[1] In England, Cavendish was a millionaire, and Bentham and Darwin men of considerable wealth. But it is becoming increasingly difficult to trust to this source of leisure as sufficient for the intellectual guidance of the Great Society. Not only does the small percentage of rich men provide a too restricted gathering-ground for ability, but the fact that they all belong to one social class is a very serious hindrance to effective thinking on those subjects on which Thought is now most urgently required.

The Great Society will, therefore, I believe, be forced to undertake the deliberate provision of the material conditions of thinking, instead of trusting to the appearance of Thought as a by-product of religion, or teaching, or copyright, or administration, or private wealth. Throughout history money has been occasionally given with the direct purpose of enabling men to live lives of disinterested Thought. Kings have had learned men about their court, and rich nobles have

---

[1] *Applied Sociology,* pp. 207 and 210. Ward complains that it is extremely difficult to find out the economic position of great men from their biographies. "If a great discoverer or inventor works ten years uninterruptedly and at last succeeds and astonishes the world, all this will be told in minutest detail without a word as to how he was fed, housed, and clothed during all this time that he was earning nothing. If a great author writes a book that costs him many years of patient unremunerative research, nothing will be said about how he was enabled to devote all these years to such a subject. The fact is that in every such case there must have been some kind of a fortune behind it all, or something equivalent to a fortune, such as a state annuity, emoluments granted to the nobility or the clergy, or some sinecure official position, or at least a well-paid position that did not exhaust all of the man's energies" (*Applied Sociology,* pp. 198-199).

supported poor scholars. But it is only in the last two generations that the endowment of Thought for its own sake has become one of the acknowledged duties of all governments, and as yet little progress has been made in discovering the most effective methods of doing it. It is easy enough to choose a dozen clever young men or women and give them yearly payments sufficient to provide food and clothing and quiet; but it is not easy to secure that they shall use those opportunities with effect. In that respect the Norwegian custom of giving travelling "stipendiums" to young writers who have already achieved something seems to produce better results from a given amount of money than the Oxford and Cambridge custom of giving all their scholarships, and nearly all their fellowships, to promising pupils who have achieved nothing.

It is convenient to treat warmth and quiet and food as material facts which aid Thought. They do so, however, by making possible certain physiological and psychological states favourable to Thought, and sometimes it is more convenient to classify such states rather than their material conditions. This is particularly the case when we are dealing with the more complex among those states of consciousness which the introspective experimentalists in psychological laboratories have observed to accompany Thought, and which they call "mental attitudes."

Because the primary process of Thought is unconscious we cannot direct it as the painter directs the movement of his hand. There will always be an element of surprise in what actually happens or refuses to happen in our minds. William James quotes Hodgson:

Volition has no power of calling up images, but only of rejecting and selecting from those offered by spontaneous association. . . . There is no seeing them before they are offered; there is no summoning them before they are seen.[1]

But we can, to a certain extent, control our "mental attitudes," and thereby, though indirectly, the course of our Thought.

Some of these attitudes, such as "attention," "inhibition," the "feeling of the problem," etc., will be more conveniently dealt with when I examine the relation of the thinker to his subject-matter. But there are others which are better treated as general conditions of thinking than as part of any method of approaching the material of Thought. Some of these more general "attitudes" are on the line which divides physiology from psychology. Take, for instance, the "warmth of the blood," the sense of mental vigour and fertility which indicates that Thought will go easily. Some men do not sit down to work unless this feeling has appeared of itself. Others struggle, as I believe most men with experience of connected thinking would advise, morning after morning against their first feelings of discomfort and distraction until, after perhaps an hour's unsatisfactory work, they get their "second wind."[2] The output of Thought, again, is not only

[1] *Principles of Psychology*, vol. i. p. 589. James suggests the substitution, which I have made, of the term "association" for "redintegration," which Hodgson here uses in that sense.

[2] As Sir Henry Miers points out in his address on *The Revival of Learning* (p. 6), a great deal more academic consideration has been given to the psychology of athletics than to the psychology of

slow to begin, but also, like the revolutions of a heavy
fly-wheel, slow to cease. A man, who is reading in
order to stimulate his thinking, finds it useful to remain
passive for a short time at the end of each chapter, and
still more at the end of each book, in order to allow
his thoughts to continue of themselves. The house-
holder who works at home finds that it pays to stop
writing twenty minutes before lunch, so as to harvest
the last gleanings of his Thought, instead of allowing
them to present themselves during the meal, and then,
having injured both his digestion and his manners, be
finally (like 95 per cent of most men's intellectual output) lost through forgetfulness. Hobbes, the father of
modern social psychology, took his own intellectual
processes in this matter with scientific seriousness. "He
walked much," says his friend Aubrey, "and contemplated, and he had in the head of his staffe a pen and
inke horne, carried always a note-book in his pocket,
and as soon as a thought darted, he presently entered
it into his book, or otherwise he might perhaps have
lost it." [1]

Sometimes efficiency in thinking seems to be connected with our choice of some particular tract of the
brain in which Thought shall take place. The records
of brain injury show that a man who, owing to the
fact that some region of his brain has been injured by

---

intellectual effort. Any handbook on golf for beginners contains
hints on the subconscious tricks of attention which would be of real
value to a beginner in mathematics or moral philosophy.
    [1] Quoted by Pogson Smith in the Introduction (p. xxii) to his
edition of Hobbes' *Leviathan*. Pogson Smith also quotes from
Aubrey a passage (p. xxv) which shows that Hobbes had no patience with those who toil to make broad their bibliographies until
they see men as books walking. "He was wont to say that if he
had read as much as other men, he should have known no more
than other mēn."

disease and accident, has, *e.g.,* lost the power of understanding and applying, though not of hearing and repeating, spoken words, may yet teach himself to do his thinking by turning his attention to the movements made by his mouth in the act of oral repetition. We apparently can, that is to say, voluntarily use within certain limits different nerves and ganglia for the same purposes of Thought. For some men, owing either to inheritance or habit, there is a definite and permanent advantage in thinking through visual or through audile mental images, or, like the boy whose button Sir Walter Scott cut off, through "kinetic" images of muscular movement. A born or trained speaker must talk if he is to think effectively, a writer must write. Cardinal Newman, in a letter to a friend, says:

> I think best when I write. I cannot in the same way think while I speak. Some men are brilliant in conversation, others in public speaking—others find their minds work best when they have a pen in their hands. But then, if it is a bad pen? a steel pen?—that is my case just now, and thus I find my brain won't work—much as I wish it.[1]

Sometimes a man may suffer all through his life from the fact that his habits in that respect conflict with his inherited nature—as happens when a very left-handed boy is brought up right-handed. Friedrich Froebel and his followers have, I believe, done an immense amount of injury to modern European Thought by causing a large number of naturally "visual" children to be taught to think almost solely through images of spoken sounds, and perhaps the followers of Madame

[1] *Life,* vol. ii. p. 315.

Montessori may do as much harm by forcing all kinds of children to use "kinetic" thought-images.

But in less extreme cases it would appear that a man may gain in intellectual fertility by a change of mental attitude which feels like the transference of work from a tired to an untired brain-tract. An artist, by looking backward through his legs, can see a landscape with a sense of creative novelty which was denied to him when he looked at it in the ordinary position. Zola, I have read, used to stimulate his slow and overworked imagination by writing long confidential letters to himself about the characters of his next book, until the characters began to live of themselves. He apparently found that he used a slightly different tract of his brain in writing such letters from that which he used in literary composition. If a lawyer desires that a client shall appreciate the full significance of a document, he makes him first read it in silence and then aloud. A business man who has sat at his desk for a weary hour holding his attention on a single problem without the least result, will often find his mind full of suggestion the moment he tries to explain his difficulty by word of mouth to a fellow human being; and one of the ways by which a solitary thinker can set his mind working is to picture to himself the arrival of an intimate friend with the cheery question: "Now then, what is it that you really want to say?"

The extension of association produced by the search for the right word in which to express a thought may often result in stimulating a new and better thought. Théophile Gautier said: "Expression *is* Thought." And when an American Professor told me: "Men of Science over here do not write books," I felt that perhaps he had given one of the causes of a certain disappointment which other professors had sometimes described to me with the output of original thinking from some of their ablest and most devoted enquirers.

Brain-physiology is still largely guess-work, and it may be that many of these facts represent rather the addition of new associations by the extension of the tract employed, than the substitution of one tract for another, or that the two processes may shade into each other. An extension of the range of association does seem to be one of the effects aimed at by modern painters and writers when they take large doses of alcohol, or of coffee, tobacco, absinthe and other vegetable alkaloids; or by the mediums attached to the ancient oracles when they sought inspiration from the hypnotic trance; or by the Germans described by Tacitus who found that they thought more fruitfully on any question when they considered it first drunk and then sober.

All such expedients, good or bad, lead of course to an attitude of "self-consciousness," the self-consciousness of the artist as contrasted with that gentlemanly unconsciousness of one's own mental processes which we English so admire in our governing class. M. Paul Blouet tells how, when he was a public-school master in England, he said to the head-master (who, like so many others, had extended his public-school boyhood unchanged into middle age): "You have a boy there who ought to speak French very well . . . his pronunciation is capital," and was answered, "Oh, I do not doubt it, he is full of affectation." [1]

And self-consciousness may have to extend from the mental attitudes which are mainly concerned with the

[1] *John Bull and His Island*, by "Max O'Rell," pp. 151-152.

physiology of the brain to those which are concerned with deeper moral states. Just as it is impossible to sing, or to speak a foreign language, well, with one's mouth and throat in a "gentlemanly" position, so it may prove to be the case that one cannot think effectively if one's main purpose in life is to be a gentleman. "Truth," I heard Mr. G. B. Shaw say some thirty years ago, "comes, not from an avoidance of the vulgar vice of lying, but from the agony and sweat in which the professional critic has to approach his work." It may even be that modern thinkers may, at the risk of priggishness, have to teach and learn the old Greek conception of moral goodness in the conduct of the intellect. In the book in which Miss Jane Addams explains the origin of her own splendid output of original Thought, she says: "As our boarding-school days neared the end, in the consciousness of approaching separation, we vowed eternal allegiance to our 'early ideals,' and promised each other we would 'never abandon them without conscious justification,' and we often warned each other of 'the perils of self-tradition.'" [1] Miss Addams can smile at this now, but if we are to trust to Thought as the main guiding force of our society, the priggishness of Rockford College, Illinois, in the eighteen seventies may be a better stimulus than the silent suppression of all serious interest which one guesses at in the atmosphere of an English twentieth century hockey-playing girls' school.

And if we really desire to increase the national production of Thought, we must give organised attention to the question whether the moral atmosphere not only of our schools and colleges, but of our social and po-

[1] *Twenty Years at Hull House,* p. 63.

litical institutions is one favourable to the stimulation of the thought process.

Historians tell us that the great periods of intellectual activity are apt to follow the coincidence of the discovery of important new facts with the wide extension of a sense of personal liberty. It has been asked what has social or political liberty to do with the success or failure of the unconscious process of individual Thought? Most men can provide an answer from their own personal experience. There are some emotional states in which creative Thought is impossible, and the chief of these is the sense of helpless humiliation and anger which is produced in a sensitive nature by conscious inability to oppose or avoid the "insolence of office." Let any man who doubts it sit down for a day's work at the British Museum after being grossly insulted by some one whom he is not in a position to resist.

Mr. M'Kenna's training has been that of a barrister and not that of a thinker or writer. His parliamentary treatment of the Court Censorship of Plays as Home Secretary in 1911 would probably have been different if he had realised that the question was not whether the Censor was likely to cut out this or that percentage of the words in any play submitted to him, but whether, when a serious dramatist knows that what he writes will be submitted to the blue pencil of the author, say, of "Dear Old Charlie," the spontaneous presentation of creative Thought may not refuse to take place in his mind. Tolstoy once wrote: "You would not believe how, from the very commencement of my activity, that horrible Censor question has tormented me! I wanted to write what I felt; but at the

same time it occurred to me that what I wrote would
not be permitted, and involuntarily I had to abandon
the work. I abandoned, and went on abandoning, and
meanwhile the years passed away." [1]

A man, again, who is dominated by the common-
sense intellectualism of ordinary speech may fail to
see any "reason" why an elementary school teacher or
a second-division clerk cannot do his work properly
after he has been "put in his place" by some official
who happens to combine personal callousness with social superiority. But no statesman who did so could
create an effective educational or clerical service.

This is one of the considerations which trouble some
Englishmen who hope that, on the whole, our empire
in India makes for good. The thousand members of
the covenanted Civil Service obviously cannot do all
the thinking required by a population of three hundred
millions living under rapidly changing social and industrial conditions. If India is to fight successfully
against the plague which ships and railways spread, if
she is to revive the arts and industries which have been
killed by Manchester and Birmingham, above all, if
she is to contribute her fair share to the world's literature and science, a much larger number of creative
thinkers must appear among her native inhabitants.
But Anglo-Indian officials do not, one fears, often produce or perhaps often desire to produce an emotional
condition favourable to the growth of creative Thought
in the natives with whom they are brought into contact. Athens during the last quarter of the fifth
century B.C. was not well governed; and if the British
Empire had then existed, and if Athens had been

[1] *Life of Tolstoy*, by A. Maude, vol. ii. p. 378.

brought within it, the administration of the city would undoubtedly have been improved in some important respects. But one does not like to imagine the effect on the intellectual output of the fifth century B.C. if even the best of Mr. Rudyard Kipling's public-school subalterns had stalked daily through the agora, snubbing, as he passed, that intolerable bounder Euripides, or clearing out of his way the probably seditious group that were gathered round Socrates.

We now come to the third of the three conditions of effective thinking which are more or less completely under our control, and therefore part of the Art of Thought in the broadest sense, viz., our relation to the subject-matter of our Thought.

I have already said that that relation may be divided into Memory and Record on the one hand, and Logic on the other, and I shall now deal with Memory and Record. We think, not in a mental vacuum, but about something, and that something is not the world as it really exists, of which we are necessarily ignorant, nor the world as we should see it if we could examine every detail of it at short range and in a good light, nor even the piecemeal world as it originally reached us through our senses, but an "environment" composed partly of Memory and partly of our direct perceptions at the moment of Thought.

Memory transforms our perceptions. Millions of individual "percepts" appear in Memory as a comparatively few "concepts" or "ideas." If, for instance, we recall a pile of bricks or a train of railway carriages, the memory of individual bricks and carriages is merged

in general ideas of "brick" and "carriage." Most of
our words are the names of such ideas, and ever since
men have begun to examine their use of language, they
have disputed as to the relation between these ideas
and the individual facts of the external world. Is the
idea of a carriage prior to the existence of real carriages, or at any rate to the sight of a carriage by the
man in whose brain the idea is found? Or does each
man independently form the carriage-idea by generalisation from carriages which he has himself seen?

As long as this question was argued on exclusively
philosophical grounds it was possible for any one to
adopt any answer to it which happened to please him.
But experimental psychology is beginning now to give
us a little outside light on the subject. We can, for
instance, watch the process by which a general idea
may be actually formed by the automatic drawing together in our memory of a large number of individual
sense-impressions into a smaller number of groups. If
a man is shown repeatedly a hundred different shades
of grey, it is found that the hundred shades will crystallise in his memory into perhaps seven or ten groups,
the number of groups being very likely fixed by the
number of names for shades of grey which he happens
to know or to be able to invent. The "idea" of each
group will represent something near the middle one of
those shades which go to form the group, and the other
shades within each group will be remembered as more
like that "idea" and more different from the shades in
the adjoining groups than they really are. If,
again, a man is told to learn by heart a long list of
numbers he tends automatically to form them also into

groups, and the numbers in each group are "displaced in memory towards the average" of each group.[1]

In these cases, therefore, of colours and numbers, the answer to the old question of priority between the individual fact of experience and the general idea, is that the fact is prior to the idea, and that the idea arises from the grouping of the facts in memory; the points round which the grouping takes place depending on the circumstances of each case. It will be convenient to call ideas so formed "artificial."

But in other cases an idea crystallises round a point which is fixed beforehand by some inherited disposition, and then it may be convenient to call the idea "natural." There are, for instance, in the world many species of animals and plants which, in the long course of human evolution, have been of direct importance to us. Any sense-impression which indicates the presence of an object belonging to one of these species directly stimulates the appropriate disposition. In Chapter IV. I argued that this stimulation has a quality of elasticity and generality. A man born with the instinct of cat-fear will be frightened, or a dog born with the instinct to fight cats will be excited, not by one particular cat only, but by any one of many cats and cat-like animals, all rather unlike each other; because if any action (grasping, hunting, spitting out, running away, etc., etc.) was originally useful when stimulated by any one individual of the species, the same action, with minor adjustments, was useful when stimulated by any other.

When our instincts are first stimulated we are nor-

[1] See Lehmann, Leuba, Xillier, etc., quoted by Pillsbury, *The Psychology of Reasoning,* pp. 73, 78.

mally unconscious of this general quality in the stimulation. A boy who sees and smells an apple for the first time, and instinctively desires it, has no preliminary idea of "apple." He desires it *simpliciter,* and not because he consciously classifies it as belonging to the species of "apples in general," any more than a youth feels when first he falls in love that he does so because the girl who attracts him belongs to the species of "girls in general." When, however, a boy has seen a large number of apples, and especially when he has learnt to use the word "apple," he acquires a natural idea of "apple" indistinguishable in memory from the artificial ideas of greys and numbers which are formed by deliberate experiment.

The "natural" idea, however, of "apple" and the "artificial" idea, say, of "nearly-white grey" have two important differences.

It is, in the first place, an "accident" whether we put any one of the ten whitest shades among the hundred shades of grey into a class of ten "nearly-white" or a class of twenty "rather-white." It is not an "accident" whether the boy classes the greenish apple on the tree with an apple somewhat redder than itself or with leaves somewhat greener than itself. The limits of the idea of apple were fixed, before our individual experience, by the fact that we have a disposition to desire apples and no disposition to desire leaves, and that therefore our instinct draws a line of separation between the green sensation which means apple and the other green sensation which means leaf.[1]

---

[1] It is this fact which was at the back of the insistent medieval belief that things have "essential" as well as "accidental" qualities. The essential qualities of those species which formed important parts of our primitive environment are those which originally con-

Sometimes our ideas may be most conveniently described as drawn not from individual percepts but from relations—the relation between the south wind, for instance, and the rain, the path and its destination, theft and punishment, the cobra and death. The point round which such relation ideas crystallise may also be "artificial" and due to accident, as in the case of the path, or "natural" and due to instinct as in the case of the cobra. It is indeed only a question of convenience whether we think of them as ideas of relations between two things or as ideas of qualities of a single thing—the quality of leading somewhere in the case of the path, and the quality of deadliness in the case of the cobra.

The second respect in which "natural" and "artificial" ideas differ is that the particular kind of grouping which our memory mistakenly imposes upon the "artificial" species corresponds to a real fact in the "natural" species. Our memory is wrong in "displacing" the shades of grey in each group, or the numbers in each list, "towards the average." It is not wrong in supposing that most apples will be more like the middle apple of the species than like the exceptional apples near the limit of the species.

Memory, therefore, which provides us with the main material of our Thought, was built up when the things

---

stituted its importance to us, and the recognition of which constituted the stimulus to our senses. The medieval thinkers were right in saying that the terribleness and teeth of a lion and the lovableness and sucking mouth of a baby were "essential attributes," and that the fact that a baby was liable to catch measles and a lion to catch mange were "accidents," even although they were "inseparable accidents." Where they were wrong was in failing to see that things which were not important parts of our primitive environment (churches, for instance, or laws or carpets) had no "natural" or "essential" attributes at all.

which chiefly concerned us belonged to certain primitive biological species, and tends to treat all other facts in our environment as if they belonged to such species. And not only the way in which Memory arranges its contents, but the quantitative limits of its recording powers were fixed by the conditions of man's primitive life. Primitive man had neither the eagle's flight nor the wolf's speed. He moved slowly over the earth's surface within a radius of a few score miles, and could therefore only see and hear things that mattered to him within a few hundred yards and smell them within a few yards or feet. His memory, after twenty or thirty years of active life, was, even when helped by the use of language, only retentive enough to enable him to recognise a few thousand familiar objects, to assign unfamiliar objects to a few thousand classes, or to forecast results by the help of his knowledge of a few thousand relations. It is with this limited and misleading Memory that a twentieth-century statesman or economist or industrial organiser has to face the tremendous task of thinking out decisions affecting scores of millions of people, of whose individual characteristics he knows nothing, scattered over continents which he will never see.

One of the most urgently necessary duties, therefore, of the art of Thought is the management and correction of Memory. It has long been known by teachers that Memory, both of "natural" and of "artificial" species, can be enormously improved in range and accuracy by conscious attention, abstraction, and inhibition. Let us take first, for the sake of simplicity, an ordinary case of an attempt to increase by education the range and accuracy of Memory in dealing with a

biological species. Take, for instance, the way in which
a boy may be trained to remember and distinguish various kinds of moths. From early childhood moths and
butterflies have naturally distinguished themselves to
him from the flowers on which they settle by the fact
that he wants to catch them, and a rough idea of moth
has sprung up in his mind arising out of that fact and
his hearing the word "moth" used. His teacher now
tells him to look carefully at all the moths which he
sees in the course of a series of walks, and to listen
while he is told their specific names. The boy finds
that, as a result of this effort of attention, he has acquired new "artificial" ideas which enable him to recognise and name, say, fifty different species of moths.
He is then taught to practice "abstraction." He con-
centrates, that is to say, his attention on particular
points distinctive of each species, and finds that, in
consequence, he can both remember species more easily
and assign newly observed individuals to them more
quickly. He can now "learn" perhaps a hundred
species with the same effort of attention with which
before he could learn fifty. Later on he is told to notice the causal relations of these distinctive points, the
connection, for instance, between the usual habitat of
each species and its colour, or between its food and the
shape of its proboscis. Then, still with the same effort,
he can remember and distinguish perhaps two hundred
species.

After some years the boy becomes a serious student of entomology and determines to do a piece of
original work. He suspects, owing perhaps to a vague
sense of discomfort of which he is conscious in applying
some of his type-ideas, that the smaller nocturnal dark-

brown moths have been inaccurately classified, and he determines to reclassify them after observing at least a thousand specimens. At once he has to make a new effort, that of inhibition. He is told to keep out of his mind the ideas which he tends automatically to form, and to prevent himself for a time from forming new ideas of the same kind, or, if he forms them, to treat them as merely shadowy hypotheses which must not be allowed to modify the sharp individuality of his memory of individual moths.

At this point he will come definitely against the limitations of his powers. If the course of human evolution had been different, he might have been able to carry in his memory a separate clear impression of each one of a thousand very slightly differing moths and to prevent those impressions from "drawing together" into types. But as it is he finds that he cannot. He either forgets his impressions or crystallises them into groups more homogeneous than are the facts. He has come to the end of the powers of Memory. He therefore proceeds to create an external Record which will neither forget nor modify what is entrusted to it; and for that purpose he forms a collection of a thousand specimens of moths, or of as many drawings or photographs, or of written figures which record perhaps twenty thousand measurements, or written words which record twenty thousand observations. If he had been dealing with things belonging to "artificial" species, fragments of rock, stories of savage customs, the imports and exports of commercial harbours, etc., the need for such a Record would have made itself felt much sooner.

Now it is upon Record, consisting for the most part

of sheets of white paper, with black ink-marks on them, and called maps, drawings, statistics, returns, etc., that the organising Thought of the Great Society is mainly based. The advantages of these paper sheets as compared with the living tissues of the human brain are obvious. They permit of an immense system of division of labour. Twenty assistants can fill their master's notebook while the thinker occupies himself with something else. The Record, when once made, waits, without the effort of recollection or the possibility of change, until he wants it, and meanwhile can be reproduced and used with confidence by a thousand other thinkers up and down the world. A few young Australian civil engineers made the other day the map on which architects in America and Germany and England based their plans for a new Commonwealth capital. If the architects themselves had visited the site and had trusted to their memory for its characteristics, that which Napoleon used to call the "picture-making" tendency would have inevitably come into operation. Memory would have made the facts more simple and more picturesque than they actually were, and their plans would have failed when they were applied to the real site.

Professor Pickering once showed me in the Harvard Observatory photographs of regions in the sky, taken at short intervals for the purpose of ascertaining the existence of variable stars. One could see on each plate perhaps a hundred thousand stars. A being might have been evolved, and possibly has been evolved on the planet Mars, who could look at that region of the sky, impress a clear picture of it on his Memory, retain that picture unchanged for a week, look then at the same

stars again, and notice by direct comparison whether
any of them had become larger or smaller. No human
being who has ever been born could do so, and as I
looked at the plates I felt that the modern astronomer's
artificial eye with its telescopic lens three feet across
and its photographic retina of superhuman delicacy was
a small thing as an aid towards Thought about the universe when compared with the artificial memory of
warehoused plates which I saw around me, whose capacity was a thousand million times greater than that
of the human brain, and which never forgot and never
transformed.

Sometimes Record can be at once used for the answering of a scientific problem by a process of Thought
which is so simple that it may almost be taken for
granted. Professor Pickering, for instance, was able
by printing positive and negative versions of successive
plates over each other, to show, in the form of unmistakable white rings, those stars whose light had varied
in any given period. But even in astronomy there is
as a rule a long interval of hard work before the daily
photographs and measurements can be made available
for the searcher after new truth. The entomologist's
collection of moths or moth-measurements must be arranged and rearranged in graded order before they can
be made to mean anything. Before raw statistics, say
as to the relation between overcrowding and illiteracy,
can be helpful to the statesman who is preparing new
legislation, the individual cases of an overcrowded room
here and a backward child there must be "drawn together" into curves and percentages. The process by
which this is done looks at first curiously like the automatic "drawing together" of perceptions into ideas in

Memory. But it is essentially different. The grouping of Record adds nothing to and takes nothing from the original facts. It is mechanical and exact, while the grouping-process in Memory is vital and inexact.

Record has, however, for the purposes of Thought, great disadvantages as well as great advantages when compared with Memory. It is necessarily abstract. If our history of the past were as full of detail as the past itself, the whole world would not contain it. The boy's moth collection tells him nothing of the movements of the living insects. Statistics of ignorance and over-crowding tell the official before whom they are laid nothing of those indications, for instance, of accompanying congenital defect, which might have automatically formed themselves into an inexact but significant idea if he had looked closely at a hundred cases for himself and had trusted to Memory for the result. The European architect, planning an Australian capital on the careful contours of a map, may miss just those hints from concrete nature which would have made the difference between inspiration and journey-work in his drawings; the colours, perhaps, and outlines of the distant hills, the hard glare of the December sun, and the reflections of the river.

Record, again, provides material which is only useful to some one who is seeking an answer to a problem akin to that which was in the mind of the man who originally selected the quality to be isolated. The really important and seminal idea may have preceded that selection, and may have been one out of a thousand ideas which automatically presented themselves, during a period of concentrated inward attention, to a fertile mind enriched by varied concrete experiences.

Even when a man is using abstract Record, the real success of his thinking may depend on the fact that it is not really abstract to him, that the figures of backwardness do bring up pictures of faces that are not only ill-nurtured but ill-born, and that the infantile death-rate suggests those who are injured by disease as well as those who are killed. This is one of the reasons why, in a government office, the ultimate decision of great questions is left to the practical statesman with experience of the outside world, rather than to the trained official. The ideas which the statesman brings as his own contribution to each problem are founded upon fewer instances and are much less well-arranged than those of the official, but they are the result of concrete experience. And this too is one of the reasons why some of us desire that officials also shall have some concrete experience and shall not, for instance, spend their lives in administering the Poor Law without ever having seen or smelt the inside of a workhouse.

Whoever, therefore, is to think with success about the Great Society must use both Record and Memory. He requires Record because he deals with facts too numerous and too distant to be covered by his inherited powers, and because he must have exactly quantitative evidence as a basis for exactly quantitative results. He also requires a well-stored Memory because Record by itself is abstract and unfertile.

So far I have taken the problem of increasing the range and exactness and fertility of our ideas as to moths and stars and children—things which we cannot change in order to make them more easy to think about. But in many cases Thought can be made more easy by changes in the facts themselves. A chemist can abstract by analysis the common qualities of various specimens of water and thereby obtain a more useful working idea of water; but he can also practise what one may call "real" abstraction by producing and employing for his experiments actual water, which possesses those common qualities and no others, and any ounce of which may be trusted to behave under the same circumstances exactly like any other ounce.

We so treat many material things which are essential to human organisation on a large scale. The great achievement of our race in that respect has been the invention of money. World-commerce, on a scale larger than the exchange of canoes or lumps of jade, only became possible when metallurgists had reduced certain metal ores to standard metal, and governments had minted coins every one of which was practically identical with every other. And on this "real abstraction" has been founded that vast mental abstraction of money-value which alone enables the modern financier to find his way in an otherwise unintelligible world.

Every year new "currencies" are being created by the "standardisation" of iron, or sugar, or rubber, or of any new commodity which enters the world market. If one looks from the terrace of the Alexandra Palace south and east over the vast new working-class quarters which speculative firms have erected for the artisans of North London, one can watch the standardisation of homes, and in a later chaper [1] I shall discuss the relation of that process to the happiness of their inmates.

Indeed, the dominant intellectual problem of the

[1] Chapter XIII. p. 332.

Great Society (a problem whose solution may form
the basis of a new science of Jurisprudence) may be
summed up in the statement that he who thinks about
the civilised world is now compelled either to stand-
ardise it in shifting Memory and abstract Record, and
so think erroneously about it, or to attempt to stand-
ardise it in fact, and so, perhaps, destroy the only conditions of life in which man is fitted to find the satisfaction of his nature.

In enquiring whether an art of Thought exists,
whether, that is to say, we can by deliberate effort increase the range and efficiency of our thinking, I have
dealt up to this point only with those factors—material
surroundings; mental attitude; and knowledge (stored
either in Memory or Record)—which the old formal
Logic often took for granted and therefore ignored.

Now I come to Logic in the narrower sense of the
term, the processes by which new inferences arise out
of our perceptions and ideas. Is there an Art here too?
Can those processes, that is to say, be made more effective by conscious effort? Or must our analysis of
them merely aim at an explanation of facts which we
cannot change?

In answering this question I must begin with the
"mental attitudes" of Attention, Inhibition, and Problem, to which I have already referred as being rather
part of the Thought-Process than preliminary conditions of its success. In describing the means by which
the capacity of Memory may be increased I dealt with
Attention and Inhibition. But we can attend and inhibit, not only when we desire to remember what we
should otherwise forget, but when we desire to draw
inferences which would otherwise not occur to us.

If while thinking we *attend* to some particular point, presented to us either by Memory or by those sense-impressions which, as we attend to them, become memories, our Thought is likely to be concerned with that point. If our attention is turned to a geometrical figure, we may, it is true, discover in our minds the answer to a riddle which we were asked a week ago, but we are more likely to discover a geometrical conclusion of some sort. The effectiveness of this voluntary control of Attention is enormously increased by habits formed in education, and, still more, by the use of language. The verbal sounds and images which all experimenters describe as normally accompanying the more unconscious processes of thought, act as a constant directing and limiting influence on the associations and inferences which we form.

Or our attitude while thinking may be one of Inhibition. We can fight with some prospect of success against associations and inferences along one line, and, with less certainty, in favour of those along another line. Or (in the attitude of consciously "suspended" judgment) we can sometimes prevent our Thought from reaching an expected conclusion.

But at the actual moment of Thought the most important mental attitude is that which the experimentalists call "Problem" ("Aufgabe"), the feeling that we have to find an answer to some question. It is the presence, conscious or semi-conscious, of this "attitude" during, as well as after, the moment of thinking which distinguishes Reasoning from other forms of Thought. "What transforms," says Watt, "into judgments the mere sequences of experiences that we discover when we analyse the processes of judgment, and what distinguishes a judgment from a mere sequence of experiences, is the problem." [1]

I have already told how Lord Russell of Killowen turned into Reasoning all the imaginative work we had done during a certain afternoon, by suddenly treating what he found in his mind as "problem-material." Watt's experiments show, as is clear enough in any case, that Lord Russell might have voluntarily adopted this attitude early in the afternoon and have held to it throughout the afternoon. In that case the total process of his Reasoning would have been different from what it was, less fertile perhaps, but probably in closer contact with the facts.

Now by combining the attitudes of Attention and Problem we can acquire the power of compelling, with more or less certainty, our mind to attack any succession of questions which we put to it; and it is with the form and order in which such questions should be put, and the methods by which the answers to them should be tested, that the rules of Logic deal.

The original invention of logical rules must have been the result of conscious effort, and the training of any individual in the use of them may be equally conscious, although, like other rules of art, they may be "picked up" by our half-conscious observation of our fellows, or, if attained by conscious training, may become (like the rules of composition which underlay Wagner's subconscious musical production) a matter of unconscious habit.

[1] H. J. Watt, "Experimentelle Beiträge zu einer Theorie des Denkens," *Archiv f. d. ges. Psych.*, iv. (1905), p. 413 (quoted by Titchener, *Experimental Psychology of the Thought Processes*, p. 120). W. B. Pillsbury (*The Psychology of Reasoning*, p. 69) uses the word "purpose" in this sense: "the purpose or momentary mental set that controls the course of association at any moment."

It is a historical fact that human thinking has been enormously improved by the invention of logical rules in the past. Aristotle's formal syllogistic scheme seems to us now so poor and clumsy that any insistence upon it is a hindrance rather than a furtherance to Thought. But that is because we have already absorbed its main results into the words and implications of our ordinary speech. How could we think to any effect about the complexities of modern life if we had no words like "principle" and "instance" or "proof" and "disproof"? The repetition of such formulas as "All A is B" wearies us now, but they stood at one time for a passionate new conviction that nature is uniform, and that the same conditions might always be trusted to produce the same results. To understand what the invention of the syllogism gave to mankind we must compare it with that world of thought which it helped to supersede, the incalculable divinities, the contradictory maxims and proverbs, the disconnected fragments of observation and experience which make the apparatus of the primitive mind. Bacon's Organon itself, and even the Four Methods of Experimental Enquiry in Mill's *Logic,* seem inadequate and almost irrelevant to a modern man of science, simply because he takes the need of testing hypotheses by experiment for granted.

The fact that we do not realise how greatly science has been helped by logical discoveries later than Bacon is mainly due to that arbitrary distinction between Logic and Mathematics which has always been a hindrance to clear thinking about scientific method. The engineer or the actuary or the astronomer is not now told that he will require for his work a more complex Logic than Aristotle's or Bacon's, but that he must

learn certain branches of Mathematics. The making
of bridges and electrical installations, the calculation of
eclipses, or the drawing of contracts for life assurance
is now done by men whose logical methods are neither
the Barbara and Celarent of the schoolmen nor the
rules of Bacon or Mill, but such formulas as

$$P = \frac{\left(R - \dfrac{E}{c}\right) \pm \sqrt{\left(\dfrac{E}{c} - R\right)^2 + 4RF.}}{2}$$

Formulas of this degree of complexity require, of
course, that the material to which they are applied
should consist of exact Record and not of inexact
Memory, and it is the vast and constantly growing accumulation of recorded observations which has made
their use possible. And though the actual use of the
formulas is now left to technical experts, it has become
necessary to invent non-technical or half-technical
terms by which the conclusions of the experts can be
made clear to lay thinkers.

The same tendency is to be observed in the moral
sciences, Sociology, Economics, Psychology, and the
rest. A special branch of mathematical method has
been developed for each. When Professor Bowley, for
instance, published an enquiry into the probable effect
of increased mobility of labour upon the rate of wages,
he occupied a page and a half of his article with mathematical formulas of which one of the shorter specimens
is:

The increase in average wage in A is $y_1 - \bar{y} = hf'_1 (x'_1) -$
$\dfrac{h^2 f''_1}{2}(x'_1 - \theta_1 h) = hf'(x'_1 + \dfrac{h^2 f''_1}{2}(x'_1 + \theta' h)$, where θ' is a proper

fraction, and where $x'_1 = x_1 - h$.   This is positive unless the cost curve is rapidly concave.[1]

And we can already watch the beginnings of such a development of language and mental habits as shall enable these methods or something like them to control in large part the ordinary intellectual work of social organisation.   Already the economic student, when he uses the word "marginal" instead of "average," or the merchant when he speaks of a "flattening price curve," implies the application of the Differential Calculus to economics; and a few generations hence social theorists may be using, and newspaper readers may be following, forms of thought whose essential principles are now understood only by Professor Bowley and his mathematical colleagues.   But if the gap between the trained thinker and the layman in these sciences is not to widen, the present rate of the invention of terms which can be transferred from the technical to the non-technical vocabulary of the Moral Sciences must be quickened considerably.   The Permanent Secretary, for instance, to the Irish Local Government Board told the Royal Commissioner on the Civil Service:

I don't say there are not second-class clerks [who are recruited at 18] equal to first-class [who are recruited at 23], nor do I say that all first-class clerks are on the same footing as regards ability; but there is undoubtedly a line of demarcation, which any one dealing with administration easily detects, between first- and second-class clerks.[2]

His phraseology is obviously unsatisfactory, but if he had merely said that "on the average" first-class

[1] Professor A. L. Bowley in *The Economic Journal*, March, 1912, p. 52.
[2] Sir James Dougherty before the Royal Commission on the Civil Service, February 17, 1913 (Qu. 26,769).

clerks are abler than second-class clerks, he would not
have told the Commission that which he wanted to say,
viz., that, if the ability of the members of the first and
of the second class were plotted on "polygons of variation in respect to ability," the two polygons would be
similar, but that the first-class polygon would be superior to, though overlapped by, the second class. This
is the kind of statement which we all want to make a
dozen times a day about sections of every biological
species from human beings to cabbages, and I know
of no existing words in which it can be said which are
both short and clear.[1]

In the physical sciences there is no sign of any reaction against the substitution of Record for Memory,
or against the consequent invention and application
of new and more complex logical rules and terms. The
most intransigeant Pragmatist does not propose to
drop Mathematics from the training of an engineer or
a chemist, or to encourage astronomers to rely on
Memory rather than Record. But in the moral sciences, side by side with the growth of the new quasi-
mathematical Logic, there has been noticeable during
the last ten years an important revolt against all Logic,
old or new, and in favour of "instinct" or "divination."

This revolt is in part due to the defects of Record

---

[1] Perhaps some such phraseology as this may become possible
in the future. "I estimate that the second class is naturally two-
thirds below the first class, and nurturally three-quarters." This
would mean that in respect of natural ability two-thirds of the
members of the second class are below the mean of the first class;
and that, when the effects of a shorter education, less stimulating
work, etc., are allowed for, three-quarters of them are, in fact, below
that mean. On the same lines, in a "feminist" discussion, an actual
clash of different estimates, e.g., as to the relative physical or mental powers of men and women, might take the place of much beating of the air by arguments about "equality" and "inequality" that
never meet.

when applied to mankind. Record, as I have already said, is abstract and incomplete unless it rests upon that artificial uniformity which I called "real abstraction," and the "real abstraction" of men is impossible. In the case of steel billets supplied to the same specification it is very nearly true that two and two make four; in the case of men it is very gravely untrue. We are apt, therefore, to feel that we are given a choice, in the Logic of the moral sciences, between the mathematical treatment of misleading statistics and the syllogistic treatment of casual generalisations.

But a more important cause of the revolt is a general spread of Anti-Intellectualism. The absence of a satisfactory Logic has helped to discredit not only the conscious rules of Thought, but the Thought-Process itself.

Of one form of modern Anti-Intellectualism I have already spoken, that represented by Mr. McDougall and, less definitely, by M. Ribot. According to Mr. McDougall, Thought is not (as I believe) an independently stimulated Disposition, but an "apparatus" which can only be set in motion by one of the "instincts." [1]

Another more common and more subtle form of Anti-Intellectualism is the view that Thought, though it can act independently of Instinct, is less efficient than Instinct as a means of drawing valid conclusions about the world in which we live. Professor James wrote in one of his last books:

All philosophies are hypotheses, to which all our faculties, emotional as well as logical, help us, and the truest of which will at the final integration of things be found in

[1] *Ante,* p. 39.

possession of the men whose faculties on the whole had the best divining power.[1]

Some of his followers go further and say or imply that our "emotional" faculties should be trusted to the actual exclusion of our "logical" faculties.

Now in what does this "divining" power of Instinct consist, and in what way does it differ from Thought? In order to answer this I must repeat what I have already said more than once,[2] that when any one of our instinctive dispositions is stimulated by our environment the process of stimulation involves something equivalent to an estimation of the fact which stimulates. I have just described the simplest form of that estimation, the "instinctive classification" by which the fact that we desire to eat an apple is equivalent to a decision that the thing before us belongs to the class of edible things. Now this instinctive estimation in its more complex forms is equivalent, not merely to an act of classification, but to the drawing of elaborate inferences as to future occurrences. If, that is to say, we use the term "Instinctive Classification" for the decision implied in the fact that a kitten seeing a bird for the first time desires to eat it and thereby classes it as edible, we are entitled to use the term "Instinctive Inference" for that which is implied in the fact that the kitten goes through a number of complex (and apparently fully conscious) hunting movements in anticipation of the probable actions of a frightened bird.

Now it is this "Instinctive Inference" which James calls "divination" and which others treat as an alternative to logical Thought. A man sitting on a mountain

[1] *Essays on Radical Empiricism,* p. 279.
[2] See *ante,* p. 201.

slope sees a rock above him move, and leaps aside. If he acts by Instinctive Inference the first thing that reaches his consciousness will be a shock of fear accompanying the movement of his muscles in leaping. The inference that danger exists may be as implicit as that which takes place when a flash of lightning stops the beating of our heart, or when a newly born infant, held over a bath, clings to the nurse's hand.

On the other hand, the climber's experience may begin with Thought. He may notice that a distant tree which he saw a few moments ago is now invisible, and may sit still for perhaps a second vaguely wondering what has happened and subconsciously arranging his ideas on the subject. He may carry his Thought to its full conclusion, and may infer that the rock is moving, and that, being in the line of its fall, he is in danger, before the instinct of Fear "values" his inference for him. Or he may only carry the process of Thought to the point of forming a clear mental image of a moving rock, and Fear may then interrupt his thinking with an instinctive "decision" to leap. If one of two men sitting together goes through the purely instinctive process and the other the full Thought-Process, an onlooker will see them both stare at the rock and both leap aside, but may notice that the man who reached his conclusion by Thought was rather slower to act, and that his face bore for an instant a puzzled and vacant rather than a frightened expression.

At the moment of action a man will in such a case probably have no choice as to whether he shall act by Thought or Instinctive Inference. But in forming his mental habits he has a real choice. An experienced climber may, for instance, advise a novice either to

trust Instinct always, and to leap before he gives himself time to think, or to train himself to keep a constant
lookout for little signs of danger, which do not excite
Instinct, but can be interpreted by Thought, and then
if Fear comes on him before Thought, to inhibit, until
Thought has had time to take place, the impulse towards instinctive action. Even when dealing with
much more complex affairs, a man may be aware of this
distinction. Bismarck, for instance, in one of his rare
moods of introspection, said, "I have often noticed that
my will has decided before my thinking was finished." [1]

Now the fact that it is still possible to argue that Instinctive Inference is superior to Reasoning in the
Moral Sciences, and that it is not possible to do so in
the case of the Physical Sciences, has come about, not
only because of the inexactness of the picture of mankind given us by Record as compared with the exactness of the picture which Record gives us of dead matter, but also because our perception of our fellow-men
stimulates in us many more instinctive dispositions and
stimulates them much more intensely than does our
perception of the inorganic world.

The number of dispositions, other than the "intellectual" dispositions of Curiosity and Thought, which
are stimulated by inanimate objects is small. A moving rock, by exception, does look terrible the moment
we see it, but the chemicals in a test-tube are not likely

---

[1] Quoted by Lord Morley at Manchester University, June 28,
1912. Note that I do not here dogmatise as to whether Thought
and Instinctive Inference may not have been developed out of the
same facts inherited from our prevertebrate ancestors, but merely
claim that, at the present point of human evolution, the disposition
to go through the process of Thought may be stimulated as an
alternative to the stimulation of the simpler disposition leading to
"instinctive" behaviour.

to produce any immediate emotional effect on us. At the most the chemist may find that the beauty of colouring in some mixture of reagents is starting in him an irrelevant access of æsthetic feeling.

Non-human animals constitute the appropriate stimulus to a greater number of instincts. A physiologist who is about to inoculate a dog will hardly do so without some intrusive painful emotion.[1] But by far the most important and extensive group of instincts are those whose appropriate stimulus is the presence or the idea of our fellow human beings. The juryman who tries to concentrate his attention on the evidence as to the guilt or innocence of a prisoner before him finds that his thinking is constantly accompanied or interrupted by pity or dislike or dread. The orator answering difficult questions before an excited audience, the general sending a favourite regiment to certain destruction as part of his plan of battle, find it difficult merely to compare facts and draw conclusions. Bentham, in that sarcastic commentary on French revolutionary thought which he called "Anarchical Fallacies," compares the cool logic of the great French eighteenth-century chemists with the welter of feeling and instinctive emotion in which Sieyès and the other French political thinkers of that time did their intellectual work. "In chemistry," he says, "there is no room for passion to step in and to confound the understanding—to lead men into error, and to shut their eyes against knowledge; in legislation the circumstances are opposite and vastly different."[2]

---

[1] A writer in *The Times* (March 13, 1914), describing the process by which a starving plague infected flea infects its host, speaks of "the wretched flea."

[2] Bentham, "Anarchical Fallacies," *Works,* vol. ii. p. 522.

The question whether we ought to train ourselves to accept or reject the Instinctive Inferences offered us by such emotions is, of course, one of morals as well as of science. The crowds who gathered in 1912 to hear Professor Bergson lecture in London did so mainly in the hope of obtaining moral guidance. They may not have accepted M. Bergson's full doctrine of the separation between the worlds of action and reason, but most of them left the room after each of M. Bergson's brilliant lectures, inclined to think that they might let themselves go, in accepting the evidence of feeling in Ethics and Theology, beyond the point which they had hitherto thought justifiable.

Reliance on Instinct against Reason has been the characteristic of conservative thinkers from the time when Aristophanes attacked Socrates and Euripides in *The Clouds;* and since the French Revolution, that characteristic has dominated throughout Europe the opposition to "logical" democracy. It was this tradition which Seeley was carrying on when he said in 1891:

I treat government not as a conscious contrivance, but as a half-instinctive product of the effort which human beings make to ward off from themselves certain evils to which they are exposed.[1]

Lord Morley, on the other hand, was following in the steps of his favourite pre-revolutionary thinkers of eighteenth-century France when he quoted Spinoza's statement:

When I have applied my mind to politics so that I might examine what belongs to politics with the same freedom of

[1] *Political Science*, 1896, p. 129 *n.*

mind as we use for mathematics, I have taken my best pains not to laugh at the actions of mankind, not to groan over them, not to be angry with them, but to understand them.[1]

In the end it is the psychological question of fact which will have to settle the ethical question of conduct. Does history show that Instinct or Reason is the better guide? It is easy enough to make out a strong case for Instinct. In the strange world which is revealed to us in Dr. J. G. Frazer's *Golden Bough* that which shocks us most is often the victory of Reason over Instinct, the killing and eating of a well-loved king because Reason indicated that in that way alone could the strength of the tribe be preserved, or the execution by an affectionate husband of a wife who brought forth twins. The history of later times is full of the tragic failures of those who, like Calvin and Torquemada, or Lilburne and Robespierre, or Joseph II., were willing "to follow Reason whithersoever she should lead," even in despite of natural feeling.

And yet if Reason has slain its thousands, the acceptance of Instinct as evidence has slain its tens of thousands. Day by day, in the ordinary direction of their lives, men have learnt during hundreds of generations how untrustworthy is the interpretation of fact which Instinct offers, and how bitter is the truth contained in such proverbs as "Anger is a bad counsellor" or "Love is blind." The proprietors of the tables at Monte Carlo and the organisers of State lotteries have learnt to calculate with quantitative exactness the degree to which the gambler's hope will distort his estimation of his actual chances. At the end of a year's work in the Law Courts one can ask the barristers how

[1] "Address to Manchester University," *Times,* November 23, 1911.

often they have been engaged on the right and how often on the wrong side. The two totals should obviously be equal, but those whom I have asked have always told me that they believed 60 or 70 per cent of their clients had been in the right, and have admitted at once that their conclusion has been influenced by their instincts of goodwill or of combat.

And in greater matters than litigation or gambling the distortion of evidence by the process of Instinctive Inference is responsible for an appalling proportion of the weary sum of human misery. Wars are often started and maintained, neither from mere blind anger nor because those on either side find that they desire the results which a cool calculation of the conditions makes them regard as probable, but largely because men insist on treating their feelings as evidence of fact, and refuse to believe that they can be so angry without sufficient cause.

In the Great Society both the danger of Instinctive Inference and the comparative reliability of Reason yearly increase. The mere growth of the scale of our social organisation has destroyed, in the case of popular decisions on national policy, the main advantage which Instinctive Inference could claim, that it was stimulated, not by abstract generalisations, but by a direct perception of our concrete environment. Those things which during a war-fever or an election now stimulate our instincts, the caricatures and posters, the flags and tunes, the cunningly constructed entities of "foreigner" and "landlord" and "agitator," even the personalities of the Kaiser or Mr. Lloyd George, make up a world at least as far removed from concrete reality as the world of Nature and Liberty, Republican Rome and the Social Contract in the mind of Robespierre. There always seems to me, for instance, something grimly ironical in Mr. Garvin's constantly implied exhortation to his readers that they should trust to their plain unsophisticated feelings to guide their action with regard to that "Germany" whose every feature is the work of Mr. Garvin's own well-practised pen.

I have already said that Instinctive Inference is implied in, is indeed identical with, all our impulses towards instinctive action. But in the Great Society instinctive action on a great scale is impossible. A hundred thousand men cannot surge passionately into Hyde Park. However completely they may be under the sway of Instinct, they will not get through the gates unless some one with a map and a list of marshals before him has worked out a route and a time-table. The vague impulses of modern nations can only result in corporate action on lines which some one, whether wise or foolish, has deliberately laid down. If in America to-day the ablest men should take Seeley's implied advice and stand by to watch passively the results of the "half-instinctive" political efforts of a population of a hundred million souls, those efforts would express themselves in the creation of new political machinery deliberately invented by less able men. Between 1832 and 1870 many Englishmen felt a "half-instinctive" anger with the local institutions that had been developed during the eighteenth century. But the only men who then seriously thought about the structure of British Local Government were a rather slow-witted disciple of Bentham called Chadwick, and an ex-lecturer on phrenology called Toulmin Smith,

and the plan actually adopted was an unworkable compromise between their two schemes.

And both the development of more delicate logical
methods and the accumulation of recorded observations
are, in fact, now making deliberate Thought about
mankind less inexact and misleading than at any other
point in history. A doctor now may honestly believe,
what a doctor in the Middle Ages must often have
doubted, that the conclusion to which he comes by observing symptoms and comparing them, in the attitude
of suspended judgment, with the statements in his
books, is more trustworthy than the first unsophisticated emotion of fear or hope that is excited by his
patient's general appearance.[1] The linen-covered files
of papers which help the statesman to form his decisions, though they are still abstract and incomplete,
yet come every year into a more real connection with
the complex human beings whom his decisions will
affect.

If, therefore, we are now forced to choose between
Instinctive Inference and Thought in the direction of
the Great Society, we must choose Thought. In fact,
however, the problem before us is not to be settled by
a single choice. At any one moment we can reject the
evidence of feeling on a question of fact, or we may
even form a habit of being on the watch to prevent
"our will deciding before our thinking is finished." But

---

[1] In medicine a certain amount even of "real abstraction" is now
possible. The tuberculosis bacillus which a general practitioner
sends to the analytical laboratory is much the same whether it
comes from one patient or another. And the letters which many
consultants daily receive from less experienced practitioners would
show, I believe, that the medieval rule (invaluable in its time) that
no man should prescribe for a patient whom he has not seen is now
constantly and wisely broken through.

our Thought must still go on in the presence of a constant accompaniment of Feeling, and the relation between them will be of vital importance to the social efficiency of both Thought and Feeling. At present that relation, even in the most conscientious thinker, is apt to be confused and accidental. Let any one who has ever seriously tried to "think out" a sociological problem for himself try to remember what actually occurred to him. Let us suppose that in 1903, when the problem of Free Trade and Protection suddenly became actual in England, he recognised with shame that his own opinions on the subject were merely the result of habit or family tradition. He rearranged his household customs so as to enable him to read with concentration on two evenings a week and to have a fire in his study on Sunday mornings in winter. He honestly tried to keep himself in the mental attitude of "suspended judgment." He subscribed to a second daily paper which opposed his own party, read perhaps half-a-dozen books on the fiscal question, and three times as many pamphlets and magazine articles, and argued daily with a friend in the morning train.

He voted on one side or the other at the election of 1906. What really happened to him during the intervening three years? He probably followed up from time to time arguments which were as purely logical as Professor Bowley's mathematical analysis of the wages problem, though less technical in form. His previous opinions may have been confirmed or shaken by them. He may have thought that some particular statement of the problem left out an important factor or that some argument involved a logical fallacy. He probably had reason to be thankful that a good deal of fragmentary

thinking got itself arranged and filled out during sleep
or in periods of wordless reverie.

But, unless he was a very unusual man, it is not
likely that he could honestly say that he reached his
final conclusion by the sole process of combining a
series of logical steps into one demonstration. The
"telling" arguments on one side or the other probably
left in his memory, not so much a series of premises
to be used as the basis of future conclusions, but a
slightly increased sense of discomfort or reassurance.
The decisive moments in the "making up of his mind"
were not when a calculation of his own was confirmed
or disproved by the Board of Trade returns, but when
he felt with a flash of hot conviction that he hated the
typical Cobdenite or the typical Tariff Reformer. He
knew what his decision was when he heard himself
saying, "I can't and won't vote for a set of men like
that."

The fact that, at the end of the three years of reconsideration, so enormously large a proportion of
thoughtful Conservatives found that they were convinced Protectionists, and of thoughtful Liberals that
they were convinced Free Traders, does not speak very
highly for the efficiency of the whole process. Even
Mr. Sidney Webb (whose name would first occur to
many English politicians in search of a type of passionless intellectuality) acknowledges in a tone of regret that "We are almost irresistibly tempted to judge,
as between different schemes, according to our own
liking for them," [1] whether that "liking" is due to a
careful valuation by feeling of purely intellectual con-

---

[1] Sidney Webb in *The Crusade* for August 1912, p. 151.

clusions, or merely to a preference, due to habit, or loyalty, or friendship, for certain lines of argument.

If we are to do better than this we must undertake a systematic enquiry into the relation between Feeling and Thought. Such an enquiry will need the time and patience and personal evidence of many students, but it will lead, I think, to the conclusion that we can consciously substitute some measure of order for mere accident in the emotional side of our intellectual life.

I have already, for instance, spoken of the relation between Instinctive Feeling and Thought in the *valuation* of our intellectual conclusions. When we have decided what the result of any course of action will be, it is our whole nature, and not merely one intellectual disposition, which must be called in to decide whether that result is good or bad for us.

Any one of our Instincts can again serve as the *motive* which impels us to undertake and continue the toil of Thought, without, if we see clearly the facts of our nature, distorting either the methods or the conclusions of our Thought. A Moltke when he is preparing mobilisation plans, or a cancer-student when he comes from the hospital to sit, tired but determined, at his microscope, may learn to make patriotism or pity the driving force in his long search for truth. Perhaps some day religion may so far escape from its present bewildering confusion between emotion and belief that the passionate love excited by contemplation of the universe may be, for those born with the religious genius, not evidence for the supernatural authority of this creed or that, but the motive which sustains them in a lifelong search for that which lies behind all the creeds.

Sometimes the conclusions of Instinctive Inference may be made the *material* of unbiassed Thought. When a man of affairs finds himself saying: "I don't *see* Smith doing that," or, while interviewing candidates for office, deliberately jots down some sign indicating his first impression, he may fairly (if he knows exactly what he is doing) treat the instinctive conclusions of real or remembered "physiognomy" as being part of the evidence for a final reasoned conclusion. And a woman may fairly use in Thought the greater natural skill in that respect which is apparently one of the "secondary characteristics" of sex.

Instinct again helps Thought by increasing the *range* of our associations and inferences. The first connection between the idea already in our mind and the other ideas which it calls up is often provided by one of our simpler dispositions. Every thinker, like every poet, knows the truth of that which Wundt, after much introspection, declared, that "Feeling is the pioneer of Knowledge," and it is often the case that "a novel thought may come to consciousness first of all in the form of a feeling" [1]—however rigorous may be the logical test to which we afterwards submit it.

But the most essential factor in the relation between Emotion and Thought is to be found in the Emotion of Thought itself. So far, in this section of my argument, I have followed the usage of ordinary speech in distinguishing between the Instincts (*i.e.* all our dispositions other than Thought and its allies) and Thought. But since, as I argued in Chapter III., Thought is a true disposition, it, like all the other dis-

[1] Wundt, *Principles of Physiological Psychology,* ii. (1893) pp. 501, 521; iii. 121 f., 625, quoted by Titchener, *Psychology of Thought Processes,* p. 103.

positions, has not only its appropriate group of stimuli and its appropriate course of action, but also its appropriate emotion—an emotion which may be heightened into passion and harmonised by the sense of ordered beauty.

It is the passion, not of Love or Fame, but of Thought itself which controls the noblest moments of Dante's *Paradiso* or Lucretius' *De Rerum Naturæ*. Milton, in 1644, drew for all time a picture of a whole nation inspired by that passion. He notes both the sworn lovers of philosophy, the "pens and heads . . . sitting by their studious lamps, musing, searching, revolving new notions and ideas," and also the "cheerfulness of the people . . . as in a body when the blood is fresh, the spirits pure and vigorous, not only to the vital but to the rational faculties," so that "our hearts are now more capacious, our thoughts more erected to the search and expectation of greatest and exactest things." [1]

"The search and expectation of greatest and exactest things" is the passion of Thought itself, unhelped and uncoloured by any lower Instinct.

[1] *Areopagitica*, pp. 92, 96, 98.

PART II

CHAPTER XI

THE ORGANISATION OF THOUGHT

In the following three chapters I shall approach my problem from a new point of view. So far I have been examining facts of human psychology with the purpose of discovering how they can be adapted to the needs of the Great Society. Now I shall examine existing forms of organisation in the Great Society with the purpose of discovering how far they can be improved by a closer adaptation to the facts of human psychology.

I shall not hope to succeed in inventing any new social system, and even in the tentative suggestions which I shall put forward I shall run the risk of discrediting a method of enquiry which may be right by connecting it with practical proposals which may be wrong. My treatment will be "insular," for my instances will be mainly drawn from those English facts with which alone I have any real familiarity. But at least I shall not have left my analysis in the air.

At the first approach to this side of my subject I must deal with a verbal difficulty which has been the cause of constant misunderstanding. Most of the terms used to express the general idea of organised association between human beings have been taken either from collocations of inanimate things, as in the case of "mechanism," or "system," or from single animate things, as in the case of "body" or "organism." If we use the inanimate terms we are apt to imply either that the associated human beings do not influence each other at all, or that they only influence each other in the simple way in which one piece of inanimate matter influences another by impinging upon it. If we use the animate terms we are apt to imply, not merely that the associated human beings influence each other vitally and consciously, but that their association itself has a conscious life of its own, apart from the many lives of the individuals who constitute it—that a community is an "organism" or "body" in the same sense in which a man is.

In order to avoid both these implications I shall use the word "organisation." By a happy accident of speech "organisation" suggests an arrangement the constituent parts of which are alive, without suggesting, as "organism" does, that the arrangement itself has a "super-life" or a "super-consciousness" of its own. Such a "super-consciousness" may of course exist, and conscious men may be related to a conscious society as individually conscious blood-corpuscles would be related to the man of whom they were part. But if any one believes that this is the case, he should say so with the utmost definiteness, instead of vaguely implying it by the use of such terms as "social organism," "social consciousness," or "social will." I myself believe that there is in fact no evidence whatever that a self-conscious society in that sense does exist.

I shall group the Organisations which I am considering by reference to the psychological facts with which they are mainly concerned. For this purpose I shall need a different psychological scheme from that which

I have hitherto used. In Chapter II. I made a classification on the plane of "structure," and on that plane divided the relevant facts of human psychology into "Complex Dispositions," Instinctive or Intelligent,[1] Now, as I there indicated, I shall cross-classify the same facts by dealing with them on the plane of consciousness, and dividing them into the "elementary" classes of Cognition, Feeling, and Conation.

Every conscious psychological event is, according to a well-known analysis, "at once" (I quote Mr. McDougall's excellent little *Psychology* in the Home University Series) "a knowing, a being affected, and a striving; or, in technical terms, a cognition, an affection . . . and a conation" (p. 61). Cognition, Affection, and Conation, as Mr. McDougall points out, do not exist apart from each other. "The affection and the striving," he says, are "consequential upon the knowing, and the character of the striving" is "in some degree determined by the affection," and "in turn the striving reacts upon the knowing and leads to modification of the feeling" (p. 61). But he adds that, although "every mental process is at once a knowing, an affection, and a striving," one of the aspects may be dominant, and we may legitimately call a mental process by the name of its dominant aspect; "thus we speak of acts of perception, recognition, recollection, reasoning, when we are predominantly cognitive; of states of emotion, or feeling, when affection is dominant; of volition, resolution, deciding, desiring, when we are vividly conscious of striving towards an end" (p. 63).

The same is true of Organisations. A conscious hu-

[1] See p. 27.

man being in carrying out the functions appropriate to membership of any Organisation is always simultaneously knowing and feeling and willing, and his knowledge and feeling and will not only interact on each other but are, perhaps, in the ultimate analysis, merely different conscious aspects of one vital process. And yet a particular Organisation may be predominantly concerned with one aspect only, and may therefore be rightly classified by a reference to that one. A Royal Commission, for instance, is an Organisation predominantly concerned with knowing. The Commissioners are directed to collect evidence and to assist each other to draw conclusions from that evidence. But the conclusions of individual Commissioners will differ, not only according to their industry in studying the evidence and their acuteness in thinking about it, but also according to variations in their desires. Every Royal Commission is therefore, to a certain extent, a Will-Organisation, a machine by which persons of different desires are enabled to form compromises and act by the votes of the majority; and some Royal Commissions prove, when they get to work, to be almost exclusively Will-Organisations, and hardly Thought-Organisations at all. A Trade Union is predominantly a Will-Organisation, concerned with collecting, welding, and enforcing the desires of its members. But the proceedings, both of its executive and of its branches, consist very largely, and sometimes predominantly, in the organisation of concerted Thought. The Organisation created by a Shop Hours Regulation Bill aims primarily at securing a feeling of comfort among those employed in retail trades. It is therefore predominantly a Feeling-Organisation or, as I shall call it to avoid ambiguity, a

Happiness-Organisation. But all legislation which shortens the hours of regular work, not only makes effective political thinking by the wage-earners more possible, and is so far part of the national Thought-Organisation, but may be intended to enable them to form and manage associations for carrying out their political desires, and may therefore be part of the national Will-Organisation.

While following this general classification on the plane of consciousness, I shall, of course, at the same time have in my mind my earlier and more detailed classification on the plane of structure. In fact without the simultaneous use of the two classifications it is extremely difficult to get and retain that concrete conception of psychological fact, which, like binocular vision, is required by any one who is to see the real world in its true perspective. The three chapters will deal therefore with "Thought-Organisation," "Will-Organisation," and "Happiness-Organisation."

The problems with which I shall have to deal in each of the three chapters will be alike in that they arise from the change of social scale which has created the Great Society. If the fact that our present society is larger than any that has existed before merely meant that it contained the same number of individuals magnified as in the field of a microscope, no new problem of organisation would result. But it means that our society contains a larger number of individuals of the same size as before, and that therefore the relation of those individuals to each other is changed. The average citizen of twentieth-century London is of nearly the same height as the average citizen of modern Andorra or medieval Florence. His eyes see no further, his memory holds no more. If he is tested in a psychological laboratory, the "reaction-time" intervening between his sensations and his conceptions is the same. And in more conscious and less easily measurable respects, such as fertility of mental association, or strength and range of affection, the Londoner and the Andorrist are both subject to similar inherited limitations, which are none the less real because they are sometimes better represented by a curve of decreasing efficiency in learning to carry out increased functions than by a hard line separating what a man can from what he cannot do.

The fact, therefore, that any particular institution works well in Andorra, or worked well in medieval Florence, creates no presumption that it will work well in London. If, in London, we retain a medieval governing body unchanged in form and numbers, its working will be changed, because brains and wills of the same size will have to deal with enormously more numerous and more complex questions. If the governing body itself is merely increased in numbers to meet the increased work, the relation of its members to each other will be by that fact changed, so that the larger body may be able to do less, instead of more, than the smaller. A change of scale in the functions of any organisation may indeed require, not merely its modification, but the invention of a new organisation on a totally different plan.

For the rest, therefore, of this chapter I shall be dealing with those institutions in the Great Society whose main function is the Organisation of Thought.

For this purpose I will first try to make clear what

I mean by Organised as distinguished from Individual Thought. Before the invention of writing, that distinction must have been easy. A man who engaged in serious and continued Thought did so either while dealing, in solitude and silence, with material provided by his own memory and imagination, or while forming one of an arguing group who constantly provided each other with new facts and diverted in new directions the course of each other's mental associations. The only type of Thought, as to which any difficulty in deciding whether it was Individual or Organised could occur, was that which took place during a "one-sided" oral communication; when a disciple, for instance, listened in silence to his teacher, or the members of a crowd too large for argument were addressed by an orator or prophet.

As soon, however, as writing was invented, it was possible for intercommunication of Thought to take place without bodily presence. A thinker could then write in solitude arguments addressed to unknown readers, or read in solitude the arguments of others. In such a case Thought is "Individual" if the moment at which it takes place is alone considered, and "Organised" if the whole process from the original writing to the final reading is considered together. In the Great Society, owing to the enormous distribution of printed and written matter, this last form of Organised Thought has become typical. We do the main body of that intellectual work which depends upon organised communication with our fellows, rather while reading books and letters in studies and at office desks than while hearing and uttering spoken words in monastery cloisters, or university halls, or political hustings, or at the meetings of "Merchant Adventurers."

It will be convenient to call this newer type of Thought-Organisation "impersonal." The older "personal" forms of Thought-Organisation in groups and committees and assemblies still, however, survive among us, owing partly to traditional habit, and partly to the more permanent fact that our psychological nature was evolved under conditions of personal intercourse, and that impersonal intercourse leaves some of our powers unused, and, therefore, some of our needs unsatisfied.

Of these older forms of organisation, the simplest and oldest is that which is constituted by a small number of persons—from two to perhaps seven or eight—who meet together for the purpose of sustained oral discussion. This form may be studied at its finest point of development in the dialogues of Plato. It is, as the Greeks knew, extraordinarily difficult. At first sight it might appear that the main condition of its success is that it should be as little "organised" as possible, that the group should meet by accident, and that each member of the group should freely obey his casual impulses both in speaking and in remaining silent. But a closer examination shows that the full efficiency of argument, carried on even by the most informal body of friends, requires not only that each should be master of the most delicate shades of the same language, and that each should be accustomed to make use of similar rules of Thought, but that they should have a large body of knowledge in common, that each should be familiar with the peculiar strength and weakness of each of the others, and, above all, that each should be influenced by the same desire to follow truth "whither-soever the argument may lead." All this requires that the group should consist, not of men of average powers who have come accidentally together, but of men se-lected (as Socrates, for instance, selected his disciples) in some way which should secure that the worst of them should possess a rather unusual share of natural ability, acquired training, and interest in ideas. And normally, the necessary discipline and concentration cannot be secured unless some one of the party is ac-cepted by the others as a leader, and does not abuse his position.

Philosophy, in the widest sense of that term, began in such group-discussions. But the elastic art of "dia-lectic" by which they were regulated became fixed and unprogressive, and its system of question and answer became, in the hands of the medieval schoolmen, as I have already said, a very inefficient code of directions for individual thinking.

In the modern world, and especially during the last two generations, the "dialectic" art has, outside the law courts, been greatly neglected; and nothing would per-haps more startle a disciple of Socrates who should re-turn to life among us, than to listen to the futile at-tempts of three or four exceptionally able English pro-fessional men to thrash out after dinner some philo-sophical or political question. Many men who now do hard intellectual work with some success have, like the late Duke of Devonshire, never acquired the power of following a verbal argument at all.[1]

[1] B. Holland, *Life of the Duke of Devonshire*, vol. ii. p. 241. "It was no doubt a difficulty for him in Cabinet Council that a decision was usually arrived at by swifter intellects before he had been able to formulate even to himself his own position." In any case, men

Philosophers and scientists, whether men or women, generally live now a long way from each other in great cities; and they are mostly married and take more seriously than did the Greeks the duty of social intercourse with their families. At the same time, even in the case of the more abstract forms of professed Thought, the decay of dialectic is largely due to the quantitative pressure of modern knowledge and modern needs. Philosophers and scientists, like other men, have now to economise time. Reading is quicker than listening, and concentrated individual Thought than the verbal exposition and counter-exposition of arguments, while the printing-press enables a man who has anything important to say to address the eyes of those interested in his subject in a whole nation or the whole civilised world rather than the ears of a few friends.

The modern scientist, again, does much of his thinking while he is closely observing concrete facts with microscope or balance, and we have not yet developed a system of oral dialectic suitable for more than two persons so occupied. When a group of men argue personally about some point of natural science, the actual material before them has generally to be provided, not by the sharp evidence of Record or of concrete observation, but by that Memory which the modern man of science is trained to mistrust.

No one desires to return to the old belief that oral dialectic is a sufficient guide to truth without direct observation and solitary Thought. But I myself believe that the degree to which we have abandoned it is un-

---

of the "audible" type of mind have a natural advantage, apart from training, over the "visualisers" (of whom the Duke was probably one) in oral argument.

fortunate. Dialectic is slow and inexact, but in many
sciences, and particularly in those whose subject-matter
is human action and feeling, it has magnificent possibilities of fertility. Here and there, indeed, a few
among those Englishmen who attempt the task of
Thought are enabled for a few months or years to sup-
plement their individual work by discussion carried on
under something like Athenian conditions. Some physical defect may have prevented them when undergraduates from devoting to organised athletics all the energy they could spare from their books, or some accident of career or of temperament may have, a few
years later, prevented them from being entirely absorbed by their several professions. If so they probably remember the hours so spent as the most fruitful
in their whole intellectual life.

But if the art of dialectic is to be revived, it must
make such use of the economies of the printing-press as
is not inconsistent with its essential advantages, and
must bring into conscious recognition a number of
psychological considerations which Aristotle, in fram-
ing his rules of Logic, could take for granted.

For the mere purpose of giving information, speaking
has no advantage over reading. A dialectical group
will, therefore, be generally wise to read some agreed
book before meeting, or to deal with some subject with
the facts of which they are familiar in their individual
work. They will find that the real advantages of
group-dialectic are those which books cannot give. One
of them is a great extension of the range of immediate
mental "association." In individual Thought the
thinker waits (in the Problem-Attitude) till some
promising idea comes into his mind and then dwells on

it till further ideas spring from it. A group of people, however, engaged in dialectic can, like a pack of hounds, follow up the most promising idea which occurs to any one of them. This means that a rule, for instance, requiring the members of such a group to speak in regular order is wrong, as it prevents ideas being brought forward at the moment of their greatest relevance. But if free interjection is allowed, it must be so managed as to prevent any member of the group causing what Socrates, in *The Clouds,* called the "miscarriage" of ideas amongst the rest. Here the art of dialectic can learn from the introspective evidence of individual thinking. Students who write down their conscious experiences while answering problems in psychological laboratories describe the verbal form of the ideas which successively present themselves and are rejected before the most relevant one is chosen for prolonged consideration, as being curiously bare and curt.[1] A member of an arguing group should generally put his first claim on the attention of his fellows into the same curt form, which takes the minimum of time, can be forgotten in an instant, and if rejected does not interfere with the subconscious process of association in the rest.

But the relevance of an idea is not always immediately apparent, and therefore, in a well-chosen group of joint thinkers, if any one is impelled, as was Thrasym-

---

[1] See, *e.g.,* the instances given by Kakise in his paper on "The Conscious Concomitants of Understanding" (*The American Journal of Psychology,* January 1911, pp. 15-64). Even when the visual and kinetic images accompanying Understanding are described as full and complex the words accompanying them were apparently few and simple. "Isolated words," he says (*loc. cit.* p. 58), "as a rule awoke richer content-feeling than those given in phrases. A single noun awoke frequently a richer content-feeling than did a short phrase." See also Marbe, *Experimentell-Psychologische Untersuchungen über das Urteil* (Leipzig, 1901).

achus in Plato's *Republic,* to "leap like a wild beast" into the discussion, he should be allowed to do so, and to indicate the intensity of his impulse by the heightening of his voice. If his conviction of the supreme, though unapparent, relevance of his ideas proves generally to be unfounded, the group can be reorganised without him. We are none of us, indeed, "unbribed judges" of our own thoughts, and a man who really tries to make use of oral discussion would do well to aim at taking, in a series of evenings, not much more than his equal arithmetical fraction of the common time.

Perhaps the greatest advantage of oral dialectic arises, however, from the relation, which I described in Chapter X., between Instinctive Inference and Thought. When friends meet together, that which is most valuable, even as intellectual stimulus, may be found in those things, too delicate for our clumsy words, which were present when Socrates sat in the inner court of Cephalus's house at the Piræus, and which are absent when a modern thinker sits down alone to review a new book or to test a colleague's experiment; the ripples of laughter, the unuttered kindnesses, the suggestion that the effort of Thought is supremely worth while and its successes supremely delightful, even the occasional silences, unembarrassed and almost unnoticed. M. Maeterlinck revealed a deep experience of personal intercourse when he wrote with deliberate paradox:

It is idle to think that, by means of words, any real communication can ever pass from one man to another. The lips or the tongue may represent the soul, even as a cypher or a number may represent a picture of Memling, but from the moment that we have something to say to each other we are compelled to hold our peace.[1]

While, therefore, the logical requirements of the art of oral dialectic in its finest form would include the common acceptance of recognised rules of Thought, its psychological requirements may be found to include the common acceptance of a code of manners, French or Italian perhaps rather than English, which will allow Feeling to play without shame round the whole process of Thinking.

And, finally, it must be remembered that while personal dialectic is, for certain purposes, still one of the best means of discovering new truth, it is no longer of importance as a means of disseminating truth when discovered. Just as its subject-matter must be now drawn in the main, not from the personal knowledge of a group of friends, but from the larger world of books, so its results, if they are to influence modern life, must be returned to that larger world for distribution.

It is singular that we English, who neglect more than other nations the personal dialectic of small groups as a means of arriving at general truths, trust much more than do other nations the conduct of our municipal and national affairs to the oral deliberations of larger and more formal Councils and Committees. This is, perhaps, mainly due to the fact that such bodies are often more efficient as Will-Organisations than as Thought-Organisations. Men who could not invent new truths by verbal discussion can yet find a way on

[1] *The Treasure of the Humble* (trans.), p. 4.

such bodies to working compromises between different
interests. The distinction between Will and Thought
may be difficult to draw at any moment in the complex consciousness of an individual councillor engaged
in "making up his mind" how to vote. But in the procedure of a deliberative assembly it is unmistakable.
An experienced listener can always distinguish between
the speaker (often, unfortunately, looked on by the
rest as a bore) who is consciously engaged in the eliciting of truth by argument, and the "practical man" who
has done any thinking that he permits himself beforehand, and is now only anxious to make his decision
prevail.

The "intellectualist" Whigs who passed the Municipal Reform Act of 1835 (on which our present city
government is based) drew, of course, no distinction between Will and Thought at all. They assumed that
the members of a council of sixty or a hundred members would be actuated by the one desire of Happiness, and would attempt by pure logic in full session
to persuade each other that that desire would best be
satisfied by this or the other expenditure; just as the
same statesmen, when they passed the Limited Liability Acts a few years later, assumed that the six
thousand shareholders of a great Railway Company
would settle the policy of the Company by logical discussion at their annual meetings.

In a large English municipality most of the actual
invention by Thought of means for carrying out desired ends is in fact done in solitude, either by the officials or by some one among the more energetic councillors. In so far as that Thought is not individual, it
is in such cases the result either of the world-wide or-

ganisation of books and newspapers, or of that smaller but still impersonal local organisation which consists of written minutes and reports read by the official at his desk or the member at home. A new idea is sometimes invented or elaborated during the discussions of a few leaders in the "Mayor's Parlour," and, less often, in the meetings of committees and sub-committees which deal with information, and mostly with actual proposals, submitted by the officials or the chairman. But, even in committee, no real "dialectic" may take place on the questions of greatest importance. When a council is divided (as of late years the London County Council has been) between parties the members of which are pledged or expected to vote in accordance with the decisions of a party caucus, real organised Thought on the main lines of municipal policy is avowedly transferred to the caucus or to a party executive. Useful committee discussion on detail may still go on, but when a point has once been decided by the party, no loyal member considers himself open to conviction, or utters, for the possible use of his opponents, his most relevant ideas or doubts. If a committee meets in public, the speeches are then either appeals to public feeling or at best contributions to the impersonal discussion carried on by the newspapers. If, as generally happens, the committee meets in private, argument on "party" questions may be merely a deliberate wasting of time until a fellow partisan arrives to vote or an opponent, who is believed to have an important engagement, goes. The best result that can be hoped for from such discussions is a slow change of feeling among the members of one or both parties resulting from a gradual habituation to the opposing point of view.

In a great modern city, again, a scheme of education or main drainage or water supply may cost millions of pounds and take perhaps ten years to work out. Unless its results are foreseen with a clearness which few men are capable of acquiring during odd hours taken from their daily business, and unless all the detailed steps are kept subordinate to the general idea with more consistency than is to be expected from a varying committee of average minds, that money and time will be largely wasted. The mere sense, therefore, of the danger of interference with complex but coherent plans is, in many English towns, already reducing the ordinary members of the Council, even when sitting in committee, to the position, either of obedient shadows, or of intriguers, on behalf of their constituents or themselves, for small concessions from the holders of real power. If a Mayor or committee-chairman or an official has the exceptional imaginative range and nervous energy which make him what the Americans call an "executive" or "big" man, he is apt to find that his plans are unintelligible to the majority of his colleagues, and that he had better trust rather to his personal influence than to his skill in argument to carry them into effect.

This discrepancy between the form of a Thought-Organisation using personal oral communication, and the fact of a Will-Organisation using for its intellectual work the vast modern system of impersonal communication, is even more clear to any one who attends a session of the English House of Commons. It was my duty not long ago to sit "under the gallery" of that House throughout a debate which was described by several speakers as exceptionally "interesting" and "informing." It was a "private members' day" and there was no sign either of party spirit or of obstruction until the end, when the motion was "talked out." Every one of the forty or fifty members present was, for nearly all the time, honestly attempting to discuss a difficult question which had not yet become a matter of party policy. But favourable as the conditions were, I had, as the hours went on, a maddening sense of the utter futility of the ostensible proceedings. When any member sat down after speaking, ten or a dozen others sprang up to "catch the Speaker's eye." Whoever succeeded, delivered a speech which might have been relevant at the beginning of the debate, but every point of which had by that time usually been made by some one else. The speeches themselves with their mixture of vague declamation, commonplace facts, and the tags by which a practised orator fills up gaps in the sequence of his thought, would never have been recognised by Socrates as belonging to the art of dialectic. One man obviously felt something strongly which had no relation to the typescript (prepared perhaps a month earlier) which he read with vibrating emphasis. Another, an experienced open-air agitator who spoke without notes, rambled on in that loose manner of trusting that every sentence will suggest another which constitutes the special disease of working-class rhetoric. Another spoke, it seemed to me, both well and to the point, but his arguments had absolutely no effect upon the prepared speeches that followed. The formal question of debate was, for most of the time, an amendment moved (as I was told across the rail which divided me from the House) by a member who had to catch a train, and who thereby secured priority for a speech which itself had nothing to do with it.

There was perhaps no one there who did not belong to the most earnest 20 per cent of the House, but the way in which their discussion was organised produced a general atmosphere of intellectual slackness. Most of the members seemed frankly to give way to it. The wigged clerk at the table, who reveals under more favourable circumstances as keen an intelligence and as fresh a public interest as any man in England, sat asleep in his chair with his head at a startlingly ironic angle. The members present were scattered in little groups about the seats, waiting for their turn, and listening good-humouredly, but with no pretence of concentrated attention, for signs that the speaker was about to perorate for really the last time. The three Labour members were, if I interpreted their feelings accurately, in a truly pathetic situation. The debate dealt with a question concerning the prevention of poverty, and at the preceding general election they had denounced the indifference and dilettantism of both the "capitalist" parties when such matters are being discussed. They were themselves therefore fiercely determined not to be indifferent, and sat there, like the deacons at an exceptionally dull nonconformist service, overcoming boredom by a sheer effort of will.[1]

At the far end of the House, in a dark recess under the Press Gallery, sat three or four officials from the department concerned, turning over papers under

---

[1] The endurance of the most earnest of the three has since given way, and he has announced himself to be a disbeliever in Parliamentary democracy.

shaded electric lights. I remembered that a Labour
member had, not long before, publicly complained that
one of his colleagues had asked a high official sitting in
that recess what he thought of the House and had been
answered, "I have seen squirrels run round in a cage
before." [1]

I strove to say to myself the best I could about the
British Parliament as a place of concerted Thought. I
remembered a few great occasions when the crowded
house had received a real intellectual stimulus from
the eloquence of a full-dress debate. I thought of the
excellent acoustic qualities of the chamber, and the
tradition of tolerance and good manners among the
members. I compared the scene before me with that
which I had watched from the huge gallery of the
House of Representatives at Washington, the rustling
newspapers, the hurrying page-boys, the speakers dron-
ing inaudibly from their manuscripts. I said that the
forty or fifty members before me were at least being
compelled to half-listen to opinions unlike their own,
that they were not allowed to read anything but the
Orders of the Day, and so must be at least half-think-
ing about the subject of the debate. I thought of the
absence of that uproar of which I read in some foreign
parliaments and of the freely whispered accusation of
personal corruption in others. But I always returned
to the point that the House of Commons was sitting
for the purpose of organised discussion, and that organised discussion was not, in any real sense of the
term, taking place.

Now in the extreme pressure of modern public life,
with its scores of competing claims on every waking

[1] F. W. Goldstone, M.P. in *The Schoolmaster* for May 20, 1911.

hour, that which is not from day to day felt to be worth while ceases to be done long before it ceases to be thought of as a duty. A busy country gentleman will think it his duty to go to church, will tell you, indeed, that he does go to church, although, in fact, he has decided to do something else every Sunday for the last two years. So it is with participation in the debates of the House of Commons. Members work now, I believe, very much harder than they have ever worked before in the history of Parliament. But they spend a much smaller proportion of their time and energy than ever before in attempting to convince their fellow-members by means of speeches in the House itself. They carry on an enormous correspondence; they make, even during the session, a very large number of platform speeches; they talk informally among themselves in the smoking rooms, the tea-rooms, on the Terrace, and in the clubs and places in the neighbourhood of the House from which the Whips, by an elaborate system of electric "division-bells," can summon them to vote. The House sits for an unprecedented number of hours, but seldom fills except for a division, and the speeches are, to an ever-increasing extent, avowedly or tacitly obstructive, intended not to convince any one, but to prevent the passing of the measure discussed, or, more often, the introduction at a later stage of some other measure.

And, as in the case of some of the larger municipal councils, so, to an even greater extent in the House of Commons, the party system has helped to deprive most of the public discussions of any kind of reality. All the members are supposed to hear all the arguments, and the decision of the House on each question is supposed to represent a majority of the decisions of individual members. In fact, though on unimportant details a free vote may sometimes be given by the few members who happen to be in the House, on all matters of importance the decision is made by the Whips (after consultation with the Minister concerned) and enforced by the votes of members the overwhelming majority of whom have not listened to any of the arguments. Every year the number of divisions in which any appreciable percentage of those who vote do so independently of party allegiance steadily diminishes.[1]

Mr. M'Curdy (Liberal Member for Northampton), speaking in 1911 on the question of Women's Suffrage, which cut across the platforms of both the great parties and was therefore being left to the unfettered decision of the House, said (to the accompaniment of "laughter" and "cheers") that:

Probably for the first time within the Parliamentary lifetime of any one present members were called upon to give their votes in respect to a measure of first-class constitutional and political importance free from party pressure. No wonder they felt embarrassed. It was so long since they had used them that their faculties of free judgment were atrophied. At last they might speak the truth, and they found their powers of truthful utterance were paralysed by long disuse.[2]

This system, of course, produces better results than would follow from the free but inconsistent voting of changing fractions of the House on all questions. It provides for a rough division of labour, by which the

[1] See Mr. A. Lawrence Lowell's admirable statistical treatise, *The Influence of Party upon Legislation in England and America.*
[2] *Times,* January 25, 1911.

Ministry deal with principles and the members are sometimes allowed to deal with details. But because it is founded on pretence, it has all the intellectual faults of pretence. An ordinary member is rather ashamed of the fact that in five divisions out of six he votes without thought or knowledge of the questions at issue, and his shame makes him less keen to think about any new question.

The real business of the House in full session is not therefore argument, but a conflict of Will, either between the parties or between the sections of the governing party. This last, I could see, was taking place on the Friday of which I write. Liberal and Labour members were whispering to each other. Would the Minister oppose or the Speaker grant the closure? If a division took place, would enough members vote for the original motion to warn the Minister that he must introduce a Bill? And the "talking out" of the motion at the end, with the consent of the Speaker, was felt to be the decision of that conflict.

An able member of the party in power, who has learnt how to think with concentration under the most unfavourable conditions, and who, though not a Minister himself, has access to Ministers and officials, can, in the House of Commons, exercise a real influence on the details of legislation. An equally able and industrious member of the Opposition can damage the Government, and can help to construct the arguments and the legislative programme which may carry the next election. But both will work mainly by correspondence and personal interviews, and will succeed in spite of, rather than by means of, the organised discussions of the House itself. And the members who go behind forms to realities, who consciously treat the House as a Will-Organisation, who concentrate their efforts on schemes for gaining the private ear of the Minister or the Whip, and who thereby influence divisions, are not always those whose intellectual processes are the most trustworthy.

As in the case of the Municipal Councils, a system of Committees has grown up in the House of Commons, and provides better opportunities of Organised Thought than do the full sessions. But the relation of these bodies to the civil servants who prepare their work (though they can take no part in their discussions) is still undefined and unsatisfactory; and strict party discipline, with its consequences of obstruction on the part of the minority and refusal to argue on the part of the majority, has already invaded most of those Committees which are not engaged on that purely judicial work of decision on "Private Bills," which ought not to be entrusted to a representative body of any kind.

In the United States, behind the Capitol at Washington, where members of the House and Senate are supposed to legislate by oral discussion, stand the new and singularly beautiful office buildings where they spend most of their time. There each member has a study in which he sits with his secretary, doing hour by hour that which seems to him to be most worth doing. His constituents still demand that he should make speeches in Congress, just as the clients of a country doctor still demand that he should give them bottles containing coloured solutions. And so he or his secretary, from time to time, writes a speech, which he either reads to the official reporter lounging on the seat in front of him, or has printed in the *Congressional Record* as if it had been delivered, and then circulated post-free among his constituents. Voting in Congress remains as important as ever, but members decide how they will vote by correspondence, by informal talks or private caucuses, by interviews, in person or on the telephone, with constituents or others interested in special legislation, by the reading of innumerable newspapers, and by occasional visits, in the case of the more conscientious and intellectual members, to the splendidly organised Congressional Library.

But because the new facts are still unavowed, the time spent at Washington, both on the old debates and on the new "business" methods, is largely lost. Pretence, there too, is a bad basis for intellectual efficiency. A representative from Indiana or Oregon begins his afternoon by leading a party of awestruck constituents past the dead statues of dead orators in the entrance halls of the Capitol, and depositing them in the gallery to watch the Congress of the United States at work. He then hurries back to his study, and dictates his letters or corrects a draft memorandum by his secretary. But he settles down into his armchair with less concentration of purpose and less simplicity of motive, and therefore with less efficiency in result, than he would have reached if the difference between the ostensible and the actual organisation of Congress had not given him a half-conscious feeling that the whole game of politics is insincere.

In the British House of Commons the evolution of legislative architecture has not advanced as far as in Washington. An unofficial member of Parliament who wishes to write a letter or read a book has neither a study nor a desk of his own, but must take his chance of finding that one-eighth part of a library table is free, and if he leaves his place, must huddle his papers together and carry them away. Even when he sits at the table the whole custom and tradition of the House make it as difficult as possible for him to secure any period of real concentration. A distinguished statesman and philosopher said to a newly elected friend of mine, "You have come to a place where you can neither work nor rest."

In the case of the British Cabinet, oral discussion is still a reality, and every possible effort is made to keep it so. Upon the degree to which the twenty or so Ministers who sit round the Cabinet table can, by spoken words, discover truth may depend the administration and finance of the United Kingdom, the making of peace and war, and the whole initiative in Parliamentary legislation.

The success of the Cabinet in concentrating into its own hands the power, not only of all the other organs of executive government (the Monarchy, the Privy Council, etc.), but also, to a large extent, that of Parliament, indicates that its makers must have contrived, consciously or unconsciously, to satisfy many of the psychological conditions of success. Of these conditions the most important is, I believe, the tacit recognition of the fact that, as I have already said, Thought itself, from one aspect, is an effort of Will, and that a certain degree of preliminary Will-Organisation is sometimes a necessary condition for the finer work of any Thought-Organisation. Party solidarity in the Cabinet, instead of making discussion unreal, is the main force which makes it real. Ministers will not effectively put their minds together unless, to adapt the late Duke of Devonshire's phrase when he refused to join Mr. Gladstone's Cabinet in 1886, they "mean the same thing." [1] The real beginning, therefore, of the modern Cabinet system came when Sir Robert Walpole introduced the practice of confining the Cabinet to members of one party, who had agreed to be jointly and severally responsible for the party action, and therefore had every motive to think closely and speak frankly as to the probable results of any proposed policy. Most Ministers now have a disinterested love for their party as a living entity which, by the wisdom or unwisdom of their decisions, they may destroy or preserve. But if a Minister is personally ambitious, his individual career, and if he is absorbed in departmental work, his individual schemes, may be cut short in a moment by a Cabinet defeat.

Party solidarity alone is not, however, sufficient to explain the advantage which the Cabinet, as a Thought-Organisation, has gained over the House of Commons and its other rivals. Another cause is the fact that Cabinet Ministers are chosen neither by the accident of heredity nor by the rough indication of popular election, but by a Premier who has full experience of their powers and training and knows exactly the duties which they will have to perform. In order that Cabinet deliberations shall proceed without friction or confusion, Prime Ministers have also been known to consider points of detail which might seem absurd to any one but a psychologist or a born organiser. Gladstone, when he tried to describe British

[1] *Life of the Duke of Devonshire* (B. Holland), vol. ii. p. 147.

Cabinet Government in a Church magazine, emphasised this point. In his sonorous Parliamentary manner he declared that:

> Every trade has its secrets. The baker and the brewer,
> the carpenter and the mason, all the fraternity of handi-
> craft and production, have, where they understand their
> business, certain nice minutiæ of action neither intelligible
> to nor seen by the observer from without, but upon which
> niceties the whole efficiency of their work and the just bal-
> ances of its parts depend.[1]

Gladstone himself, like a London hostess who is preparing a dinner party of professed talkers, used to draw
up "a plan . . . showing the position of the table and
how his cabinet was to be arranged around it." [2] Even
the table, he thought, might interfere with the mental
attitude most suitable for concerted thought. Henry
Sidgwick in 1885 described him as saying that "the
Cabinet now sit round a table, whereas they used to sit
on chairs in a circle; he thinks the change a mistake, as
leading to a less steady concentration of attention." [3]
Apparently on the same ground, refreshments, during
Cabinet meetings, are, we are told, confined to "Cap-
tain's biscuits and a carafe of water." [4]

That Cabinet Government has worked better in
England than elsewhere may be due in part to the traditional form of speech, which even those members of
the English "governing class" use among themselves
who, in public, adopt the flowing rhetorical style of the

---

[1] *Church of England Quarterly Review,* January, 1877. Reprinted
in *Gleanings of Past Years,* vol. i. p. 87.
[2] *Cornhill Magazine,* January, 1904, p. 50. "No. 10 Downing
Street," by Sir Algernon West.
[3] *Life of Henry Sidgwick.* p. 425.
[4] Sir Algernon West, *loc. cit.* p. 50.

early Victorian decades. That speech—short, colour-less, and almost brutally unemotional—is exactly that which would be chosen by a psychologist who desired that a dozen brains should search in concert for the means of attaining ends on which all are agreed.[1] At the same time some of the defects of British policy may be due to the fact that this manner of speech is an un-suitable medium for the suggestion of the finer humani-tarian feelings and values. Japanese generals and staff officers must, one supposes, have by this time invented some such form of speech for councils of war or for the stern military administration of Korea or Formosa, in place of the courteous periphrases of their normal social intercourse. Nothing, for instance, could be more exactly typical of the raw material of thinking as it comes into the mind of an able and unsentimental man than the saying attributed to Lord Melbourne, after his tired Cabinet in 1841 had at last decided to go to the country with a proposal for a fixed duty in-stead of a sliding scale in the taxation of corn. He called, we are told, after his departing colleagues, "Stop a bit! Is it to lower the price of bread, or isn't it? It doesn't much matter which, but we must all say the same thing."

But no observer of the effect on the British constitu-tion of the development of the Great Society can feel sure that the Cabinet will long retain, without serious modifications in its form and methods, its efficiency as a Thought-Organisation. The enormous increase in the work of the State, the multiplication by perhaps a score during the last fifty years of the number of ad-ministrative, legislative, or quasi-legislative decisions

[1] See *ante*, p. 246.

which come every month before the Executive, has
vitally changed the conditions of the problem which
Walpole's invention of the Party Cabinet originally
solved. Already in 1878 Gladstone complained that:

A protracted experience of public affairs, not unat-
tended with a high estimate of the general diligence, devotion and ability of the Parliamentary as well as the civil
servants of the Crown, has long convinced me that, of the
more difficult descriptions of the public business, apart from
simple routine, it is only a small part that is transacted
with the requisite knowledge, care and thoroughness. We
have undertaken in the matter of Government far more than
ever in the history of the world has been previously attempted by the children of men.[1]

In 1875, when discussing the suggestion that an English king might resume the practice of presiding at
Cabinet meetings, he wrote:

Now such is the mass, detail, and technical difficulty of
public affairs in this great Empire, that it would be an
absolute cruelty to the Sovereign to put him through these
agonies; for it is no trifling work and pain to hammer into
form the measures and decisions which are, when promul-
gated, to endure the myriad-minded, myriad-pointed criticism of the Parliament, the press, and the country.[1]

Since Gladstone wrote, the work to be done by or in the
name of the Cabinet may have been multiplied by ten.
From time to time Prime Ministers have been tempted
to meet the new demand by increasing the Cabinet far
beyond the number of ten or twelve at which organised

[1] "England's Mission," W. E. Gladstone, *Nineteenth Century* for
September, 1878.
[2] "Review of Prince Consort's Life," *Gleanings of Past Years,*
vol. i. p. 85.

oral discussion is most efficient. The Cabinet of 1858 had thirteen members, that of 1868 sixteen, that of 1900 twenty, and the present Cabinet (1914) twenty-two.

And the fact that of late years, owing to the extension of democracy in England, Cabinets are no longer composed only of members of a small governing class, with one habit of speech and one social tradition, must mean that Cabinet discussions, though they may cover a wider range of reality, require for full efficiency a longer time and a greater expenditure of nervous energy.

Different Cabinets, of course, and even the same Cabinet in different years, vary greatly, and Ministers are bound in honour not to tell the outside world whether their own Cabinet is working well or not. But it is clear that Cabinets do often fail in the difficult task of discussing by methods, both informal and orderly, the questions brought before them. Walter Bagehot, several of whose intimate friends were members of Palmerston's last Cabinet, wrote in 1867 that Cabinets were often "like a rather disorderly Board of Directors where many speak and few listen." [1] In 1899 Lord Rosebery, who had himself been Prime Minister four years before, described Cabinet meetings as "the collection of the heads of departments at sparse intervals to discuss hurriedly topics for which they are often unprepared." [2] The revelations resulting from Mr. Chamberlain's resignation in 1903 seemed to show that members sitting at one end of the table did not know that the resignations of the Duke of Devonshire and

[1] *English Constitution*, p. 14.   [2] Rosebery, *Peel*, p. 36.

Mr. Chamberlain were being discussed at the other end.[1]

Administration must be carried on, and therefore if for any reason oral argument in the Cabinet is inefficient, and if the inco-ordinated individualism of the Departments breaks down, some other instrument of discussion, or at least of decision, must inevitably be used. That instrument may be, and has often been in the past, the written correspondence of Ministers among themselves. The sincere and heart-searching letters, for instance, exchanged by the members of Peel's and Palmerston's Cabinets are admirable organs of thought. But such correspondence is even slower than oral discussion, and when letter-writing fails to produce enough concerted thought, the Cabinet may practically surrender to the personal power of the Prime Minister. Pitt, in his best days, reduced his Cabinet colleagues to nonentities, and Lord Morley declares that "Walpole was undoubtedly an example of the important political truth . . . that no administrations are so successful as those where the distance in Parliamentary authority, party influence, and popular position between the Prime Minister and his colleagues is wide, recognised, and decisive."[2]

If Britain were now to engage in a great war, either under a Premier whose energy was not diminished by age or under a weaker Premier dominated by some vigorous and popular Secretary of State, it is safe to say that the Cabinet would soon be in all important matters that which the American Cabinet

---

[1] Sidney Low, *The Governance of England*, p. 40.
[2] J. Morley, *Walpole*, p. 164.

has always been, a body of officials advising a single chief.

If the war took place fifty years hence, Britain might fight merely as the most important member of a group of states, less than half whose white population lived in the United Kingdom. In that case the rapid and intimate negotiation on which Imperial military organisation would depend could hardly be carried on by a body as large or, from the point of view of the Dominions, as irresponsible as the present Cabinet. Its place, for the things that mattered, would be taken by the Prime Minister sitting in the imperial Committee of Defence.

And even if the threatened world-war does not take place, and the Powers settle down to a period of prolonged sanity, there are causes already active in home politics which may make it difficult for the Cabinet to retain its present authority. The two-party system may, for instance, come to an end, and it may become exceptional for any one organised party to control an actual majority of the House of Commons. If so, the Prime Minister (through the Chief Whip who serves him personally) will be the single official link which holds together the coalition on which the retention of office by the Cabinet must depend. The really important decisions which make and unmake governments will then tend to be taken by him, or by some one who controls him, after receiving confidential advice, not only from the members of the Cabinet, but from the chiefs of the supporting groups. Under such circumstances it would be extremely difficult to retain at its full strength the present Cabinet tradition of solidarity and candour. An ambitious minister would no longer feel that his whole future depended upon the coherence and success of his party. A Cabinet defeat, leading not to a General Election but a regrouping of forces in the Commons, might give him his best chance, and at any moment of strain he might begin unofficial advances to those who would be his future colleagues.

In any of those cases the Cabinet, as an organisation for concerted and responsible thought, might sink into insignificance, although no change whatever had taken place in the legal structure of the British constitution, and no intentional and foreseen change had taken place in any of its functions.

But even among Prime Ministers men with the driving power of Peel and Gladstone are rare; and under most circumstances a decline in the intellectual efficiency of Cabinet discussion would transfer the real work of systematically organised national thought neither to the Premier nor to the politicians in the House of Commons, but to the high officials in the Whitehall offices. The number of "first-class" British officials is about the same as the number of members of Parliament, and the two bodies discuss much the same questions. From the point of view of economy in time and effort, the official organisation is immeasurably superior to the Parliamentary. The six or seven hundred officials, instead of all thinking, as members of Parliament are supposed to think, of only one question at a time, think of six or seven hundred different questions at a time. In a well-organized office every responsible administrative officer is, at any given moment, attacking some one problem with complete concentration. He collects his material, spends whatever time may be necessary for making up his mind, and then records his conclusions in writing. He can always stop, as an orator in the Commons or a minister at the Cabinet table cannot, to find the best instead of the second best phrase; he can correct what he has written if, as he writes, he alters his views, and he can carefully check all his statements of fact. When he has finished, his minute will go before some other and higher official who will consider it with equally concentrated attention, not at a time fixed by ballot or by the accident of the "Speaker's eye," but when, having been considering other questions of the same class, he is best prepared to think fruitfully on the subject.

In the Government offices that division of responsibility for principles and for details which is the accidental result of party organization in the House of Commons is openly and deliberately provided for. Small questions are dealt with by one, or perhaps two, minor officials. Large matters go up the hierarchy to men chosen because, by natural endowment or acquired training, they are most capable of taking wide and long views, and are finally decided by them in consultation with the political chiefs who have the widest experience and bear the public responsibility.

Yet a Government office has serious intellectual defects of its own. If the House of Commons suffers because its ostensible organization does not correspond to the real motives at work, a Government office suffers because the motives at work in it are often poor and inadequate. Not only are the training and experience of the official apt to be narrow and "bookish," [1] but the problems which, consciously or subconsciously,

[1] See p. 208.

he sets himself to solve may be less comprehensive than those raised in a search for the public good. He may consciously avoid, or half-consciously flinch from, the tormenting effort of new thought. He may be influenced by a desire to snub a pushing subordinate or a rival office, or be guided by the probable effect of the proposal before him on his own accumulated skill or his future career. The written debate which goes on in a Government office does not put such a strain upon the temper as does the spoken debate of Parliament or a committee. A man whose "unclubbableness" would make him impossible if he were sitting at a committee table may be a very fair official if he spends his day at a desk. But this very absence of strain may prevent an unclubbable official from acquiring that minimum degree of consideration for the feelings of others which oral intercourse produces in all but the most thick-skinned. The total effect, therefore, of a modern official organization based solely on writing is the combination of great efficiency in the handling of detail on established lines, with the existence of an "official atmosphere" which may be incompatible with some of the finer intellectual requirements of government, and has, in fact, often produced a general dislike of official methods among the outside public.

I do not propose to discuss here whether the main outlines of representative democracy in central and local government are likely to survive the increasing intellectual pressure of the Great Society.

But it is clear that a conscious psychological analysis of our social institutions, if it is at all widely undertaken, must ultimately lead to changes both in the details of our representative and official Thought-Organizations and in the spirit in which those organisations are worked. The first and most obvious of these changes would follow a consideration of the purely quantitative question as to the best size of deliberative assemblies. Any final decision in that respect must, as I have pointed out elsewhere, be the resultant of many independently varying conditions.[1]

But in almost every case I believe that the size of those bodies ought to be so reduced as to secure more efficient deliberations, and that all duties which the reduced body cannot carry out without make-believe should be abandoned. In the House of Commons the resultant number would probably be still too large to permit of the effective oral discussion of the detailed clauses of a Bill in full session. If so, the "Committee of the whole House" should be at once abolished. The House as a body might meet perhaps twice a week for the discussion of the "second reading" of important Bills, or of what the French call "orders of the day" affecting the policy and existence of Ministers. The rest of its business might be done in committees, varied in size and composition according to the work to be done; using standing orders [2] which frankly recognized the existence of printing presses and voting machines; and attended from time to time by professional officials with the right both to submit written memoranda and to speak. Under such conditions the House might be able to deal with some of those arrears of urgently

[1] *Human Nature in Politics,* pp. 144-145.

[2] A comparative psychological study of the "rules of public business," used in different countries and for different purposes, is urgently needed as a basis of invention in that respect.

needed legislation which every one admits and every one laments.

If the methods of the House of Commons require reconsideration, still more do those of the present or any future, and smaller, House of Lords. *A priori* it would seem certain that the procedure of a chamber whose functions are mainly revisory, that is to say, quasi-scientific and quasi-judicial, should be different from that of a chamber whose functions are mainly original. The procedure, therefore, of the Lords should be less of the nature of a public meeting than that of the Commons, and more of the nature of a public enquiry. One conceives of a possible "Second Chamber" as a sort of panel of Royal Commissions, with sections sitting as often out of London as in London, and developing methods of enquiry as unlike as possible to the stereotyped system of question and answer by which most of the Royal Commissions of to-day save themselves the trouble of thinking about method at all.

In both Houses every facility should be given for individual members to work with their books and papers and private secretaries, and to argue in private and informal groups.

There is less make-believe about the present organisation of the Cabinet than about the organisation of the Houses of Parliament. But Mr. Sidney Low, in his admirable analysis of Cabinet Government,[1] points out several respects in which the Cabinet has failed to make use of modern aids to concerted thought, and particularly that it has no efficient record of its proceedings. The distinction which he draws between the

[1] *The Governance of England* (1904).

present "secret" meetings of the Cabinet and the "private" meetings which might take their place,[1] is illustrated by the existence of those Cabinet Committees which have already been developed in order to deal with the ever-increasing work, and which keep careful minutes and provide an opportunity for real dialectic, not only to Ministers but also to the high officials and outside experts who attend.

More important is the fact that, while every other Minister is served by an organized official department, the Premier, by a curious historical accident, has only an unrecognized and insufficient body of private secretaries to assist him in exercising such a general oversight over the work of government as would enable him effectively to guide the deliberations of the whole Cabinet.[2] If the Premier had a small department of his own, consisting of officials "seconded" in early middle life from other departments and including the Government draftsman and his assistants, the gain in the intellectual concentration and efficiency of the Cabinet work would be immense.

In the case of the Government offices, most of those who have had dealings with them would say that they need to be "humanized." The official should be a man, should be known as a man, and should be expected to behave as a man. From the beginning he should do part of his work by oral methods. If, however, half a dozen clerks are merely placed round an office table and then told that they are to think with the same kind of effort that would be made by a newly elected

---

[1] *Ibid.* chap. ii.

[2] The Premier is First Lord of the Treasury, but the Treasury has now become mainly the department of the Chancellor of the Exchequer.

Town Councillor, or a Cabinet Minister faced with the opportunity of his lifetime, disappointment will inevitably follow. Civil servants require, not only opportunities but motives for Thought.

Even an official Board meeting in a Whitehall back room can, it is true, be sometimes kept in the mental attitude of effortful Thought by an appropriate use of official discipline. Sir John Briggs, in his delightful book on *Naval Administration,* describes Sir James Graham's way of doing this when he sat, as First Lord, at the head of the Board of Admiralty.

> It is no easy matter for a First Lord to keep the attention of the various members directed to the particular subject under discussion. This can only be accomplished by occasionally putting questions to them, which, if they were not paying due attention to what was passing, it would be impossible for them to answer. Sir James did this with such adroitness as to excite the admiration of those who were silent listeners, and could plainly perceive the force and object of the interruptions when attention and interest were beginning to wane.[1]

But a much better stimulus than mere discipline would be provided if the public and personal responsibility of civil servants were from time to time secured by sending administrative officials, who now spend all their time in Whitehall, to hold public "enquiries" into questions of local administration, or to do local work themselves, or by requiring them to make oral statements before Parliamentary or Cabinet Committees. In the process by which Samuel Pepys, the son of a tailor and the hanger-on of a nobleman, the amateur of undignified temptations, became perhaps the most

[1] *Naval Administrations* (1827-1892), p. 42.

wide-minded and self-respecting of all British officials, an important incident was his being summoned as Secretary of the Navy Board to defend the action of his Board before the House of Commons on March 5, 1667-68. When he had delivered his four hours' speech, "with full scope and all my reason free about me," and had been congratulated by every one from the King to "Progers of the Bedchamber," he wrote in the diary which he meant no one but himself to see, "for which the Lord God make me thankful! and that I may make use of it not to pride and vainglory, but that now I have this esteem I may do nothing that may lessen it." [1]

The mere published signature from time to time of an official Report by its actual author might do something to dispel the "official atmosphere," and to diminish the authority of the official tradition represented by the phrase, "I shall be blamed if it goes wrong and shan't be praised if it goes right."

Any improvement of the Thought-Organisation of English municipal bodies would involve the reduction of the size of each body, the adoption of methods of work which corresponded to the real fact that the members do not now directly administer, but criticize the proposals of professional officials, and, above all, a complete change in the way in which those officials are appointed, their professional organization, and their responsibility to the Council.

It may not perhaps be fanciful to suppose that a wider extension of psychological self-consciousness may also ultimately affect the personal mental attitude of elected persons, whether in Parliament or on the mu-

---

[1] Wheatley, *Diary of Samuel Pepys*, vol. vii. pp. 350-353.

nicipal bodies. I have myself, during the last twenty-five years, sat through perhaps three thousand meetings of municipal committees of different sizes and for different purposes, and I am sure that at least half of the men and women with whom I have sat were entirely unaware that any conscious mental effort on their part was called for. They attended in almost exactly the same mental attitude in which some of them went to church—with a vague sense, that is to say, that they were doing their duty and that good must come of it. If they became interested in the business it was an accident. Of the remaining half, perhaps two-thirds had come with one or two points which they wanted to "get through," and meanwhile let the rest of the business drift past them, unless some phrase in the discussion roused them to a more or less irrelevant interruption.

Those committees were by far the most successful as Thought-Organisations which were attended by three, or at the utmost, four persons dealing with some isolated "non-party" question on which their decision was likely to be final, and where the automatic and half conscious stimulation of "interest" could be trusted to take the place of the deliberate effort of "attention." Here, if the members were fairly experienced and good-tempered, it happened not seldom that they each ceased to think of the rest as constituting a committee. Their colleagues became and remained individuals—Brown, or Smith, or Miss Jones. Personal goodwill half-consciously asserted itself, and was helped by the habits acquired in social intercourse. Brown would say afterwards, not "I attended a meeting of the sub-committee yesterday," but "Smith and

Miss Jones and I had quite a nice time yesterday afternoon arranging about the new North Ward school."

Fifty years hence, when the language and conclusions of psychology have penetrated into the education of the ordinary man and the books and newspapers which he reads, both members of Parliament and Town Councillors may consider a definite effort of attention (in the absence of such automatic "interest") an obvious condition of effective deliberation.

Any serious psychological enquiry into the form and methods of political Thought-Organisations would soon be extended to the quasi-political, quasi-philanthropic voluntary Boards and Committees of which we English make such large use, and must ultimately affect the still larger question of the intellectual organisation of industrial and commercial business.

A student of sociology on the lookout for a Thesis subject could hardly do better than to examine, from the point of view of intellectual efficiency (even if he left the great worlds of business and politics untouched) the constitutions and standing orders by which the Hospitals, the Charities, the Clubs, the "governing bodies" of schools and colleges, the associations of party politicians, and the various religious organisations of a large provincial town are managed.

He would have to remember that such bodies are Will-Organisations as well as Thought-Organisations, and that a committee whose constitution was absurdly ill-adapted to enable its members to think in concert may be admirably adapted to secure that the policy of those who manage it should prevail. But, even after making that allowance, he would, I am convinced, discover at once that able and public-spirited men and women will often involve themselves in an almost incredible waste of time and temper from mere indifference as to the machinery of discussion. Some of them have unworkable standing orders. Others recognise no standing orders at all, and do their work by "conversational" methods which prevent any question from being either closely discussed or finally decided. And if he found that some committee with a constitution outraging all his preconceived ideas of efficiency nevertheless worked well, or another with an apparently excellent constitution worked badly, he might find himself on the track of a genuine social invention.

Sometimes the mere asking of the question as to the intellectual relation of the ordinary members of an organisation to the discussions by which its policy is directed would at once reveal the fact that no such relation exists. I was in America during the spring of 1910, when the Republican party throughout the Eastern States was, with very good reason, anxious about its political health. In Massachusetts a public dinner was given to the Republican legislators as a sort of tonic. After dinner Speaker Walker [1] said: "The party should get together and squarely face the situation which confronts it." "The candidates," he said, "and the policies of the party must be discussed and decided upon in the open. Every Republican must be made to feel that he is wanted and is welcome, that he is free to speak and free to exercise such influence as he may have in the councils of the party." His advice was cheered, but, popular as it was, it did not help much in the process of "squarely facing" the situation of a body containing some hundreds of thou-

---

[1] In American Legislatures the Speaker is a political leader.

sands of nominal members distributed over a whole State. Later in the same evening, Chairman Hatfield, whose management of the party committee was apparently considered to have been reflected upon by Speaker Walker's address, is reported to have "outlined a few of the troubles which always confront the men charged with guiding the destinies of any organised and scattered body of men." [1]

The ordinary members of a political party cannot "get together." The real party organisation must consist of a few men, whose work it is to issue appeals to the others and to calculate as closely as they can the chances of their appeals being successful at the polls.

The Thought-Organisation of business requires a special study of its own, and a large body of able, though empirical, literature exists on the subject.

The intellectual relation between the shareholders and the directors in those Joint Stock Companies which are the typical forms of the Great Industry and the Great Commerce is obviously in a state of transition, and no one would attempt seriously to defend its existing phase. The relation between the Directors and Managers of big businesses is often equally inefficient. The Thought-Organisation, on the other hand, which is composed of the manager of a big business and his salaried subordinates is much more efficient. In its economy of effort, in its rejection of oral discussion among more than two persons, and in the practice of throwing the responsibility for Thought on each question upon a single mind, it is the very antithesis of a typical organisation in politics and philanthropy.

[1] *Boston Herald,* February 15, 1910.

But, though no one would desire to introduce Parliamentary methods into a London Bank or Railway office, and to settle the day's business by motion and amendment with the manager in the chair, yet my impression is that business organisation might often gain on its intellectual side by the wider adoption of means for concerted discussion, and by a close examination of the methods by which those who work in a small section of a business can be induced or empowered to think about the business as a whole.[1]

So far in this chapter I have dealt with those forms of Thought-Organisation—Councils and Committees and Offices and Parties—which consist of a limited number of persons, brought into relations with each other for the sole or main purpose of concerted Thought. But only a small part of the Thought of the Great Society is done in these specialised personal Organisations. The really typical Thought of our time is that which, as I have already said, must either be classed as Individual Thought, or as part of that vast impersonal Thought-Organisation which has been created by modern means of communication, and to which almost every adult member of the Great Society in some degree belongs. That our more personal

---

[1] Professor Marshall dealt incidentally with this point in an address to the Royal Economic Society in 1907, and gave as an instance of invention in that respect "the congresses" and other opportunities for submitting their ideas to the judgment of brother experts, "which are organised by the chief owners of the trusts" for their superior officials. But he ended (like President Wilson in his New Freedom) with the conclusion that nothing effectual could be done unless the more extended forms of this Great Industry itself were broken up, and we returned to the system of small independent businesses and "the bracing fresh air which a strong man with a chivalrous yearning for leadership draws into his lungs when he sets out on a business experiment at his own risk" (Economic Journal, March, 1907, pp. 16-17).

newspapers and newspaper placards, and of a much smaller number of magazines and books. The newspaper is taking to a large extent the place of conversation, and often copies the discontinuity and familiarity of conversation without securing that which is its essential value as an intellectual instrument, the stimulus of one mind by free association with another in the process of following up a train of ideas.

But just because a vast quantity of passive reading is inevitable in the Great Society as we know it now or as we can conceive of it in the near future, it is of the first importance to consider how the large ill-organised system which supplies it can be made more effective. No one now knows whose interests direct the avowed or suggested policy of newspapers, whose shares are for sale in the open market, and which cannot exist for a week except by the favor of great advertisers. Books, being signed, are less dangerous in that respect, and perhaps a larger extension of the practice of signing articles may introduce a larger element of responsibility into journalism. The life of a writer of "best-selling" books is indeed short, and his temptations and disillusionments are many, but, at any rate, fractions of the influence which his writings have created cannot be bought as a matter of daily business on the Stock Exchange. And an able journalist with a reputation for independence, who signs his articles, can, provided he is at first content with perhaps a third of the salary which he could otherwise earn, even now get an opportunity for responsible utterance; just as a dramatist with something to say can get some sort of a hearing even in the syndicated theatres. That deepest form of sincerity, which requires long consideration before the declaration of opinion, is, of course, almost impossible for a writer who has to comment each evening on news which may be only half an hour old; and one already sees that signed daily journalism may become the special province of the neurotic partisan whose emotions can be trusted to react immediately to the weakest stimulus. But the practice of considered signed writing on the events of a week or a month rather than on those of a few hours may become, as it is becoming in the press of the United States and France, more common than it is now in England.

More permanent in its influence is the enormous cheapening of the production and distribution of books in which writers with a reputation to lose give their estimate of the main tendencies of their time. Among all the rawness and disorganisation of life in the straggling mining villages of the Rhondda or Don valleys, one feels one's feet for a moment on something like a firm foundation when one sees in the windows and doorways of the little tobacconist-newsagents' shops, piles of *Home University* and *Cambridge Scientific* treatises at a shilling, resting against rows of serious and penetrating criticisms of society in the form of fourpenny or sevenpenny novels. An old pitman once said to me: "It makes me groan to think o' the thousands of hours I've spent i' reading the wrong books"; but the authority of the editors of the new cheap series, the widespread knowledge of the names of important writers, even the advice of officials in Free Libraries (though, in that respect, England is far behind the United States) gives the working-class student an enormously better chance in that respect than he had when he was forced to trust to the titles on a barrow-load of second-hand volumes.

All this, however, still remains passive reading. If non-official Thought is to become effective it must also use the oral interchange of ideas. And since, in our urban communities, nothing can be done effectively which is not done deliberately, we must provide at least as carefully for the Organised Thought of the ordinary citizen as we are now beginning to provide for his Individual Thought. Now that the streets are cut off from the fields, we are coming to understand that for the "working man," as well as for the school-master or professor and his pupils, silent Reading Rooms, intelligently arranged museums, shorter hours of Labour, better housing, and even seats in public parks, are necessities of intellectual life. And much more complex material and social arrangements will be needed if we intend that working men and women shall form effective dialectical groups. Some of the lines on which such arrangements may be made are already beginning to reveal themselves. Educationists are claiming that the working-class child shall learn in school, not only the power to read and write, but the power to express his own thoughts in intelligible words. The scholarship systems are beginning to enable those who are naturally fitted for a life in which Thought plays a real part to discover their own powers and to come into touch with their equals. The rise of local universities unhampered by the social traditions of Oxford and Cambridge, and able to resist the tremendous centralising force of London, has made, at any rate, a beginning of intellectual self-respect in our provincial cities. University teachers and organisations

like the Workers Educational Association, or the Adult
School Association, are discussing with a new note of
seriousness the methods by which, in Seminar or dis-
cussion-class, dialectic may be an aid to or a substitute for the passive process of learning from lectures.[1]
Local repertory theatres and provincial coteries of
young writers and artists seem no longer an impossible
hope either in England or in America. The United
Kingdom has a population of forty-five millions and
the United States one of a hundred millions. The
Norway of Björnsen and Ibsen and Grieg had a population of two millions, and the Italy of Dante and
Petrarch one of perhaps four millions. No one even
dreams that the first-rate intellectual output of the
English-speaking world of the twentieth century will
be twenty-five times that of nineteenth century Norway together with fourteenth century Italy. But our
wealth and knowledge and organising power may perhaps make us together equal to one of them.

[1] See, for instance, an interesting article on Adult Schools in the
Manchester Guardian of September 26, 1912, which describes, more
exactly than any book which I have read, not only the conditions
of effective dialectic, "the sense of freedom," the "facing the real
problems with which men of the day are wrestling," "the confidential
friendship between the classes and their leaders," but also its dangers—the possible presence of the undialectical "man of one idea,"
and the possible failure of the leader to "guide and inspire" the class
like Socrates, "by sheer weight of superior knowledge and force of
character."

CHAPTER XII

THE ORGANISATION OF WILL

In this chapter I shall deal with the Organisation of Will in the Great Society.

Again, I must begin with a warning against our tendency to ignore the difference between a human society and an individual human being. We constantly speak as if nations and cities "will," or "desire" or "intend" or "decide" to carry out corporate action by the same simple process as that which in a single human being precedes his individual action.

But the Organised Will of a modern society only comes into existence as a result of the formation of difficult and always imperfect social machinery. When we say that "Russia intends to make war on Austria," we form in our mind a picture either of a single Russian with a conscious intention to make war, or of a vaguely enormous number of identical Russians, all having the same conscious intention.[1] Neither picture of course corresponds to the facts. It may be "true" that Russia intends war, when a dozen statesmen have agreed among themselves upon an aggressive policy, and when they have reason to believe that their policy will be supported by the organised force of the nation. Only two per cent of the Russian population may in

[1] See my *Human Nature in Politics,* p. 139.

that case consciously dislike and fear the policy of
Austria, but the statesman may know that a much
larger proportion of the population can be made to
hate Austria as soon as an open quarrel occurs, and
that the army has been trained to obedience of almost
any orders from above. On the other hand it may be
"untrue" that Russia intends war even although an
actual majority of the population desires it, if a majority of the persons who are in a position to control
the national policy are opposed to it. Or Russia may
be in such a state of political disorganisation that no
Organised Will on the subject can be said to exist, and
the nation may drift into a war which no one intends.

The events indeed which we ascribe to the corporate
decisions of communities are usually the resultants of
a number of interacting causes—the Wills of those
persons whom the machinery of the community has
brought into organised relation with each other, the
unorganised Wills of individuals, and the circumstances of the case, which no one may have realised
and whose effects no one may have expected. When a
thousand individuals run to the side of an overcrowded
ferry-boat, their Wills are entirely unorganised and
the result of their action entirely unintended. When a
million families migrate from the country to the town,
the action of each family is probably due to a more or
less organised relation between the Wills of the members of that family, but the action of the whole body
of migrants is unorganised. If a general war should
break out in Europe, the action of each nation in the
proceedings leading to war would probably be due to
the rather highly organised Wills of its politically important members, but the outbreak itself might (owing

to the absence of a European Will-Organisation) be undesired by any nation. And even when the action taken by a large community is directed by an Organised Will in that community, yet, owing to the imperfection of human knowledge and of the Thought-Organisations of human societies, the unintended results of that action may prove to be more important than its intended results.

Yet, however carefully we try to remember this, the false analogy between a community and an individual still persists, and often creates in us a feeling of personal resentment against any community which seems wantonly to refuse to direct all its actions by a definite purpose. When we read Mr. Wells's complaint, "A world that had a collective plan and knew what it meant to be doing would do a sight better anyhow," we are apt to blame "the world" as we would blame an individual man, who can always, if only he will take the trouble, form a plan and know what he means by it; and who does not require first to provide himself with new eyes, or ears, or new lobes to his brain. We forget, that is to say, that "the world" can only have a "collective plan" or collectively "mean" anything in so far as machinery exists enabling certain definite persons, whether many or few, to consciously formulate their desires on some point with the expectation that "the world" will carry those desires into effect.

If we are to blame mankind, we should blame them, not for being without a collective plan, but for being without the machinery which would make a collective plan possible. When Sir Valentine Chirol writes from India to the *Times*, "Over and over again, reflecting

Civil Servants have said to me, 'What are we here for?' If only I knew that, I should know how to order my life and my duty," [1] we blame ourselves or "the Government" without asking whether any constitutional machinery exists by which the inhabitants of the United Kingdom can form any purpose with the expectation that it will guide the action of the officials and soldiers whom they send to India. It may well be that the Civil Servants are sent there "for" no purpose at all, and that without important changes in the constitution of the British Empire that must remain the case.

In the Great Society, however, men are continuously compelled, if they are to enjoy the advantages of civilisation, or indeed to exist in anything like their present numbers, to act in ever larger units, industrial and political, national and international, and experience daily shows that the action of these units should as far as possible be the intended result of an Organised Will.

Almost the whole of what we call 'the social question," for instance, consists in the controversy as to what Organised Will should direct the enormous industrial units of our time. The three chief Will-Organisations whose claims are put forward for that direction are Private Property, the State (organised at present on the basis of locality) and non-Local Associations (mainly on the basis of common occupation). The exclusive fitness of each of these to be the main or sole Industrial Will-Organisation suited to the Great Society is advocated by a special group of thinkers, the claims of Property by those who call themselves Indi-

[1] *Times,* June 28, 1909.

vidualists, of the Localised State by those who call themselves Socialists or Collectivists, and of the Non-Local Associations by those whom I will call, though some of them would reject the name, Syndicalists.

The Individualists, in claiming that the general interest of the community is best secured when the Great Industry is directed by the Will-Organisation of Property, have on their side the great advantage that the institution of Property is based upon a true human instinct.

The details of the Property Instinct vary rather widely both among individuals and races, partly, perhaps, because a single line of our ancestors went through several evolutionary phases in that respect, and partly because different human stocks (which are now interbred) had evolved somewhat different instincts. But the main outlines of the instinct are clear enough. From a point in his evolution long before he became human, man has not lived, as most of the fishes live, by consuming every day food which he finds that day in an environment which he makes no attempt to change. He has always to a certain degree accumulated food, and later on tools, and weapons, and clothing; and has constructed or adapted shelters against enemies or the weather for himself and for the women and children of some kind of family group. Intrusion into the chosen shelter, or consumption of the accumulated goods by persons not in the family group, is instinctively resented. Within the group, co-operation in the production and accumulation of possessions is instinctively undertaken by the male and female adults and the younger children. On adolescence the young males, and to a lesser degree the young females, develop an individual impulse to produce and accumulate, which is absorbed a little later in a new family impulse.[1]

It is this body of facts which has led almost every critic of society during the last two thousand years to think of agricultural "peasant proprietorship," where a definite piece of land is tilled and its fruits stored by the labour of a family group, as the most "natural" form of industrial organisation. Both production and accumulation seem to organise themselves automatically in such a group: since the father and the mother toil without external compulsion both to support their children in infancy and to make provision for their future, while the children, with little or no compulsion, help, until the *Wanderlust* comes upon them, in the work of their parents.

When, a hundred or more years ago, economists began to discuss the first beginnings of the Great Industry, they still thought of unrestricted Private Property as the most effective form of industrial organisation, and of family accumulation as the main impulse by which it should be directed. But as soon as the "factory system" took the place of the "domestic system" in those textile trades which so greatly influenced economic thought, it was seen that, in a highly organised industry, family accumulation is inevitably separated from family co-operation. It was still assumed that the main motive of the employer as "economic man" would be to accumulate wealth for himself and

[1] For certain purposes, *e.g.* common defence, men seem also instinctively to co-operate in the larger unit of the tribe. But tribal co-operation is not instinctively "economic," *i.e.* aimed at the production and accumulation of the necessaries of life. In this respect human instincts differ from those of the ants and other social insects, among whom in this sense the family and the tribe are one.

his family. But it was no longer assumed that that wealth would normally be produced by the co-operative labour of himself and his family. The modern capitalist would, it was recognised, normally direct the labour of large bodies of hired servants. But the most efficient capitalist, it was argued, would direct the largest body of workmen, and his efficiency would consist in offering to the general body of consumers the most valuable commodities and services.

Pure Individualism now represents, however, a rapidly shrinking body of opinion. The substitution of concentration for competition has destroyed in the largest and most characteristic modern industrial units the old presumption (never very sound) of identity of interest between producer and consumer. When Sir Edgar Speyer (the organiser of the great industrial combination called "The Underground Electric Railways Company of London") was reported in the *Times* as saying: "The fear had been expressed in some quarters that a concentration of traffic facilities would tend towards an increase of fares, but he maintained that the true safeguard against any possible abuse was that the interests of the shareholders and of the travelling public were identical," [1] his statement sounded to us merely absurd.

The separation of family accumulation from family co-operation has also brought about an enormous and growing hereditary inequality in the ownership of wealth, and few economists think with satisfaction of the degree to which the less urgent desires of the minority who have inherited wealth are now satisfied

[1] *Times,* February 25, 1913.

before the more urgent desires of the majority who have not inherited it.

As the second and third generations of "captains of industry" grow up, the presumption also that the accumulation of private property from family motives would necessarily lead to industrial management by the ablest and most energetic members of the community is seen to be no longer well founded. A great capitalist may leave the management as well as the profits of his business to a stupid son, or the stupid son may choose a stupid or dishonest manager.

Accumulation and co-operation are even more clearly separated in the joint-stock system, whose Will-Organisation is as incoherent as its Thought-Organisation. The inheritor of shares in a large joint-stock business has normally little or nothing to do with its management. It is easier for a shareholder in Sir Edgar Speyer's company to prevent fares being raised by agitating politically for a general Minimum Fare Bill than by attending the annual meeting of his Company; and a clerical holder of brewery shares can vote more effectively for Sunday Closing as an elector than he can as a shareholder. But the present complete legal responsibility and actual irresponsibility of the shareholder are in some of the largest and most important forms of industrial organisation, not likely to remain unchanged. Either the main capital value of those companies which are intimately concerned with the public interest will come (as in America) to be represented by non-voting bonds and debentures, while voting power is concentrated in the hands of a "boss" who can negotiate with the holders of political power, or control by the State will so extend that the shareholder will become, as the East India stockholders became towards the close of the East India Company's existence, in fact the receiver of fixed interest on a State debt.

And, finally, even if the desire to accumulate for oneself and one's family were sufficient to secure both the maximum energy of the owners of modern capital and the direction of that energy towards the maximum good of the community, most men now have an uncomfortable feeling that that desire is not under present conditions sufficient to secure the best results from the working employee, who is no longer either a son of the employer or an apprentice adopted into the employer's family and expecting to become an employer himself. In so far as the lifelong workingman in a large industrial unit is identical with Archbishop Whately's economic man, concerned only with his own pecuniary advantage and that of his own family, it seems difficult now to find arguments which would convince him of the unwisdom of the deliberate restriction of output, or even of deliberate injury to his employer by "sabotage" or "ca' canny."

In fact the institution of Private Property only now works tolerably as the main organising force of the Great Industry because it gives scope for other impulses besides that of personal or family accumulation, and because it is constantly checked and modified by other forms of Will-Organisation. Rich men now continue to make money after they have provided for the future both of themselves and their children, not only because the instinct of accumulation has no clearly defined limits, but because they are influenced by the desire for admiration and power (the Give a Lead instinct), or by the need of outlet for their energy, or by Love for human beings outside their family. If Sir Edgar Speyer were to submit himself to cross-examination in a psychological laboratory as to his motives for not immediately raising fares on the London Electric Railways, it would probably appear that he was influenced, not by a simple calculation that in a purely individualist society he would make more money for himself and his family by adhering to the existing fares, but rather by a very lively sense of the possible interference of Parliament or the Railway Commissioners, by the realisation that he might need the support of public opinion in a future struggle with the Railway Men's Union, and perhaps by a vague and half-ashamed feeling (which Professor Murray would call Aidos) that he would like to behave decently to those who use his railways.

If we assume, therefore, that the growth of the Great Industry in Europe during the nineteenth century was inevitable, the reaction from the Individualism of the beginning of that century to the Collectivist Socialism, which became the most important political movement at the end of it, was equally inevitable. Given that the choice was between a Will-Organisation based solely upon Property and one based solely upon Representative Government, the argument in favour of Collectivism in the Great Industry seemed irresistible. Collectivism substituted a direct aiming at the public good for a very hypothetical calculation that the public good might indirectly result from individual and family accumulation. It encouraged and depended on conscious public spirit, instead of a blind property-instinct distorted by the disappearance of its original environment. Above all it seemed that a democratic government would necessarily use the enormous wealth-producing power of the Great Industry so as to lessen instead of increasing economic inequality.

Wherever, therefore, during the last fifty years, the Great Industry has developed among a nation of European origin, it has been followed by an insistent demand both for representative democracy and for the State control of production; and that demand has already resulted in a transformation towards democracy of the majority of European governments, and in the enactment of a growing and generally accepted mass of "socialistic" legislation.

But the continued growth of Collectivism depends on the continued efficiency and acceptability of the machinery by which the collective Will is ascertained and enforced; and the dissatisfaction with the actual methods of democratic representation which I discussed in my last book [1] seems also to be growing.

In particular the methods by which the less eager working-class voter is induced to go to the poll are felt to an increasing extent to offend against a vague but deep-seated sense of the terms on which alone men can live permanently together. A proportion of the electors sufficiently large to turn any election will, if they are left to themselves or to the spontaneous exhortation of their neighbours, stay at home. It is therefore necessary that they should be visited on some organised system, both during the campaign and on the day of the election. In America the system adopted consists of an elaborate arrangement by which

[1] *Human Nature in Politics* (1908), *e.g.*, Introduction, and pt. ii. chaps. i. and ii.

some one, who in social or industrial life has acquired influence over the voter, calls on him and tries to use that influence by making him vote. Sir Edwin Cornwall, M.P., in a lecture at the National Liberal Club (reported in the *Daily Mail* of October 17, 1908), proposed that this (which was the rule in eighteenth-century England) should again become general among us. "The confusion," he is reported to have said, "which generally prevailed at elections was unwarrantable and unjustifiable. What was the good of sending a violent Nonconformist to canvass a violent Churchman? Send a Nonconformist to canvass a Nonconformist; a Churchman to a Churchman. If a man were influenced by his landlord, send the landlord to him. If a man never went to Church on Sunday, but took his dog for a walk instead, let him be interviewed by the man who went for walks with him."

But most men, if they are asked to use systematically the influence gained in religion or business or personal friendship to make neighbours, who do not like to refuse, promise that they will vote for or against, say, Imperial Preference, are likely to feel that the process is not quite "fair," and that feeling will probably be shared even more strongly by those whom they visit.

In the English cities, since the great Reform Acts of 1867 and 1884, "canvassing" has normally taken the form of the house-to-house visitation of whole streets by persons who are strangers to those whom they visit. This is not felt to be unfair, but it is felt to be unpleasant. One of the most necessary duties of the professional ward-agent at an English election is to go from time to time from the inner to the outer committee-room, and to tell the politicians whom he will find there, engaged in a natural and pleasant discussion of their candidate's chances, that they must each go out with a bundle of canvassing cards. The men and women whose public spirit compels them to obey do so with a conscious shrinking, not so much from muddy pavements and sore feet, or from the reading, with matches that continually go out, of door-numbers in dark "model-dwellings," as from the sense that they are somehow offending against good manners. The last time I went canvassing I spent half an hour trying to teach an old street-hawker to fill up a specimen voting-paper. Every few minutes he implored me to let him alone. "I have been wet through three times to-day," he said, "I am tired and angry." (The phrase pleased him, and he repeated it half-a-dozen times.) "This sort of thing ought to be left to them that is apprenticed to it." I felt that I was outraging every possible social code. The political canvasser can indeed see himself as in a glass when a week or two after the election he is called on by a commercial canvasser of books or milk. The creature before you, with his nervous smile and his hurried anxiety to get into any kind of conversation before you shut the door in his face, seems to have lost some of the proper dignity of a man.

Though the political leader ignores all this, the working-class voter sees it at first hand. He or his wife is canvassed perhaps a dozen times during the election, and if a speech or a newspaper article rouses his public spirit and sends him to the committee-room of his party, there is nothing for him to do except to go canvassing himself. No wonder that, in a working-class district, "politics" are often looked upon as rather a disreputable fad, which the best kind of man, the man who "keeps himself to himself," will not touch, and that the burden of organisation is so largely left to the professional agents who enjoy their own professional skill, and boast, like the secretary of the Budget Protest League, that they "have succeeded beyond all expectations in introducing the true twentieth-century note into the ever-fascinating art of political propaganda." [1] And no wonder that the questions which really interest politicians so seldom really interest the majority of their constituents.

The candidate himself, though, if he is sufficiently important, he may be allowed to confine himself to the wholesale Organisation of Will, and may leave the retail work to others, yet often looks back on the election as a period of intense moral discomfort. All his instincts were adapted ages ago to life on a smaller scale, and to a more spontaneous and less mechanical contact with his fellows. He hates, in his moments of fatigue or depression, to thrust himself on the attention of thousands of men who despise him for doing so. He would like to be silent or to speak his own thoughts in his own way. [2]

But if he is to stimulate and to express the feelings of a large constituency, an ordinary man can no more be "natural" than can an actor on the stage. Some few men, it is true, find an exalted sense of reality in

[1] *Daily News*, August 7, 1909.
[2] The social life of American University undergraduates is often very largely based upon a system of election to various clubs and societies. A very clever novel, *Stover at Yale*, by Owen Johnson, lately described with great vividness a feeling among certain undergraduates, with which every politician will sometimes sympathise, that it is better to be and to do, than perpetually, in order to win "popularity" and ultimately votes, to seem to be and to seem to do.

the whole process of electioneering. Gladstone could step on to the platform of a great meeting with the same sense of consecration to the purposes of Providence with which he had knelt that morning at the eucharist. The management of his splendid voice, the well-graced movement of his body and features, the skill with which the "old Parliamentary hand" (as he was proud to call himself) made twenty thousand people feel that his sonorous phrases expressed their varying aspirations, while he yet left himself free; in these things Gladstone had no more sense of unreality than had Disraeli in his calculated audacities, or Lassalle in the gestures which he used to rehearse before his mirror.

But all men are not so tempered, nor perhaps any man in all his moods. Lord Rosebery told the Liverpool students in 1910 that "Politics at best are a gruesome study. We like them much better at eighteen than at fifty-eight."[1] And Huxley, when at a Royal Society Dinner it was suggested that he should enter Parliament, replied "that all his life he had been consumed by a passion for the discovery of truth, and not for its obscuration; hence he had never had any ambition to enter on a political career."[2]

I have tried, so far, to take instances where the feeling of unreality and discomfort in politics arises from the difficulties of honest men trying to create and organise a common purpose among their fellows. But the graver dangers of representative government arise from the fact that the manipulation of other men's wills for ends believed to be good for them may

[1] *Daily Chronicle,* November 15, 1910.
[2] Article by Edward Clodd in *T. P.'s Magazine,* October, 1910.

shade imperceptibly into practices whose end is the advantage of the manipulator. This danger is always near in a country where democracy co-exists with great social inequality. Political organisation is expensive, and it is impossible to induce poor men to subscribe small sums to electioneering funds as long as they know that rich men can give great sums without a sense of loss. On both sides in any contest those who pay for the Organisation of Will are likely to influence its direction in accordance with their own opinions. But when a rich class feels itself attacked as a class, it is apt to go further. There are always plenty of counsellors who tell them that they should subscribe to the propagation of opinions which they do not hold, that they are not using "their enormous money power in a scientific way," [1] and that "whatever policy may be best designed to enable" their party "to keep and to gain seats . . . must be adopted without hesitation." [2] They were urged, for instance, in the *Observer* of November 13, 1910, to subscribe to the Tariff Reform League. "Tariff Reform is what the masses understand. . . . The Tariff Reform League is the agency by which the masses can be most effectually moved." The Tariff Reform League had "learnt by experience to make a consummate use of money." Mr. T. W. A. Bagley, the Secretary of the League, after "an adventurous life in West Africa and elsewhere," had organised a body of men who, with a recollection of West Africa, he called Missionaries: "These men move through the constituencies, live in the villages, engage individuals in casual conversa-

[1] A. A. Baumann, *Fortnightly Review,* October, 1909.
[2] *Observer,* November 13, 1910.

tion. . . ." The boundaries of what would be considered mere common honesty in ordinary life are here, most men would say, definitely overstepped.

And there is another danger which does not depend upon social inequality. The progress of Collectivism, by extending the functions of Government, has increased the payment by Government for work done, and such payment may become a source of corruption. When I heard an Irish policeman in Boston say to a friend with whom he was discussing a personal grievance, "Man, I tell you it's dhurrty politics," he was using the word in a sense that would be understood right across the United States. In France elected representatives are said to be overwhelmed with correspondence arising out of political patronage. In the central executive service of the United Kingdom we are, for the moment, more fortunate, but there are few workmen in a provincial town who do not know of cases where men have interested themselves in elections for Guardians or Borough Council with the expectation of a job if their candidate gets in.

Socialism began to be preached in England in 1884, a generation after the death of Robert Owen's movement under that name. In 1888 the *Fabian Essays in Socialism* were written. The article on the relation of Representative Government to Industry was entrusted to Mrs. Besant, and I have re-read it, in order to see what we then considered to be the collectivist position. Mr. Ritchie had in that year passed the Act creating County Councils, and Mrs. Besant wrote that:

In perfect unconsciousness of the nature of his act, Mr. Ritchie has established the Commune. He has divided England into districts ruled by County Councils, and has thus

created the machinery without which Socialism was imprac-
ticable. . . . It remains to give every adult a vote in the
election of Councillors, to shorten their term of office to a
year; to pay the Councillors, so that the public may have a
right to the whole of their working time; . . . and to remove all legal restrictions, so as to leave them as free to act
corporately as an individualist is to act individually.[1]

After this is done, argued Mrs. Besant, the universal
adoption of Socialism will be certain, "No one will
care to face the worries, the harassments, the anxieties
of individual struggling for livelihood, when ease, freedom, and security can be enjoyed in the communal
service." [2]

No member of the Fabian Society, when this essay
was first read, expressed, as far as I can remember,
any doubt of Mrs. Besant's orthodoxy in this respect.
But now, after a quarter of a century's further experience of representative government, it is probable that
no present member of the Society would take it for
granted that "worry" and "anxiety" would be completely absent from a community where every man's
wages and employment and the whole conditions of
his life depended upon the absolutely uncontrolled dis-
cretion of a local council, elected annually after a
contest the preparation for which would occupy at least
eleven out of every twelve months.[3]

In England, during the forty or fifty years since English democracy began, any working man who has be-

---

[1] *Fabian Essays,* p. 152.   [2] *Ibid.* p. 158.
[3] One gets an exhilarating sense of a really enormous advance
in the accumulation and analysis of economic knowledge from a
comparison between the admirable Report of a Fabian Committee
on the Organisation of Industry, published by *The New Statesman*
in 1914, with the corresponding sections of the *Fabian Essays* written
in 1888.

come disappointed with the machinery of representation has usually voted Conservative, owing largely to a feeling that the established order of employer and employed ran itself without humbug. But of late years in France and America and, to a less extent, in England working men have been offered, under the name of Syndicalism, a revolutionary movement which, like Collectivism, promises equality and "the abolition of the wage system," but which acknowledges and indeed exaggerates every charge that can be brought against the present organisation of representative democracy.

The Syndicalists ascribe many of the evils of Parliamentary government to the fact that it is "geographical," that the constituencies, that is to say, consist of voters merely related to each other as inhabitants of local areas. Even if men so related belong to one party, their appearance of solidarity is, they say, superficial. M. Challaye sums up many syndicalist criticisms on this point in the words, "A political party is an aggregation of heterogeneous elements held together by the artificial bond of similarity in opinion. In such a party men from all the social strata elbow each other, exchange vague and sterile platitudes, and attempt to harmonise by insincere compromises their essentially antagonistic interests." [1]

The Syndicalists therefore look for a Will-Organisation which has behind it some stronger emotion than that produced by the accidental residence in a few score of adjoining streets of a few thousand men who have adopted a common party name for their opinions.

[1] Challaye, *Le Syndicalisme révolutionnaire et le Syndicalisme réformiste*, p. 14.

This Will-Organisation they find in the fact of common industrial employment. The Trade Unionist, they argue, is joined to his fellow-workmen by a bond of things and deeds not of words, and one for which experience shows that he is always ready to risk his own livelihood and that of his children. "Whereas," says a writer in *The Syndicalist* of April, 1912, "it is a comparatively easy thing to get men to go out on strike for the success of their unions, . . . it is paradoxically almost impossible to get them to vote for a revolutionary candidate, to give a vote which costs them neither trouble nor pain, merely thought."

Some of the more systematic Syndicalist thinkers have worked out a full scheme for a Syndicalist State, whose electoral constituencies and administrative units are Trade or Industrial Unions, and whose Parliament is a National Committee of Union delegates.

Others refuse to look further into the future than the prophecy of a general revolutionary strike. Indeed, throughout the Syndicalist literature, one continually comes upon denunciations of systematic constructive thought, and references to the *élan vital* and the other terms of M. Bergson's anti-intellectualist philosophy. "If one reflects too much one never does anything," [1] one should trust the "philosophie de l'action qui donne la première place à l'intuition." [2]

The intellectualist logic by which the rise of European democracy was directed assumed that all votes (like all golden sovereigns, or all quarters of No. 1 Northern Manitoba Wheat), are equal to each other, and that therefore the addition and subtraction and

[1] Griffuelhes, *Bibliothèque du mouvement social,* i. p. 57.
[2] Lagardelle, *Ibid.* i. p. 8.

comparison of them must produce exact results. The Syndicalists insist that feelings and actions are more real than votes, and that feelings and actions are not equal. An energetic and passionate minority have, they say, both the power and the right to coerce by violence an inert and indifferent majority. They advocate, therefore, and justify frequent strikes among those classes of workmen, like the transport-workers, or the electricians, or the coal-miners, who, though they are themselves in a minority, can, they believe, cause such general inconvenience as to compel the rest of the community unwillingly to interfere on their side.

Though the combination of the Syndicalist programme with modern "anti-intellectualism" is new, there is nothing new about the programme itself except its name. The "Socialism" of Robert Owen in 1834, Louis Blanc's plan for the "Organisation of Labour" in 1848, and even many of the ideas of Lassalle and Marx and William Morris were Syndicalist, in the sense that they proposed to create a community, the industrial or political basis of which should be the "self-governed" workshop or the "self-governed" craft.

Many cities in medieval Europe even passed through a stage of actual Syndicalism, the last remains of which were not abolished in industry till the French Revolution, and still survive in the privileges and discipline of some of the learned professions.

The history indeed of the late-medieval gilds shows both the strength and the weakness of the Syndicalist form of Will-Organisation. The gild-brother, whether painter or weaver or lawyer, lived a vigorous and interesting life, and his close association with his fellows tended to maintain a high technical standard in the use, and sometimes, perhaps, the development of traditional methods. But even in the organisation of industry the Gilds proved unable to adapt themselves to radically new methods, or to arrange effective compromises between the various crafts, or, where the two became distinct, between the craftsman and the merchants. They constantly tended, in accordance with a narrow interpretation of the pecuniary interest of their existing members, to restrict the entrance into the gild of "strangers," and even of their own skilled assistants, and to make themselves into a body of hereditary monopolists, enjoying as employers the "rent" of the harbour or trading centre in which they were situated.

And even in the medieval city the management of Industry was not the sole function of the Organised Will of the community. Police, public health, and above all the management of the external relations of the city, had to be provided for. If in such matters the citizens avoided or neglected as unreal the process of compromise by which alone the inhabitants of a ward could elect a common representative on the city council, they only created the more difficult task of arranging compromises later on between organised and hostile interests. Cities which could enter into no binding agreement that did not bear the seals of twenty jealous gilds, and which could not keep order in their own streets during a trade dispute, proved too weak to stand against the more highly organised national states which began to appear during the sixteenth and seventeenth centuries. It proved to be more important that under Syndicalism men loved each other less as citizens than that they loved each other more as Gild-brothers.

If Syndicalism ever became the sole basis of organisation in the Great Society all these difficulties would remain, and other difficulties would arise from the change of scale which has taken place since the Middle Ages. If the whole management, not only of manufacture and trade, but of foreign affairs, religion, education, health, and the thousand functions of a modern State, depended upon elections in constituencies consisting of whole industries, those elections would soon become as much a matter of specialised skill as the present local contests, while the successful candidates would be equally liable to acquire the insincerities of the platform. And however insistently the syndicalist agitators had preached intuition, the nature of things in a modern Syndicalist state would throw all real power into the hands of the men of calculation.

Neither Individualism, therefore, nor Socialism, nor Syndicalism, affords by itself a single sufficient basis for the Will-Organisation of the Great Society. It may be that no satisfactory Will-Organisation of human beings with their present limitations, in a society on so vast a scale, is possible, and that we must ultimately choose either to live on a smaller scale, or to pay for the advantages of the larger scale by constant dissatisfaction with our relations to each other. But the effort of inventing a better Will-Organisation than now exists is at least worth while.

That invention will require the co-operation of many minds and the experience of many years. It is clear, however, that it will have to contain all the three elements which I have just discussed. Socialist thinkers both in Germany and in England seem to me to be realising this. They seem ready to allow scope both for the instinct of Property in its original and simplest form, and for the co-operation of men and women, whether as consumers or producers, on different bases from that of local residence, and they seem anxious to invent machinery which need not involve complicated plans of "Proportional Representation," but which should weigh votes as well as count them, would allow, that is to say, greater proportionate influence to the strong desires of minorities (whether local, or racial, or religious, or consisting of a smaller body of producers opposed to a larger body of consumers) than to the weak desires of merely numerical majorities.

The Syndicalists themselves, whether they use that name, or are merely "Old Trade Unionists," or ultra-loyal members of such bodies as the British Medical Association or the National Union of Teachers, seem to me to find it more difficult to realise the limitations of their own special formula. Perhaps some of them would be more likely to do so if they could accustom themselves to discuss the rights arising out of common employment in relation to other occupations than their own. It is probable, for instance, that during the spring of 1912 two out of three of the Fellows and Tutors at Oxford would have signed with equal readiness a petition in favour of the forcible suppression of Syndicalist action, and one in favour of the unrestricted ownership and control of the Colleges and University by those who taught in them. If Dr. Charles Wray had carefully considered the ethics of "ca' canny" in the case of the railwaymen in 1911, he

would perhaps have been less willing to write to the
Lancet in January, 1912: "The doctors if defeated
(over the Insurance Act) may treat patients, but they
will be under no obligation to prevent malingering nor
the prescription of good drugs if expensive. Those
under the whip must retaliate according to their
power. . . ."[1] Even the Conservative Press itself may
begin to find it difficult with equal whole-heartedness
to denounce Syndicalism and support Professionalism.

It is still harder for those who are trained to think
of social relations in terms of Property to realise the
limitations of their instrument. Since the Roman and
Byzantine jurists worked out the details of the convention of property, those who deal with it, whether
as owners or business men or lawyers, have come to
think of it, not as an expedient to be adapted to varying human needs, but as an indefeasible and unchangeable "right." The advantages of that habit of thought
have been great. Nothing, not even the convention
of money, has done more to make the high organisation of modern industry and commerce possible than
the rigid convention of property. But at present its
disadvantages are, I believe, still greater. As soon as
an ordinary well-to-do man begins to talk about the
"rights of property," he removes himself into an atmosphere where it is impossible for him either to
understand the ˚habits of thought of the majority of
his fellow countrymen or the necessary conditions of
any great improvement in social machinery. The present Archbishop of York, for instance, is a man of
unusual force and elasticity of mind. In the autumn

[1] Letter signed Charles Wray in *Lancet* of January 6, 1912, p. 53.

of 1912 he had the splendid opportunity of addressing (at a meeting which preceded the Church Congress of that year) a great audience of working men.
He told them that the industrial unrest of the day
included an "honest desire to open a wider chance of
a decent human life to a larger number of the people
of this country. In that business he wanted to be
their comrade." He then proceeded to define social
justice. "There were rights of property, and they must
be defended, whether the property was that of the
landlord, the manufacturer, the investor in the co-
operative societies, or even that of an ancient and
venerable church. Those rights were things which
should be defended, but they were co-related to their
duties, and it was the business of the Church of Christ
to say to the landlord, the manufacturer, the investor,
or the building society, and to any branch of Christ's
Church, 'You are bound to discharge the obligations
to the public good which the ownership of property
imposes upon you.' . . . The rights of labour had
also to be defended. He had been a lifelong adherent
of their great Trade Unions, but the Church of Christ
was not worthy of its name if it was to be afraid at
any time, at the cost of any popularity, to stand up
before honest men and to say that labour had its
duties. If it was the right of labour to seek for shorter
hours and higher wages, then the more was it the duty
of labour to see that it worked harder during the
shorter hours and honestly earned the higher wage." [1]

As long as Dr. Lang assumes the identity and equal
indefeasibility of the property rights of a landlord, a
manufacturer, a religious corporation, and a co-opera-

[1] *Times,* October 1, 1912.

tive society, and the consequent injustice of any read-justment of wages or hours which alters the distribution of the existing product to the disadvantage of any receiver either of rent or profits, so long will he be intellectually incapable of "comradeship" with the average working man. Even the Syndicalists find themselves in a hopeless confusion of mind as soon as they borrow the convention of property, and claim that the miners should "own" the mines or the railwaymen the railways.

It may be argued that in all modern democratic communities this breaking-up and re-combination of the simpler forms of Will-Organisation is already, both in conception and in fact, rapidly taking place. Not only do Parliamentary Governments interfere freely with "the rights of property," but they themselves are checked and guided by a Civil Service and a Judiciary which are not elected and which hardly any one now proposes to elect. Although the French Revolution identified the idea of democracy with the abolition of professional privileges, yet of late years every profession except the Church has, in the most democratic countries, received increasing statutory powers. The "recognition," both by the State and by organised property, of Trade Unions and other voluntary, but in practice coercive, associations of employees steadily grows. Above all, the electoral system itself is, it may be argued, so elastic that it can and does constantly adapt itself to meet new social developments. If Joint Stock companies, or Trade Unions, or Co-operative Societies, or Professional and Official Associations come to represent a more important body of Organised Will,

that fact automatically influences the choice of candidates, and the success or failure of policies at every
election.

And yet it is this "automatic" process which creates
the most urgent need for a deliberate analysis of the
situation, leading to the invention of new forms of
Will-Organisation. Democratic Government is sure
to degenerate if we drift into a position in which the
only, or the most effective, means by which the servants of the State can get their special ideas, or their
special prospects, attended to is by canvassing indifferent electors; or if the privileges of large property-
organisations are permitted to exist, but are exposed
in every session of the legislature to ignorant or interested attacks, and are allowed to defend themselves
by huge subscriptions to party funds. All States, again,
now employ a growing number of professional lawyers
and doctors and engineers, but in every section of the
State service one may find friction arising from the
fact that no one has thought out the relation between
the professional "expert," who is influenced by the
traditions and discipline of a great outside association,
and the "administrator," whose training and corporate
feeling are bounded by the service.

For this work of invention there exists a vast mass
of history on the various forms of association, which
at least indicates certain preliminary conclusions. It
seems clear, for instance, that some of the privileges
enjoyed by those older professional organisations,
whose traditions date from the Middle Ages, should be
transferred to authorities directly or indirectly representative of the community at large. Of these the
most important is admission to, or dismissal from, the

right of employment. In England, for instance, the General Medical Council, a body in effect representative of the doctors, has the legal right to remove without appeal names from the medical register on the ground of "infamous conduct in a professional sense." Of late there have been cases of this penalty being inflicted on persons whose conduct no layman would dream of calling infamous, but who were held to have acted in a way inconsistent with the interests of the present body of registered practitioners.[1] The Benchers of the Inns of Courts have in England the unchecked power of refusing admission to the profession of barrister; and in 1909 two Indian candidates were refused admission and one expelled, avowedly on the ground that their political opinions and actions were displeasing to the Benchers. Perhaps these privileges would be more easily abandoned if their supporters were required to argue in Parliament that it would also accord with the permanent interest of the community and the permanent efficiency of the teaching, or railway, or postal service, that the National Union of Teachers or the Unions of the Railwaymen or Postmen, should have both a statutory monopoly of employment and the right through their Executive to dismiss any of their members for any reason which seemed good to them.

The case of the relation between the Organisations representing property or common employment and the actual process of electioneering is more difficult, but

[1] See, for instance, the cases of Mr. Axham and Mr. Wallis, who were removed from the Register for administering anæsthetics to the patients of Mr. H. A. Barker, an admittedly skilled, but unregistered manipulator of joint injuries (*Times*, December 4, 1911, and elsewhere).

one can watch the emergence of certain principles from experiments tried in France, the British Colonies, and elsewhere, in delegating both the details of pay and discipline of any classes of public servants large enough to have an important effect upon elections, and the details of pecuniary arrangements with important financial interests, to bodies which, while under the ultimate control of a democratic government, are yet in a position enabling them to adhere to a considered policy against the pressure of individual legislators.

In Europe, it is true, for the moment all industrial politics are overshadowed by the struggle between the vague and easily confused economic aspirations of the newly enfranchised masses, and the vigorous and conscious self-defence of those property-owning classes which have hitherto considered themselves to constitute the community. Until the fact of greater social equality has led to a relaxation of this social tension, other advantages of political structure may often have to be postponed, in order to secure the clearest statement and most rigorous enforcement of majority rule. But even in England, where the process of social adjustment is now most actual, and the need of majority rule most obvious, one can watch instances (mainly as yet in the less exciting regions of public administration) where machinery has been invented to secure a combination of ultimate public control with the discouragement of any undue interference, either of the politician as such with the details of administration, or of the official as such with the work of politics.

Some, for instance, of the most interesting of these experiments have taken place in the reorganisation of English "Secondary" and "Higher" education, which followed the Education Act of 1902. No attempt has been made to create bodies which in the last resort are independent of the central and local control of Parliament and the Municipal Councils. Every grant out of the taxes must be approved by a majority of the House of Commons, and any rate must be levied by a majority of some Municipal Council. But in the case, for instance, of the new provincial Universities, instead of the School Boards of 1870 (directly elected by an electoral system which encouraged the conflict of organised interests under the form of local representation) a large permanent body is generally created, on which the majority of seats are filled by the State or by county or city councils, and a minority by professional organisations and the teachers in the University. This body elects the Principal, and gives the final decision, unless Parliament or the Law Courts interfere, on all important questions which may be submitted to it. At the same time the teachers themselves (acting either through their Faculty organisation or through a "Senate" or "Academic Council") are mainly responsible to the Court both for the direction of the teaching and for the development of the various sciences which are taught.

Less complex, but perhaps even more informing (as bringing in the problem of private property) is the process by which a secondary school, founded and controlled by a Joint Stock Company, secures "recognition" and aid from the State. The original shareholders become receivers of a fixed annual sum; but, if the purpose of their association was in fact public-spirited, they are sometimes given a temporary right to a minority of seats on a new "governing body."

If ever the "nationalisation" of Railways or Mines takes place, it may be that schemes of this kind, while apparently more complex, may prove in the end to correspond more closely to the needs of the Great Society than direct administration either by Parliamentary Committees, or by nationally elected Boards, or even by an ordinary Government department under the uncontrolled direction of a Parliamentary Minister.

And if ever the problem of a "Second Chamber" is satisfactorily settled, it may be found that as long as finance and the power of dismissing that executive Government which can alone use force is reserved to the "geographically" elected Chamber, the representation of other forms of Will-Organisation may play a useful though subordinate part in the work of legislation.

A similar analysis might be extended to the inchoate but all-important Will-Organisations which now occasionally make possible the co-operative action of the whole civilised world. There are, indeed, few books which are more needed than a description and classification of the forms of "ecumenical" co-operation which already take place. The writer of such a book would have to go behind the simple conceptions of majority rule and the legal rights of professions and property-owners. He might begin by considering the conditions under which nations have been successful in arranging among themselves for the voluntary mapping of the heavens, for the voluntary introduction of uniformity into scientific terminology, and for the international distribution of scientific honours. He then might examine the cases where the coercive action of States over individuals is required for international purposes (whether that coercion is exercised by State officials or by delegation to professional or mixed bodies) for "the rule of the road" at sea, the enforcement of quarantine, or the preservation of threatened animal species. Finally he might approach the cases where the whole body of States coerces or threatens to coerce one or more of its constituent members; the Concert of Europe, for instance, or the tendency of late years to bring diplomatic pressure to bear in order to secure the reference of irritating but not vital questions to The Hague Court. In all these matters he would find material which would lead him not only toward a clearer conception of the complex conditions of international co-operation, but also towards the invention of means of organising the conflicting Wills of individuals and classes within each nation more effective than reliance upon any single "principle," whether Representation, or Property, or Professionalism.

CHAPTER XIII

THE ORGANISATION OF HAPPINESS

In considering how the Great Society can be so organised as to produce the maximum amount of Happiness, I must begin by referring back to Chapter VII. I there argued that Happiness is not identical either with the sensation of Pleasure or with the feeling-tone of Pleasantness. A happy life will normally contain many Pleasures and much Pleasantness; but the state of consciousness which we call Happiness is distinguished from either sensation or feeling-tone by the fact that it contains (though they are not always consciously recognised) Memory of the past and Imagination of the future.

Happiness, I further argued, is a much better indication than either Pleasure or Pleasantness that a man is living a life which would be declared by Aristotle's imaginary jury of "the wise" to be socially good. And yet we cannot, I regretted, be sure that by aiming at Happiness, "like archers with their mark before them," [1] we shall attain social good. Conduct, merely passive contemplation for instance, may produce real Happiness without leading to the ultimate good either of society or the race.

[1] Aristotle's *Ethics*, i. 1 (2).

The question, however, whether the Great Society is efficient as an Organisation for producing Happiness, though it does not necessarily lead to a final judgment as to whether the Great Society ought to exist, yet does lead to a more complete survey of the problem than the questions whether the Great Society is an efficient Organisation for the improvement of Thought, or for the carrying out of Will. I can remember that, a quarter of a century ago, while I was reading at Woolwich, with a small class of working men, Mill's chapters on "The Three Elements in Wealth Production, Land, Capital, and Labour," the lesson suddenly turned into a discussion of the wisdom or unwisdom of one of our number who had thrown up an easy and well-paid job in the Arsenal because it was too easy and therefore intolerably monotonous. We seemed to be using a much wider and more fruitful method when we discussed his production of Happiness than when we confined ourselves to his production of Wealth. Two types of industrial organisation might, it became clear, be equally efficient in the production of wealth, and yet life under one might be happy and under another unhappy.

And formulas like the current definitions of Socialism or Individualism, though they go behind the mere production of commodities, may yet fail to indicate essential factors in the production of Happiness. At about the same date as my Woolwich class, I was talking to a middle-aged artisan who had fought for the Paris Commune. He said to me, "There can be good socialisms and bad socialisms." He explained that he could imagine himself very happy and very unhappy in two countries, in both of which the means of production, distribution, and exchange had been nation-alised.

Before criticising the Great Society as a Happiness-Organisation, or trying to get at a point of view from which improvements in that respect can be invented, I must also repeat that one must be careful not to exaggerate the Unhappiness involved in the present facts.[1] The Great Society has resulted in a degree of discomfort and uncertainty which was unexpected by those who helped to make it. Its successes have rather been in the removal of certain specific causes of Un-happiness than in the production of positive Happi-ness. But those successes have not been unimportant, particularly to those who live in the unfriendly natural environment of a Northern climate. Life is much longer than it was, and disease less terrible. Poverty no longer means the Hunger which Langland describes in *Piers Plowman,* that made a man "look like a lan-tern all his life after." [2] However clumsy and me-chanical the organisation of the Great Industry may be, it does not involve chattel slavery or predial serf-dom. We have escaped, also, from that evil which the Hebrew prophets were never tired of denouncing, and which modern observers sometimes describe as the main curse of Eastern village life, the oppression of the weak man by the strong neighbour from whom he cannot escape. Those of our dispositions, like Crafts-manship or Love, whose normal stimulus is close asso-ciation with familiar objects, are often confused and tired by our present environment. But other dispo-sitions, like Curiosity and Ambition, find a richer satis-faction than before. When I was once asked by a

[1] See *ante,* p. 6. [2] *Passus,* ix. l. 174.

Norwegian lad in the Romsdal whether he ought to
stay and inherit his father's land, shut in, as he complained, "by the mountains, always the mountains,"
or venture landless into the new world of America or
England, I did not dare to tell him to stay.

That, indeed, which chiefly angers and excites us
now, as we contemplate the society in which we live,
is not a conviction that the world is a worse place than
it has ever been, but the feeling that we have lost
grip over the course of events, and are stupidly wasting
the power over nature which might make the world
infinitely better.

The most obviously and immediately important instance of the relation between the Great Society and
human Happiness is to be found in the working day
of men engaged in the mechanical and subdivided
Great Industry. Are they normally happy, or at any
rate in a state of pleasant feeling-tone, during their
actual hours of work? The general impression which
I have formed on this point is confirmed, as far as
the evidence goes, by the answers which, at my suggestion, were given a year or two ago by the working-
class students of Ruskin College, Oxford. These, as
summarised by the Principal of the College, were:

With regard to pleasure in work. Engineers say generally it is all toil. They admit there is a certain pleasure in
a job well done, but they say the bad conditions knock the
pleasure out. Coal-miners generally say the work is all toil.
But one man said he would sooner be at work than be idle,
another that he can take pleasure in the work for half-a-
day when he knows he is going to have a half-holiday. A
third says that there is a certain pleasure in digging out the

coal when you have a good place, but that pleasure is just in the expectation of making a good wage. Factory workers, *i.e.* textile, bootmaking, etc., agree that the work is all toil. One man remarks that he has known girls of good position work ten hours a day for 9s. a week, but he believes that the attraction is purely the independence thus obtained. Ashby, our agricultural labourer, was very emphatic with regard to the pleasure to be obtained from agricultural work.

I shall refer later to what is here said about the feelings of working girls. For the rest, this piece of evidence amounts to the statement that there is less pleasantness or happiness in work the nearer it approaches to the fully organised Great Industry. The work of which Mr. Ashby (who had been an agricultural labourer and was incidentally a writer on country life) had experience did not, of course, belong to the Great Industry at all.

Compare this with any account of skilled craftwork done either before the Great Industry had been invented, or in conscious reaction from it.

Mr. Coomaraswamy published in 1906 a translation from the Sinhalese of an ancient traditional song describing the potter's art. The song obviously had the practical purpose of enabling apprentices, in the absence of text-books and written directions, to remember certain operations in their due order. But throughout the detailed rules there runs an indescribable sense of delight in the work. Here are a few extracts:

Waking before the dawn, carrying the basket, he fares to the place-of-clay;
After cleaning the basket and clearing the place-of-clay, he worships his guardian god;

Wearing only a loin-cloth, and gladly taking the basket
in hand he goes down into the pit;
Not breaking down the two sides of the pit he digs the
clay from the middle and fills the basket.

     *   *   *   *   *   *

The next day, waking at dawn, he sweeps and tidies the
workshop,
And having all the balls of clay close at hand, sits before
the wheel.
He takes with the right hand the balls of clay one by
one and sets them on the wheel,
With the left hand he turns the wheel, with the right
hand he moulds the vessel,
Knowing the size and shape required he presses down
the hand;
Then when the right shape appears, he stays the form
and moulds the rim.
Having stayed the form and turned the rim, he turns the
wheel very fast,
And looking now and then to see if it is smooth, he
amends with the finger tip any unevenness,
Sprinkling a little water he polishes the pot, then takes
it carefully with open hand,
Duly keeps it standing by, and takes it up again after
thirty hours from the time of making thus.

     *   *   *   *   *   *

Having drawn round it lines, flower-petals, cocks, par-
rots, pigeons, selalihini. . . .
Swimming cranes, flying lihini, fair kiñduro, and honey-
bees,
Great boas, fierce serpents not a few, sharks, tortoises,
and golden peacocks.
Beautiful damsels whose ever-swelling breasts are like
golden swans,
Nor does he forget to draw dear delightful children.[1]

[1] *Spolia Zeylanica,* vol. iv. pts. xiv. and xv., December 1906.

     *   *   *   *   *   *

Or take this from William Morris:

How nice it will be when I get back to my little patterns and dyeing, and the dear warp and weft at Hammersmith.[1]

And:

Indeed I have been ashamed when I have thought of the contrast between my happy working hours and the unpraised, unrewarded, monotonous drudgery which most men are condemned to.[2]

It was true that Morris, for all his greatness, never faced the fact that we cannot both eat our cake and have it, cannot use slow methods of production and also turn out without overwork large quantities of consumable wealth. Once, while I listened to him lecturing, I made a rough calculation that the citizens of his commonwealth, in order to produce by the methods he advocated the quantity of beautiful and delicious things which they were to enjoy, would have to work about two hundred hours a week. It was only the same fact looked at from another point of view which made it impossible for any of Morris's workmen, or indeed for anyone at all whose income was near the present English average, to buy the products either of Morris's workshop at Merton or of his Kelmscott Press. There is no more pitiful tragedy than that of the many followers of Tolstoy, who, without Tolstoy's genius or inherited wealth, were slowly worn down by sheer want in the struggle to live the peasant-life which he preached.

[1] Quoted in *Fabian Tract,* 167, p. 8.
[2] Letter to *Manchester Examiner,* March, 1883, quoted in *Fabian Tract,* 167, p. 12.

But allowing for all this, and for the fact that the society to which the old Sinhalese potter-poet belonged contained a large proportion of men who were too stupid, or too crippled, or too hungry, or too oppressed, to take any joy in their work, yet the fact that the working-day in our most successful industries was not, according to the Ruskin College students, anything but a dull toil for any one of an exceptionally healthy, intelligent, and energetic body of young men, must be seriously considered if we are to judge the Great Industry by the criterion of Happiness.

And that serious consideration is the more necessary because it is as certain as any sociological prophecy can be, that, largely owing to the growth of psychological science, those characteristics of the Great Industry against which Morris and Tolstoy specially protested will be enormously developed. A group of extremely able thinkers, mainly Americans, have set themselves during the last three or four years, to work out, on lines to which they have given the name "Scientific Management," the conditions of maximum productive efficiency in highly organised industry. Their thinking is based on conditions which we are beginning to take for granted, but which in fact have only come into existence during the last generation. They assume that a large body of workmen are dealing with material—iron, cotton, etc.—so exactly assimilated or graded that any portion of it labelled in a particular way is equivalent to any other portion so labelled. They also assume that it is easy to make large numbers of tools and machines which, however complicated, are exactly identical with each other. The workmen cannot be so assimilated, but they assume that it is possible to classify with considerable accuracy their natural and acquired characters, and to ascertain by experiment the "curve" of the behaviour of each class under varying conditions. The most important curves for their purpose represent the increase of fatigue in the workman while performing different series of bodily movements.

The "scientific manager" then sets himself the problem of ascertaining the maximum output of this body of workmen, the necessary arithmetical calculations being done by an elaborate "slide rule," by which the relation between the recorded curves of increasing and decreasing efficiency due to changes in the raw material, in the shape, size, and speed of every part of the machines, in the character and speed of the manual movements of the workmen, and even in rates of wages, is ascertained. Sometimes the conditions of a particular industry are sufficiently simple for the result to be arrived at by exhaustive mathematical methods. More often the number of independently variable factors is so great, and the labour of discovering by experiment all their possible curves so enormous, that a good deal of the thought of the scientific organiser must consist in the invention, by skilled guesswork, of probable hypotheses to be tested afterwards by quantitative experiments. The whole method of enquiry requires indeed so much experience and ability that it has been mainly applied hitherto, not by works-managers, but by experts specially called in to help them.

The economic effect already produced by Scientific Management has been so remarkable (the output per employee having in some businesses been trebled) that its wide extension in the near future is, as I have said, certain. But its main defect will probably be found to be that which it shares with the classical political economy, the over-simplification of the problem by using the subordinate end of maximum output in dealing with factors where the more ultimate end of maximum human happiness or human good would be more appropriate.[1]

The element of Happiness and Unhappiness, or at least of immediate Pleasantness and Unpleasantness, does, it is true, enter into the rather unreliable figures which Mr. F. W. Taylor and the other "scientific managers" present to show the percentage of increased wages which is said to be found necessary in order to induce workmen to submit to the unpleasant processes of a diminution of personal liberty, the formation of new habits, and the putting out of increased effort.[2] But the most important economic effects of a diminution of the Happiness of a whole class take long to reveal themselves, and cannot easily be balanced against an increase of wages. If, as Mr. Taylor seems to assume, the proportion of the total product which falls to the owner and employer is (in spite of the moderate rise of wages which he advocates) to be increased, and if the effort of the working day is made markedly more severe, it will require the exchange of impressions and thoughts for some years before that fact is consciously appreciated by organised working-class opinion. When that has happened the result may

---

[1] See an admirable article on Scientific Management by Mr. J. A. Hobson, in the *Sociological Review* for July 1913.

[2] F. W. Taylor, *Shop Management*, 1911, pp. 25-27, and his *Principles of Scientific Management* (special edition for the Society of Mechanical Engineers, 1911), p. 43.

be a greatly increased impatience with "the wage system" as a whole, and such a growth of the spirit of "ca' canny" and "sabotage" as may be inconsistent even with the maintenance of the increased production of wealth. Such results, whether they are good or bad, are too serious to be incurred merely for the sake of experiment, and those who wish to avoid them must form hypotheses about more distant effects than the profits of a single business for a few months or years, and must make some use of the more or less *a priori* methods of general psychology and sociology.

In such a sociological investigation of the probable ultimate effect of Scientific Management either upon social good or upon the narrower problem of the Happiness or the Pleasantness of the working day, some help may, as I have already urged in my chapter on Habit, be gained from the history of the arts. In so far as the organisation of the Great Industry involves for each worker a complex series of ordered manual acts based upon the experience of others, and only acquired by him with difficulty, it does not necessarily differ in principle from the older crafts or create a new cause of permanent discomfort. The Sinhalese potter owed much of his happiness in his work to the fact that he had painfully acquired the "right" methods of turning the wheel and "throwing" the clay. The violinist, during the act of playing, is (even if we put aside such factors as his prospects of applause or money), in a more desirable state of consciousness if he has been rigidly taught the "right" use of his bow than if he has been left to please himself in his technique. The cause of this is that the arts of pottery and violin-playing have been slowly adapted to a number of nervous and muscular conditions which make for permanent as well as immediate efficiency. If therefore any one discovers the series of movements by which a bricklayer working for a month can lay most bricks, there is no necessary presumption that the adoption of that series, instead of those now traditional in the trade, may not, without any permanent increase of painful effort, increase his output during twenty years, or may not actually increase his sense of comfort while at work.

The painful effects of monotony come not from the repetition, but from the exact repetition of series of movements. In the traditional arts, although the artist constantly carried out his purpose by repeating the same preordained series of actions, repetition was never exact. No touch of the "thrower's" hand on the revolving clay, no sweep of the violinist's arm was precisely like any other, and they obtained larger possibilities of variation by playing different tunes and making different classes of pots. Such an avoidance of exact repetition is also a possible condition of highly organised machine industry. The machine-tender need not be merely a part of his machine. Eighty years ago men used to write of mechanical cotton-spinning as being, owing to its complete monotony, the most destructive among all occupations of the worth and happiness of life. But the "minder" of a large modern cotton-spinning or lace-making machine never intends any of his customary actions to be precisely like the last. He has to correct minute variations in the running of his machine and not to imitate its uniformity.

If, therefore, the day's work of the textile or boot-making machine-tenders at Ruskin College was "all toil," it was not necessarily unimprovable toil. A scientific organiser who considered the Happiness as well as the "efficiency" of the workman would consider carefully how to retain this element of intelligent variation in machine industry by leaving all exactly uniform movements to the machine. If in any particular operation he failed to do so, he would be wise, even at a certain loss of immediate efficiency, to vary from time to time the character of the machines used by a particular workman or the grade of material which he handles. If, as is said, rail-lifters work best when their rhythmic movements are adjusted to a musical tune, care should at least be taken to vary the tune. If unavoidable work is still exceptionally monotonous, it may be found worth while to alternate it with other work. At present one often has the impression that, even from the point of view of the most economical production of the most desirable commodities, subdivision of labour is carried (often by mere inertia) to a degree inconsistent with full efficiency. Streets would be pleasanter to live in if architects allowed more initiative to their assistants, and furniture would be pleasanter to use if skilled workmen were encouraged, at perhaps a slight increase of expense, to develop such opportunities of invention as are consistent with the use of machinery.

But during the working day a man's direct relation to his work does not occupy all his consciousness. His comfort, for instance, largely depends on his relation to his fellow-workmen and to the system by which his work is tested and judged.

In his relation to his fellow-workmen, the most important factor to be allowed for is the quantitative limitation of our powers of forming that kind of subconscious and complete acquaintance with other human beings upon which ease of intercourse depends. A man may "love" his whole species, but he only "likes" those whose names and faces and characters he can recall without conscious effort. If he is employed in a business with two thousand other hands, and if his relation to no one of them is more permanent and particular than his relation to any other, there will be no one whom he can "like." The number of his fellows with whom a man can maintain easy personal intercourse varies with individual variations, with the conditions of work, and with the time which any body of workmen spend together. Perhaps it does not often exceed eighty, and is normally about twenty or thirty. I do not know of any important attempt to organise mechanical work in relation to that fact, though sometimes the success of a "gang system" may accidentally depend on it. An American engineer said, I was once told, that the only piece of work which he had thoroughly enjoyed was the making of the Key West Railway, where each pier was placed upon a separate rock in the sea, and was erected by a small and separate group of men who came to know each other thoroughly. In armies it is found necessary, if any measure of comfort and contentment is to be secured, that the officers in each regiment and the men in each company or platoon should be deliberately formed into groups, generally numbering about twenty-five; and one of the responsible organisers of a great Insurance Company told me that he consciously aims at bringing groups of twenty or thirty officials into regular social intercourse. Those Universities are most successful where, by an arrangement of "colleges" or "dormitories," the students are divided into somewhat larger groups; and if no arrangement of the kind has been made by the authorities, clubs or cliques, in forms sometimes inconsistent with other conditions of desirable social life, spontaneously make their appearance.[1]

The same quantitative limitations which fix the possibility of informal social intercourse among a body of men engaged in a common occupation also affect their comfort while their work is being inspected, and indirectly the comfort and efficiency of the inspector. If one enquires, as I from time to time have done, into the happiness or unhappiness of the employees in a big commercial business or government office, perhaps the most frequent complaints turn on this point. A man who has to inspect the work of five hundred, or even a hundred, others, must do so superficially. He knows nothing of the life and character of the man before him, and must judge by unimportant or accidental details observed at the moment of inspection (in a superficially organised army, for instance, mainly by the condition of a man's clothes or by his look of "smartness" on parade). Under such conditions, as a school teacher complained to me, "only the coarser and more obvious forms of success pay." Work (to use only words which I have written down after actual conversations) becomes "mechanical," "inhuman," "red-

---

[1] This limitation of the possibility of effortless intercourse is one of the considerations which make advisable that occasional transference of officials from centralised to decentralised work which I have already advocated (p. 274). The number of persons whom an official deals with in decentralised work is not too large for unforced personal acquaintance. An ex-official of the State of Victoria said to me: "I have heard several men now promoted to the Melbourne Offices speak of their time in country towns, when in daily contact with settlers, as the part of their work in which they had taken most interest."

tapish," and those who have to do it become "system-sick" and suffer from "Potterers' Rot."

What is worse is that the defects of any system of inspection which ignores the quantitative limitations of personal intercourse can be "played up to" by the baser kind of employee. A Washington civil servant was, I believe, typical of many thousand others when he complained to me: "The low-class man who cares only to draw his pay and intrigue for promotion is happy. The man of public spirit or with the crafts-man's love of his work is unhappy." "If one tries to succeed," said an English municipal official to me, "one is ashamed of doing so."

But the discomfort of an attempt to produce a good impression by other means than good work may exist independently either of the baseness or nobility of the official concerned. I remember once in Washington visiting, in company with one of the Assistant Secre-taries to the Treasury, a department under Treasury control. The Assistant Secretary had been, in the American fashion, only some ten months in his post, and was not likely to remain there more than twenty months longer. He was an exceptionally able man, given power over a much larger body of officials than he could possibly know, and unprovided with that trusted hierarchy of high permanent officials by which he would have been assisted in Europe. This was his first visit, and would perhaps be his last, to the depart-ment. The Head of the department was also, I judged, an able official. But the agony of his efforts to produce a good impression in the hour or so of his in-tercourse with the Under-Secretary was almost un-bearable to myself, who had watched the same sufferings in English elementary teachers on the occasion of the old set annual visit of a Government inspector. If a man's success in life is really to depend upon an hour's "window-dressing" talk, it is clear that the faithful performance of his duties is not the only or the best way to prepare himself for that ordeal.

Much has been done in almost all great businesses and services to prevent the more obvious faults of superficial inspection. The head of a great business is often warned that he must neither blame or praise an individual workman for what he happens to see in a visit to the works. Confidential "dossiers" are sometimes kept of a man's whole career, which are consulted before any step is taken to promote or degrade him. But success in the art of "human" as compared to "mechanical" direction is, I believe, still largely a matter of accident. The best output, both of Happiness in the producers, and of the commodities and services which they produce, apparently now takes place when, perhaps, from ten to thirty of them are responsible to a higher officer,[1] who knows his men without the effort of remembering them, who inspires loyalty, and even

[1] The number of subordinates with whom an official can maintain that complete and subconscious ease of acquaintance which is necessary for "human" (or "humane") direction, varies, like the range of acquaintance of a workman with his fellows, greatly with the conditions of the service and the idiosyncrasies of the superior official. Mr. Phipps of the English Board of Education, in giving evidence before the Royal Commission on the Civil Service (question 9384) refers to "heads of clerical sections" in his office who are "kept in close touch from day to day with the Chief Clerk," and says, "there are eleven of these heads of sections—not more than the Chief Clerk can keep in touch with." Another very successful and humane directing official whom I know, is by exception, able to keep in touch, in Mr. Phipps' sense, with a much larger number, perhaps thirty, direct subordinates, and to have a real knowledge of some hundreds of their subordinates. The limit of men's powers in this respect depends, to a quite important degree, upon their natural "memory for faces," and, if Professor Muensterberg's plan of psy-

affection, among them, because, rather than "give away" a subordinate by allowing him to be punished for a fault which was not one of character, he will take the blame on himself, and who in turn is known and trusted by those above him who are responsible for the general organisation of the whole business.

In this difficult task of adjusting the vastness of the Great Society to the smallness of individual man, one of the most useful ideas to be kept before the inventor of an organisation is the "self-respect" of those who are to be organised. An important means of preserving that self-respect is, as I have just said, such a system of inspection and control as shall secure that a man is judged on his whole character and by his best work. Another, in the case of the more important public officials, is that degree of recognition of their personal work and responsibility for which I pleaded while considering the Organisation of Thought.[1] But even in the case of the ordinary journey-man or clerk or teacher, more could be done than is now done to bring him into conscious contact with the service which he does to the community, and therefore into conscious recognition of his own social worth. Each particular point in that process might seem small, and yet the total effect on Happiness might be large. Boys and girls at school might learn the history and wider aspects of the staple industry of their district, technical education might aim at breadth of social outlook as well as preparation for more varied processes, Trade Unions

---

chological tests for office is ever generally adopted, a test of that type of memory might well be applied to candidates for certain kinds of directing work. I, myself, if I were submitted to such a test, would be certainly rejected.

[1] See *ante*, pp. 274-275.

might attain to something of the medieval craft-pride, while escaping the monopolist narrowness of the Medieval Gild. The English National Union of Teachers is not a perfect body, but I have watched for thirty years the process (still grievously incomplete) by which it has made self-respect possible in the profession of elementary teaching. An English bishop once related that when he was inspecting schools in the late eighteen-fifties, and was staying with a clergyman, he said, "That was a nice-looking lad who brought me my boots this morning," and was answered, "Yes, he is my schoolmaster." Even the most autocratic clerical "manager" of a country school would not say that now, and the change involves an enormous increase of Happiness. Perhaps a corresponding change may take place during the coming generation in the position of those employed in organised retail trade. Professor Muensterberg's treatment of the psychological problem of retail shopkeeping seems indeed to me to be a marked instance of the danger, even in a purely economic calculation, of ignoring all factors except the pecuniary profit of the employer. The same increased psychological self-consciousness that would bring about, according to his calculations, an increase in compulsory lying [1] might easily also help to produce a strong Shop Assistants' Union, the members of which

---

[1] "The effects which we have studied so far were produced by inanimate objects, posters, or displays, advertisements or labels and packings. The economic psycho-technics of the future will surely study with similar methods the effects of the living commercial agencies. The point is to enhance the impulse to buy and to suppress the opposing ideas. . . . The voice may win or destroy confidence, the statement may by its firmness overcome countermotives, or by its uncertainty reinforce them" (Muensterberg, *Psychology and Industrial Efficiency,* pp. 294 and 296). See *ante,* my Chapter VIII. p. 115.

would be able to resist orders to lie with unction, just as a member of the National Union of Teachers is now able to resist an order to black the clergyman's boots.

The percentage of men who are not the better for some measure of self-respect and for some sense of origination and responsibility in their work is, I believe, extremely small. Mr. F. W. Taylor assumes that men can be found to handle pig-iron, each of whom "more nearly resembles in his mental make-up the ox than any other type." [1] But the Chinese experiment of building the Great Wall by the labour of six hundred thousand prisoners, who had been surgically reduced to the condition of oxen, has not been repeated.

When one turns from the position of the men at present employed in the Great Industry to that of the women, one is immediately conscious that the whole problem is changed, and changed in a way which is unintelligible unless one substitutes Happiness for Wealth-Production as the criterion. The wages paid to women even for work of the same grade are generally smaller than those paid to men, the grade of work is, as a rule, less interesting and more monotonous, discipline is often more mechanical and "trying." But women and girls seem to judge their working lives by reference, not to these things, but to other and "non-economic" considerations.

I have already quoted the Ruskin College student, who had "known girls of good position work ten hours a day for nine shillings a week," and who believed "that the attraction is purely the independence **thus**

[1] *The Principles of Scientific Management*, p. 59.

gained." Wage-labour, that is to say, in the Great Industry is felt by many, if not most, of the women and
girls engaged in it to represent a deliberate choice of
"independence" as against the dependence of an unpaid member of a family. And even for those who
come from homes where the men receive high wages
the alternative of dependence is now becoming more
consciously intolerable.

The very existence of the Great Industry means that
most of the commodities and services which used to
be produced by the unpaid and unorganised work of
the female members of the average household are now
produced, with an enormously increased economy of
labour, by the paid and organised work of men and
women in factories, laundries, schools, offices, and hospitals. In the four-roomed tenements which are the
typical homes of the new industrial cities [1] there is
nothing for the girl to do who has left school and has
not gone to work, which she feels, or her mother feels,
to be really worth doing, and therefore .compatible
with self-respect. Everything that was interesting,
even though it was laborious, in the women's arts
of the old village is gone. Clothes are bought ready-
made; food is bought either ready-cooked, like bread,
and jam, and fish, or only requiring the simplest kind
of cooking. There is no room for more than one pair
of hands at the little stove, and nothing is left for
the unmarried daughter but darning and sweeping.
Above all, in the noisy living-room there is no possibility either of privacy or of free and intimate com-
panionship. There results, therefore, a mass of inar-

[1] The British Census of 1911 showed that a larger number of
families (almost exactly two million) lived in four-roomed tenements than in tenements with any other number of rooms.

ticulate unhappiness, whose existence has hardly been indicated by our present methods of sociological enquiry.[1]

When I was in Boston, U. S. A., in 1910, a lady, who collected the stamps which represent the elementary savings of girls and women in the Boston laundries and poorer kind of factories, most kindly consented, at my request, to ask those of them whose confidence she had gained whether they were happy. The answers at the time surprised me greatly. I expected to hear those complaints about bad wages, hard conditions, and arbitrary discipline, which a body of men working at the same grade of labour would certainly have put forward. But it was obvious that the question, "Are you .happy?" meant to the girls "Are you happier than you would have been if you had stayed at home instead of going to work?" And almost every one of them answered "Yes."

At —— Laundry, "dismal and murky, but fair in management," six Irish girls,[2] between sixteen and thirty years old, were asked if they were happy and why. "They answered emphatically—Yes." "One said that work 'took up her mind,' she had been awfully discontented." Another that "you were of some use." Another "thought it was because the hours went so much faster. At home one could read, but only for a short time. Then there was the awful lonesome afternoon ahead of you." "Asked a little girl with dyed hair but a good little heart. She enjoyed

---

[1] The same causes, combined with a rising standard of self-respect, have made working-class girls in America, and to a less degree in England, prefer factory-labour to the domestic service where the dependence of their home is largely repeated.

[2] The word "girl" is used in America for a larger proportion of the female sex than in England.

her work. It made her feel she was worth something."

At —— Laundry the first six girls asked all gave as their first reason for happiness that the work "takes up your mind," and generally as the second reason, "It's awful lonesome at home," or "There is an awful emptiness at home." On the other hand, a girl with nine brothers and sisters was happy in the collar-packing room just because "it was so awful lonesome," and she could enjoy her own thoughts. "So far only one girl has said that she was happy at work because of the money."

At the —— Laundry an Irishwoman, who had married an Italian, said, "Sure I am always happy. It leaves me no time to think."

At the —— Laundry one girl was weeping quietly. Her father had sold the house, and was moving, apparently into a better position in another city. "She would not work now, but would stay at home with her mother, where it would be so awful lonesome." "I was awful happy in the laundry and I knew so many girls, but now I won't know no one." "Two little Italian girls told me they were happy, but they would be happier if their mother let them go out evenings now and then. They never go out except to work. Italian girls are so strictly kept."

At the —— Hosiery three girls said they were very happy at work. "The reasons they gave were the usual ones." "It took up one's mind—doing nothing made one nervous" (*i.e.* produced the condition which, in Chapter IV., I called "baulked disposition"). "Another girl said that 'when she didn't work, she was always thinking of dead people, but work always made her cheer up directly.' "

The reasons given by the comparatively few girls and women who said that they were not happy were nearly as informing as the "usual" answers. Some of the older women, most of them apparently married, had "trouble at home" so serious that they were unable to forget it at work. At one extremely rough laundry "a dear little Englishwoman" said that she was not happy "because the place was so narsty and the girls were all loose (which is true) and none of them 'ad deep feelin's. I'm just by me self." One "fat and lazy Jewess," by exception, hated the physical exertion: "Me happy? No. How could I be happy and work so hard?" But the most important exceptions were two girls who had imagination enough to conceive of a life which was neither that of the home as they knew it nor that of the factory. "A nice girl in ——— Hosiery said she was not always happy. 'I'd like to be away some day. I don't mean home alone, but I could have a companion and go off in the country some day. I'd like it better than working.' " "A Russian girl from the power-machine room at the ——— Factory came to see me last night. I asked her, and she said No. At first she could not tell why. I asked her if she would like to do nothing. She said, 'Oh, no; I am not happy idle.' In the course of the conversation I mentioned the phrase 'ladies and gentlemen,' and she said, 'Now I can tell you why I am not at work happy. I am not among ladies and gentlemen.' She was afraid she was not hearing the best English, and they did not know how she felt."

I believe that in England, or any other industrial country, an enquirer with the same genius as my Boston informant for inspiring confidence, and the same patience in eliciting truthful descriptions of complex states of feeling from those whose psychological vocabulary consists perhaps of twenty or thirty words, would obtain much the same results.

The problem which such evidence raises has two different sides. In the first place, women are clearly now entering, to an increasing degree, into the organised paid work of the Great Industry, and the Great Industry must be judged by its effects on working-women as well as working-men. Though women see the bad conditions of their work—low wages, monotonous occupation, and the rest—against the background of worse conditions at home, yet those bad conditions exist, and must be improved.

And in the second place, the background itself, the domestic environment of the Great Society, must be submitted to a new analysis. Part of that analysis will involve the whole tremendous problem of sex-relation. Our confused sexual instincts seem to correspond to a confused history of the evolution of various instinctive or conventional sexual arrangements in the distant past, which only had in common the fact that sexual intercourse was frequent, and that the majority of human children, like the majority of the offspring of other animals, died young. From the beginning of civilisation philosophers and legislators have attempted to contrive schemes which should secure that the sex-relation should be regularly and rationally organised, and that all children should be both well-born and safely brought to maturity. Those schemes have either never been adopted or have failed. At the end of life most men have looked back upon their own sexual history with shame, and many women upon theirs with anger. It was when the Athenian Greeks were at the height of an experiment in social organisation, which in other respects was one of the most brilliantly successful ever known, that Euripides, who understood better than any other man of his, or, perhaps, of any succeeding time, the woman's point of view, makes Medea say, "Of all beings born to life and intelligence we women are the most unhappy." [1] If we are to succeed at a point where the Athenians failed, we shall require not only all the knowledge which is being accumulated by the physiologists and psychologists, but all the courage and flexibility of Plato's imagination, and more than Plato's sympathy with the hard-pressed and disinherited of both sexes.

Both the fact that an increasing number of women are now in the paid service either of the Great Industry or the State itself, and therefore find that their economic prospects depend on State policy, and the increasing urgency of the political problems affecting marriage and the family, make, I believe, Women's Suffrage one of the necessary conditions of any successful adaptation of the Great Society to our inherited nature. The immediate effects of Women's Suffrage will not be wholly good. If as large a proportion of women are enfranchised as of men, it will mean the instant doubling of the constituencies by the addition of millions of voters without experience, largely indifferent, and of whom, at present in England, a greater proportion than of the present male voters

[1] Euripides, *Medea*, 231.

cannot be brought to the poll except by the sort of "whirlwind campaign" which is so expensive that it can only be organised by the great capitalist "interests." If not more than a fraction of the women are to be immediately enfranchised, the only proposals which seem to have any chance of acceptance would confine that fraction to the comparatively small body of unmarried or widowed householders who now enjoy the Municipal vote. I have fought as candidate five London Municipal elections under the existing law, and I know that in a poor district that body of women includes a serious proportion who are more bitterly anti-social than any other class, who hate the very idea of the central or local State, of rates or taxes, and of paying for the education of "other people's children" or the improvement of "other people's houses." Many of the differences between men and women voters are due to circumstances and education. Some of them (though the secondary psychology of sex has received very little serious attention) may be found to be due to a difference, showing itself rather by the average of large groups than by the comparison of individuals, in their inherited type. Common speech suggests, and my own limited experience of women in public life goes to confirm it, that an able woman is more likely to be influenced by that tendency to substitute feeling for calculation in what I have called "instinctive inference" [1] than an equally able man, that she feels more keenly on personal questions, and that "principles" are apt to be for her solid entities adhered to without exception and with passionate loyalty, rather than working indications of conduct in a world where

[1] Pp. 218 et seq.

every instance differs from every other. The women followers of Marx or Kropotkin in social agitation, or of Froebel in education, are apt to be more intransigeant than the men.[1] One sometimes fears their influence in the adjustment of the relations between Church and State, and in the ever-pressing danger of European War. But when the question is the simple one of Vote or No Vote, these considerations, important as they are, seem to me to be less important than the need both of the consent and of the active assistance of half the human race in the task of organising human Happiness.

The same difficulties are involved in the possession by women of the powers arising from private property as of the powers arising from the vote, and in most civilised states it has been found necessary to assimilate the position of the two sexes in that respect. The fact that many women now hold railway shares in their own name may ultimately alter in some degree, not the position of women shareholders as compared to those of men shareholders, but the position of all shareholders, men or women, in relation to the professional railway managers or the associations of railway servants. And it may also ultimately happen that the possession of the vote by women may alter, not the

[1] One's judgment in this respect is due, of course, to a vague estimation of many hundred instances. But it may be illustrated by the position held by Frau Rosa Luxemburg ("die rote Rosa") in the German Social Democratic Party; or by that of Miss Emma Goldman among the American revolutionists; or by the part played by Saint Theresa in the Counter Reformation. Mr. Keir Hardie puts the feeling about women, which I have tried to express above, in a more optimistic form when he says, "Whilst her influence in politics will be humanising, it will also be strengthening, and much of the chicanery and knavery of political life will go down before her direct march upon the actual" (*The Case for Women's Suffrage*, 1907, p. 83). In a vast and complex society that which is instinctively felt to be "actual" may in fact be very abstract.

relation of women voters to men voters, but the relation of all voters to the other factors in the national
Will-Organisation. If, for instance, the joint constituency of men and women proves to be more bound
by abstract formulas and less ready to allow for the
imperfection of human nature than was the constituency of men only, that may be an added reason
against the direct election of judges, or against the
direct responsibility of members of representative
bodies for the administration of such nationalised industries as the Post Office or the Railway system.

But while in such matters as the ownership of land
or railway stock, or the bare act of electing a candidate, the woman is merely a substitute for a man who
would otherwise exercise the same rights, in many
important respects the entry of women into the larger
life of the Great Society constitutes an addition and
not a substitution of social force. Women are fed and
housed and clothed already, and no one proposes that
they should either be exterminated or should consume
less wealth than they do at present. If they do more
work, think more thoughts, and offer a larger contribution of skilled organisers than they do at present
to the grievously insufficient personnel by which the
Great Society is held together, we shall be drawing a
larger dividend from the same body of human capital.

But the position of men and women in the Great
Industry is only one of a multitude of problems in
the Great Society whose solution is best approached
by the criterion of Happiness. In applying that criterion it is often convenient to use Aristotle's quantitative conception of the Mean. Although particular

Pleasure-sensations are caused by the stimulation, whether weak or strong, of particular dispositions, the feeling tone of Pleasantness, and still more the state of consciousness called Happiness, may accompany the stimulation of all or any of our dispositions, provided that that stimulation takes place neither in excess nor defect but to the right or "Mean" degree. If we use this formula, it becomes easy to see, for instance, that, outside as well as inside the hours of industrial employment, failures in the organised production of Happiness are often due to the fact that "Division of Labour" has been carried to a point where, in respect of some particular function, the mass of mankind have too little given them to do for Happiness, and a few responsible persons too much. The old objection to the "dull uniformity" of Socialism, which has always seemed so absurd to the Socialists, and which nevertheless so constantly reappears, is due to a half-conscious generalisation in the ordinary man's mind from innumerable cases where, under public or philanthropic management, the function of Thought has been loaded on to a single overworked brain and denied to the many who in that respect are underworked. One sees the girls from an orphanage file along the street. Each girl walks by a companion, not chosen by herself with all the painful-delightful scheming of girlhood, but by the tired mistress who gives a general order that the girls nearest to each other in height should walk together. They all wear clothes and boots and carry umbrellas of the same pattern. A uniform hat-ribbon may be necessary for recognition and discipline; but one feels that if each girl had chosen her necktie and umbrella, even from a dozen equally cheap patterns, both the choosing and the wearing would have been a source of positive Happiness. If a committee of each class in such an institution chose dinner daily from the list of possible dishes, six girls would spend ten minutes each in the effort of Thought instead of one matron spending ten seconds. But the girls would enjoy their effort and the matron does not.

The fact, again, that there is a Mean in our powers of forming intimate acquaintance, that it is a joy to know enough people and a weariness to know too many, affects not only the group-organisation of the Great Industry, but also the life of the industrial worker during the now slowly lengthening interval between his work and his sleep. The young unmarried artisan, or shopman, or clerk generally lives either in a one-roomed lodging with a defect of intimate association or in a great boarding-house with an excess of it. Outside his factory or office, he may either know no one to speak to or have a hundred nodding acquaintances and no friend.

Many opponents of the socialistic tendency in modern politics are honestly convinced that this departure from the Mean in the use of human faculties is a necessary result, both of the collectivist type of organisation, and of dependence upon exceptional public spirit as a directing social force. The representative or the philanthropist is, they believe, compelled by the nature of his being to do his fellow-men's thinking for them, and to think of them as if they were all alike. It is only when you leave mankind as far as possible "free" to direct their own lives that they will, it is argued, each for himself, contrive a working approximation to the Mean. At this point the anarchist-communist and the individualist defender of property are often in very real sympathy. Hodgskin and Proudhon were perhaps the two ablest leaders in the nineteenth-century revolt against property as the enemy of freedom. But both of them ended in believing that their ideal would be best attained by the defence of property against the State. In England to-day Mr. Belloc and Mr. Chesterton, while attempting to re-create the ideal of Catholic peasant proprietorship in a world of railways and factories, often find themselves in alliance with those interests which have no ideals beyond the rapid making of large fortunes.

The present form of the doctrine that Happiness is better attained by Laissez-Faire (secured either by the existing rights of property or by some kind of anarchism, or by such a combination of the two as the "Associative" or "Distributive" State) than by either the Representative State or organised philanthropy, may perhaps be put most effectively if it is divided into two arguments. The first would be that which I have just indicated, that new social arrangements to meet the needs of a new environment cannot be invented for the mass of mankind by a few professed thinkers and politicians, but must be the result of innumerable experiments in which as many individuals as possible have freely taken part. The second argument would be that no new arrangements which are invented can work well unless they are based upon the permanent freedom of each individual to manage his own life and to use or abuse his own property.

Both arguments include a real and important element of truth. With regard to the first, it is true that Happiness depends upon so subtle and complex a

harmony of innumerable factors that the mind of the
single thinker is a poor substitute for the intimate
experiences of the many minds for whom he thinks.
But yet the very complexity and interconnection of
all modern social problems make it almost impossible
for social invention to proceed by individual experiments, founded upon the individual needs of the inventor and his family, and imitated by their neighbours. If any large proportion of the young clerks and
apprentices in a great modern city are to form the
right kind of friendships, it is not enough, though it
is important, that boys or parents should look out
for chances. Some one possessed of special power or
knowledge or devotion must also cause "overtime"
to be so regulated and restricted that the lads can
make and keep appointments with each other after
work. And now that the streets are nearly as noisy
and as full of moving machinery as a factory, some
one must arrange the provision of quiet places (class-
rooms out of school hours, clubs, gymnasiums, or
parks) where lads can talk and play together; or tram-
committees or railway companies must grant new facilities for carrying them to the spots from which
country walks can begin. We now take the continuous discovery and immediate spread of mechanical inventions for granted, because we grant patents for
them, and a patentee can make a fortune by pushing
his ideas. But no patents are granted, because no
monopoly is possible, for inventions in social organisation. Though it may occasionally pay a railway company to advertise the general notion, say, of country
walking, the inventors of the Boy Scouts had to spend
unrewarded years in laborious propaganda, and in the

still more laborious collection of subscriptions, before their ideas could be made effective.

While, therefore, it is true that social (as distinguished from mechanical) inventions are not likely to be made at all in the Great Society unless the feelings and experience of many individuals are brought to bear upon them, it is not true that such social inventions will often be effectively made unless that experience is interpreted by organised effort, inspired by "non-economic" motives. And those motives are not now likely to be sufficiently strong and lasting unless they are made either by individuals of exceptional public spirit or by a government whose direct purpose, however imperfectly carried out, is the general good. It is this fact which renders every increase in the articulateness of working men and women, in the power, that is to say, of the more public-spirited among them, to bring their feelings and experience and ideas into the common stock so important. I believe, to take one instance, that no more fruitful field of social invention now exists than that which concerns the customs of average family life in the new industrial districts. Ought the sitting and cooking room of a family of six persons, with an income of thirty-five shillings a week, to be combined? If a separate sitting-room exists, should it be used and if necessary warmed every day, or be kept tidy and unused for special occasions? Should neighbours "call" on each other, or should a respectable girl (like the Boston laundry-worker whom I quoted) have reason to fear that in a new city she "won't," except by chance accident, "know no one"? If calling customs exist, should the social intercourse of youths and maidens approach

the system current in the American middle class, where
the young men call on the girls, or the English and
Scottish tradition that the call must be ostensibly on
the parents?   How, in the typical tenement, is a certain measure of privacy to be secured for an unmarried daughter, either spending the day at home or
coming home after her work?   If she is engaged in paid
outside work, what proportion of her wages should she
give to her mother? and if she stays at home to help
her mother with housework and the care of the younger
children, what pocket-money or dress-money should
she have?   The circumstances of every family differ,
of course, from those of every other, and vary themselves from month to month.   But the main outlines
of the problem are at least as uniform in an industrial
city dependent upon one or two standard trades, as in
a country village, or in the "residential districts" inhabited by the payers of income tax.   The rural villagers had a generation ago their own social customs,
adapted to conditions which have now disappeared.
Handbooks containing the social customs of the well-
to-do can be bought for a shilling by those who have
lately joined that class, and the deliberate reform of
those customs is discussed with extraordinary concentration and skill in scores of "problem novels" and
plays.   But in spite of the admirable writings of Miss
Jane Addams and Lady Bell,[1] one feels that thought
about social customs in the average street has not yet
either been directed by sufficient knowledge and ability, or so recorded and compared as to prevent the best
ideas being forgotten before they become effective.

[1] Cf. Jane Addams, *The Spirit of Youth and the City Streets,*
and Lady Bell, *At the Works.*

The problem of inventing new social customs in working-class homes involves, indeed, like the problem of inventing social opportunities for the young independent worker, a much more complex and difficult series of factors than does the corresponding problem under middle-class conditions. A well-to-do family can live where they like, and in a house, within wide limits, of any shape or size that they choose. The working-man has to live near his work in a house built by a great company, according to plans narrowly controlled by local by-laws. An annual fortnight's holiday for any large number of families may require an elaborate agreement between the local education authority who teach the children and the manufacturing firms who employ the parents. The question whether it ought to be the custom for daughters to go for evening walks depends upon the opening and shutting and lighting and policing of the nearest public park.

If, therefore, a branch of the Workers' Educational Association, or of the Co-operative Union, consisting about equally of men and women of the working-class, would work on this problem with a trained woman sociologist who had access to the customs of other countries, a philanthropic employer, and a member of the local municipal council, the best conditions of invention might be attained; and they might even find themselves making an important beginning in the invention of social customs for that possible English society of the future, where, as now in New Zealand or parts of Switzerland, almost the whole population would belong to one "class." [1]

[1] The working population of the great American cities, consisting as it does so largely of recent immigrants, is far less articulate

Such an enquiry would enable those who took part
in it not only to think with effect upon the customs of
the average home, but to remember that which it is so
easy to forget, the quantitative relation between a city
and its inhabitants.

Convenient city quarters cannot be created by each
family choosing a site for itself, any more than healthy
city houses can be built without by-laws. The width
and direction of streets, the size and position of the
public buildings and parks, as well as the height and
material of the buildings, must be finally fixed by some
one acting on behalf of the whole community. The
science of City-Planning is therefore rapidly developing into the Master-science of the material conditions
of modern life. But when one looks, for instance, at
the beautiful drawings which have been lately prepared by a body of citizens for a new Chicago, one
feels that they are suited to giants and not men, or
at least only to the gigantic qualities of mankind. It
is a good thing that every citizen's heart should be
occasionally stirred by seeing the tower of a tall municipal office against the skyline, or by standing beneath the enormous dome of a museum. But ten parks,
which the inhabitants of ten quarters can reach in a

and self-directed than the corresponding population in an English
city. The middle-class members of the hundreds of American "settlements" undertake, therefore, the task of thinking out many problems which English settlement-workers would leave alone. The
book, for instance, on *Young Working Girls* (Houghton, Mifflin Co.,
1913), written by R. A. Woods and A. J. Kennedy, from the results
of an enquiry undertaken by two thousand "social workers," contains
curiously minute suggestions for the invention of games that parents
can play with their children (p. 71), exhibitions of craftsmanship by
immigrant mothers so that their American-born children may respect them (p. 73), the relation between fathers and daughters (p.
78), the pocket-money of girls, and the exhibition of "model tenements" with model household arrangements (p. 158).

twenty minutes' walk, are better than one park ten times as large which few can reach without losing a day's work; and if a working-man's wife is to buy the family supplies in comfort shopping streets must be neither too distant for her feet nor too broad for her eyes.

The second problem, however, in the relation between Freedom and social invention is the more important. Ought all social enquiries to be based on the assumption that Freedom is the absolutely essential condition of human Happiness, and, if so, what does Freedom exactly mean? In considering this second problem, it will be convenient to project Freedom on to the same plane as Happiness, to think of Freedom, that is to say, not as an external social arrangement, but as the state of consciousness which is expected to result from certain arrangements, and which can be studied in relation to the state of consciousness called Happiness. Common speech has always insisted on the close connection between Freedom, in this sense, and Happiness or Pleasantness. A man feels "free" when he acts at his "pleasure." And those who agree with Tolstoy and Ibsen and Mr. Shaw that Freedom is a necessary condition, not only of Happiness but of Goodness, sometimes express that opinion in terms of "pleasure." When I was in America in 1910, a quarrel took place between Mr. Conners of the New York State Democratic organisation and Mr. Charles Murphy of Tammany Hall. Mr. Conners issued a short *apologia pro vita sua* in the form of a newspaper interview. In the course of it he gave as the main justification for his claim to be a better citizen than Mr. Murphy: "I am just a natural man.

. . . Murphy is a politician for profit, and I am a politician for pleasure; and I propose to have my fun out of it." [1]

A man feels "free" when his acts and sayings and thoughts seem to him to be the expression of his most real and spontaneous motives. It is true that some men will never in that sense be "free," never enjoy what Mr. Conners calls their "pleasure," even though they are as completely released from external compulsion as a modern dividend-receiver with three thousand a year and a motor-car. They may remain the slaves of convention; their minds may be "the disused rabbit-warrens of other people's opinions and prejudices." [2] Or they may be (as Mr. Conners accused Mr. Murphy of being) the slaves of money, unable to distinguish the getting of money for its own sake from that free activity to which money is only a means. Or they may be the slaves of animal passions which they feel not to be their real selves. Other men, as the later Stoics were never tired of pointing out, may feel as "free" as Epictetus, even though they are in a state of economic slavery almost as complete as that of Epictetus. Marcus Aurelius would say that such men "follow nature," and Mr. Conners that they are "natural men."

But, even if such Freedom is possible in every form of society, the actual organisation of a society where Freedom is held to be all-important will be different from that of a society in which Freedom is held to be only one element among the conditions of Happiness. The most critical point in that difference will be found

[1] *Boston Evening Transcript*, February 23, 1910.
[2] Jane Harrison, *Homo Sum*, p. 25.

in the use of force to regulate social organisation. The man against whom force is used—who is arrested by a policeman, or sentenced by a judge, or shot by a soldier—can, at the moment, be only called free by the most paradoxical of Stoics. And not even a Stoic can call the policeman, or judge, or soldier who uses violence in obedience to orders and without inner impulse free in any sense of the word. In a society it is therefore sometimes argued, where the relation of Freedom to Happiness, and therefore to social good, is rightly understood, no one will consent or be asked to put himself in such a position. Violence will only be used by those who at the moment feel a personal impulse to punish or defend. And the whole cold-blooded machinery which makes men alternately inflict and suffer violence in the support of wars which they do not desire, or property rights in which they do not believe, would come to an end. It is this that Mr. Shaw means when his Cæsar says, after Rufio has killed a murderess, "Had you set yourself in the seat of the judge, and with hateful ceremonies and appeals to the gods handed that woman over to some hired executioner to be slain before the people in the name of justice, never again would I have touched your hand without a shudder. But this was natural slaying." [1]

This point of view makes Mr. Shaw an admirable influence, both destructive and constructive, in a society whose main task is to adapt a new intellectual and material environment to the permanent facts of human nature. He asks us in effect, "Do you, as the world now is, really want to go to church, or keep the ten commandments, or whip your children, or return

[1] *Three Plays for Puritans*, p. 198.

fifty calls a month, or send this thief to prison? And
if not, why do you do these things?" There is no one
who is not the better for being required, on pain of
feeling himself to be ridiculous, to answer such questions. But the formula of the Mean covers, I believe,
even the feeling of Freedom; and that feeling must
be measured against other conditions of Happiness.
If we treat it as the one absolute and limitless condition, we are soon driven back upon the ancient fact
that we are not happy if we always do what we want,
however really we may want it. The most "natural"
and independent peasant proprietor on a fine day in
August knows that the brutal conditions of the material world will compel him to gather in his crop,
although he desires with his whole soul to go fishing;
and his feelings are not essentially different from those
of the railwayman who goes to work because he must
obey his foreman, or of the foreman who must obey
his manager. Even in the use of actual violence the
want of inner impulse may sometimes be compensated
for by other factors of the problem. A good-tempered
and disciplined policeman is a dangerous thing, and
Mr. Shaw does well to remind us of that fact. He may
obey orders as cheerfully in a bad cause as in a good.
His head-breaking is not "natural." But the justification of his existence under proper political control
is that he breaks so few heads. A soldier who is bleed-
ing to death may draw comfort from the knowledge
that the man who shot him was really angry, and that
his was a "natural slaying," yet he may, on the balance
of advantage, prefer not to be shot at all. And, if he
is a man of exceptional intelligence, he may know that
the "natural" anger of his opponent was created by

the "artificial" calculations of his opponents' prime minister.

In the Balkans, during 1912 and 1913, Europe had an excellent object lesson on the whole problem. There was much slaying, and nearly all of it was "natural." The Bulgarians when fighting the Turks, and, later on, the Greeks and Bulgarians after their quarrel, genuinely hated each other. Future historians may declare that that fact lent a reality to their actions which was wanting in the cold and impotent compromises of the European Concert, just as the fact that they were intellectually sure of what they were fighting for greatly increased their military efficiency.[1] And yet to me the most hopeful event of the year was the appearance at Scutari, in 1912, of a small but well-equipped international force of good-tempered blue-jackets, who turned the Montenegrin garrison out with a maximum of compulsive power and a minimum both of anger and of casualties.

In applying Aristotle's formula of the Mean, we must, however, remember that Aristotle himself inevitably over-simplified it. He proposed with regard to each human disposition in each relation of life a single type of "mean" conduct which all men should aim at. He further taught that the single environment in which men could reach the Mean was that of the Greek city-state. To us, however, in our complex and changing world, there are, in the use of each of our dispositions, innumerable different Means adapted to different individuals and different circumstances. The differences between individuals may be due either to inheritance or training; either, as the Eugenists say,

---

[1] See *ante*, p. 77.

to "nature" or to "nurture." To every man as he is born the personal conditions of a happy life are different, and they are changed by everything that happens to him from without. Whatever his upbringing may be, the man of poetic genius will be unhappy as a manual labourer; and, whatever his natural tastes may have been, the trained student (however unhappy he may be as a student) will be also unhappy for years, if not for life, if he is made a manual labourer. If, indeed, a man's "nurture" has not corresponded to his "nature," the possibility of anything like complete Happiness may have been destroyed for him before he is thirty.

Already, therefore, throughout the Great Society, the organisation of public education is being steadily, though slowly and insufficiently, turned, with the help of such psychological knowledge as is now available, to discover in time the special faculties of children, and to start them on that course of life for which they are best fitted. All social reformers are also aiming at such a manipulation of the taxation of accumulated wealth (through death-duties and the like), that no man shall be made extremely unhappy either by a sudden alteration of life-long habit or by such initial poverty as shall prevent him from developing his powers. And meanwhile we are a little ashamed of the insistence, for instance, of the average sedentary journalist, that what is the mean for him must be the mean for every one else, and that a working man who finishes on Saturdays at 1 P.M. a fifty hours' week of hard manual toil, ought to play football, instead of looking on at it, from 3 P.M. to 4-30 P.M.

Not only, again, is the Mean different for different

men according to their nature and nurture, but for each man the Mean consists, not in uniformity, but in variety. The dinner which was my Mean yesterday will not be my Mean to-day, simply because I had it yesterday. When men at different times in their lives seek Happiness in different types of good conduct, they may not be "inconsistent." If they would realise this, many men would be saved a great deal of unavailing regret for their own past, and of useless censure of those who do not for the moment accept their present ideals. Lord Rosebery, when in 1912 he unveiled the statue of a public-spirited county councillor, said: "Any reflecting mind could point out the enormous advantage that there was in local service, where one could live at home and enjoy one's own neighbourhood and the company of one's lifelong friends in working for results which one saw immediately fulfilled all round one, as compared with political service, which occupied one in a close and often intolerable metropolis, co-operating nominally with many with whom one politically differed, for purposes which one was not likely to see realised in one's lifetime, and which it was not always certain that one particularly wished to see fulfilled. . . . There were daring and ambitious spirits wishing to mix in the turmoil of the world and raise themselves high above the common herd who would always prefer the last, but the tranquil and contented philosopher would, like Sir Robert Dundas, always prefer the first." [1] Lord Rosebery probably remembered that in his own youth he would have shrunk from the idea of life-long service as a Mid-Lothian county-councillor. And yet both he, in preferring na-

[1] *Times,* January 18, 1912.

tional politics in his youth and local politics in his late middle age, and a county-councillor who had preferred local politics in youth and national politics later, may have been consistent in aiming at the Mean. And not only in the arrangement of our whole lives, but also in the choice of work and recreation for each week or year, we approach nearest the Mean when we can enjoy such a degree of variation as is consistent with the use of our new powers over nature. As Mr. Wells says: "The human spirit has never quite subdued itself to the laborious and established life; it achieves its best with variety and occasional vigorous exertion under the stimulus of novelty rather than by constant toil." [1] The "Sabbatical year," for instance, of the American professor may slowly extend (perhaps as more frequent Sabbatical half- or quarter-years) to many other occupations.

Sometimes, however, one seems to be brought nearer to the quantitative conditions of human Happiness by the conception of Economy than by that of the Mean. Few of us can now conceive of a social organisation which will be so successful in attaining the Mean that it will not be necessary for men and women to work harder and more continuously, and to think more painfully, than is consistent with the complete Pleasantness of the moment, or with the complete Happiness of a whole life. We are so placed in the world that, even under the best social arrangements which we can invent, it will only be by a painful excess of effort in our production of wealth that we shall avoid a still

---

[1] *Daily Mail*, December 20, 1910. See also Mr. Roosevelt (*American Ideals*) with respect to political duties. "Accordingly we ought, as far as possible, to have a system requiring on the average citizen's part intermittent and not sustained action."

more painful defect in our consumption of wealth. Our aim, therefore, must be the Economy of that excess of effort rather than its abolition. The most obvious and most urgent form of that Economy is a nearer approach to equality. In a community whose members started life with approximately equal opportunities of satisfying their desires, the severity of the average working-day would be a fair measure of the average desire for wealth. It may be that we should find ourselves in such a community working harder on the average and producing more than at present, but my own expectation is that we should work somewhat less hard, even if, in consequence, we produced rather less.

Another Economy would result from that better adaptation of individual natural and trained faculty to individual function for which I have just argued. The man whose work fits him will do many times as much of it without painful excess of effort as the man who is, by temperament or training, or both, unfitted for it. The particular form of effort of which this is most true is, perhaps, that kind of organising Thought which is the special need of the Great Industry and the Great Society. To be a "good man of business," a man must be able to interpret written or printed documents as easily as concrete persons and things, to think intensely on a series of unconnected and superficially presented problems, not because they interest him, but because they must be immediately dealt with; and to inhibit his thinking on each point the instant that it is time to deal with some other point. Some men will do such work for four or five hours every day with a sense of mastery and delight, even although they find it necessary to work another three or four hours daily

against the grain. To others even the shortest spell
of it is an agony. This is often the case with the men
of artistic temperament and training, who are accustomed to get their results by waiting, in the attitude
of creative effort, upon their subconscious intellectual
processes.[1] Liszt, who did more creative work in a
day than would, if it had been spread over a week,
have been sufficient to kill an average stockbroker,
used to say: "Art is easy; Life is difficult."[2]

If we more often used Happiness instead of efficiency
as our social criterion, it might be easier than it is
now for specialised business-men to realise, in this
respect, the limitation of their ordinary fellow-citizens.
The English National Health Assurance Act of 1911
and the regulations founded upon it have resulted in
the issue to the general public of a series of printed
papers which a trained official working at full speed
would master in a quarter of an hour, and the creation
of a number of recurring duties to which he would give
two or three minutes a week. But the mass of helpless irritation and suffering which these requirements
have created in the untrained public is so large as to
make it possible that the whole course of English
political development may be diverted by it for a generation.

The National Insurance Act is only one instance of

[1] See *ante,* Chapter X.
[2] I have read that in some parts of India the natives call this
type of Thought "bunderbust," and, being themselves incapable of
it, are amazed that the sahibs can endure so much of it without
suicide. But the evidence, as in Æsop's fable, comes from the
"hunter" and not from the "lion," and one is left even in this case
with a doubt whether an increased economy of effort would not
result in India from an arrangement by which a larger proportion of "bunderbust" were left to those natives who are specially
fitted for it, and a less proportion to the admittedly overworked
sahibs.

a danger which continually attends the present socialistic trend of the Great Society, and of which those
who believe that that trend is both necessary and good
must take careful heed. As long as the Great Society
continues, even under the most carefully reformed
conditions, and, still more, as long as we are engaged
in the process of its reformation, we must submit to
the Division of Labour; and the Division of Labour
will involve, if it is to be effective, a certain degree of
compulsion. That compulsion may be direct, as when
we compel all parents to send their children to school,
or all landlords to keep their houses in a sanitary condition, or all youths to serve in the army; or indirect,
as when the Poor Law Guardians offer work to unem-
ployed persons, or secondary schools offer education to
qualified children, under stated conditions, or when an
election or referendum is based on the assumption that
every citizen will think and vote. In either case the
man who draws up the necessary regulations is a
trained and specialised enthusiast, a keen "education-
ist," or doctor, or military officer, or politician. They
all believe that the efforts which they require, and
which are so easy to themselves, will make those from
whom they require them both better and happier. But
all their requirements converge on to the unspecialised
child or citizen to whom none of them are easy. A
spread of the spirit of Economy in this respect, a com-
monsense which shall prevent each specialist from asking or obtaining more than his fair share of his neighbour's painful effort, is a very real necessity at our
present stage of democratic evolution.

Yet the conceptions both of the Mean and of Economy, necessary as they are for every Organisation

which regulates our relation to our neighbours, still leave something undescribed which we feel to be an essential condition of the good life. Aristotle, in one of those conversational flashes which lie in wait for his readers on almost every page of the Ethics, says: "Virtue is rightly defined as a Mean, and yet in so far as it aims at the highest excellence, it is an Extreme." [1] No social Organisation is, we feel, good which does not contain that element which Aristotle here calls the Extreme.

If I try to make for myself a visual picture of the social system which I should desire for England and America, there comes before me a recollection of those Norwegian towns and villages where everyone, the shopkeepers and the artisans, the schoolmaster, the boy who drove the post-ponies, and the student daughter of the innkeeper who took round the potatoes, seemed to respect themselves, to be capable of Happiness as well as of pleasure and excitement, because they were near the Mean in the employment of all their faculties. I can imagine such people learning to exploit the electric power from their waterfalls, and the minerals in their mountains, without dividing themselves into dehumanised employers or officials, and equally dehumanised "hands." But I recollect also that the very salt and savour of Norwegian life depends on the fact that poets, and artists, and statesmen have worked in Norway with a devotion which was not directed by any formula of moderation. When I talk to a New Zealander about the future of his country, and about the example which she is creating of a society based upon

---

[1] *Ethics*, bk. ii. vi. 17, κατὰ μὲν τὴν οὐσίαν καὶ τὸν λόγον τὸν τί ἦν εἶναι λέγοντα μεσότης ἐστὶν ἡ ἀρετή, κατὰ δὲ τὸ ἄριστον καὶ τὸ εὖ ἀκρότης.

the avoidance both of destitution and superfluity, I
sometimes feel that she may have still to learn that
the Extreme as a personal ideal for those who are
called by it is a necessary complement of the Mean in
public policy.

But here we reach the point where our examination
of the conditions of Happiness, and, indeed, the whole
method of psychological analysis, ceases to be a sufficient guide to life.   It is rather through Philosophy
than Psychology, rather through a general interpretation of the universe, than through a detailed study of
so small a part of it as our own minds, that the call of
the Extreme makes itself most clearly heard.

INDEX

371

THE END

Printed in the United States of America.

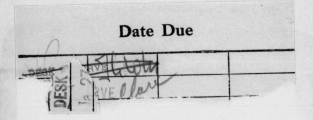

Date Due